FROM EVERYWHERE TO EVERYWHERE

International Study Centre
Canterbury Cathedral

From Everywhere to Everywhere

A World View of
Christian Witness

by

MICHAEL NAZIR-ALI

Collins
FLAME

William Collins Sons & Co. Ltd.

London · Glasgow · Sydney · Auckland

Toronto · Johannesburg

First published in Great Britain in 1990 by Flame

Flame is an imprint of
Collins Religious Division,
part of the HarperCollins Publishing Group,
77-85 Fulham Palace Road, London W6 8JB

Printed and bound in Great Britain
by Bell & Bain Ltd., Glasgow

Contents

Part One

CHAPTER ONE

Mission is God's Mission

God is Love. In Christian thought this has not meant merely that God loves us or even that he loves the world. It has meant primarily that the very internal relationships of the Godhead are characterised by love. The Father loves the Son, the Son loves the Father and their mutual love is the power that is the Holy Spirit.[1] It is important to remember that St Augustine, who first thought of the Trinity in this way, was a firm advocate of the tradition which emphasised the unity of God and sought to understand the distinctions within the Godhead in the light of the unity. Elsewhere, he speaks of the human mind, its knowledge and its love as being analogues of the Trinity. As with the human personality, so with the Godhead, these aspects are real and yet not isolated from each other. The mind that knows and loves may also be spoken of as knowledge and love. The knowledge of such a mind will be a loving knowledge. The love of such a mind will be a love which knows.[2] And yet, says Augustine, it is particularly appropriate to speak of the Holy Spirit as Love, because Scripture does so (Romans 5:5 and 1 John 4).[3]

Already in Augustine the Holy Spirit is associated with Creation.[4] The Love of God is limitless and "spills over" into Creation. Creation may be seen as an act of love which elicits a response of love, at least from human beings. If this response is to be authentic as a response of *love,* however, then it must be free and cannot be coerced. This much is basic to a biblical understanding of human freedom. At the same time, it needs to be emphasised that the Bible recognises humans as being open to divine communication and as possessing an innate *potential* for responding to divine love and being in fellowship with God.

God's Creation of the world and of human beings may be regarded as the beginning of the *missio dei,* the mission of God. If the order in the Universe and in our own thinking reflects the Logos, the divine Word, then the power and the personality of God so evident in Creation may be attributed to the work of the Spirit.[5] Particular passages of Scripture such as Genesis 1, Psalm 33 and Proverbs 8 have been understood by Christians as referring to the relation of the different Persons of the Trinity to Creation. Similarly, New Testament passages such as John 1, Romans 8 and Hebrews 1 relate the Persons of the Trinity to Creation and to its renewal. Human freedom is, as we have seen, an integral part of God's purpose for his Creation. It is, I suppose, possible to imagine a world where human freedom was always exercised in ways consonant with God's will. As a matter of fact, however, this is not so and we live in a world where the exercise of this freedom has more to do with selfishness, greed, hatred and envy. Not only have individuals become corrupt and rebellious but whole societies have come to behave in this way. Our predicament, therefore, has not only to do with the selfish exercise of our individual wills but with our inescapable participation in the corrupt structures of human society, whether it is the family, the tribe, the business conglomerate or the nation. This is not to say, of course, that these structures are inherently corrupt. Indeed, they may be God-given and necessary in order that human beings may flourish, but they have become tainted with human sin and need to be redeemed and restored, just as individuals do.[6]

The human predicament is not limited to human society. The Bible and Christian tradition have long recognised the impact which it has made and continues to make on the natural environment (Genesis 3:14–19). The environment too needs redemption and restoration (Romans 8:19–25).

The *missio dei* then is not just about the Love of God bringing Creation into existence. It must also be about the redemption, restoration and, indeed, further development of human beings and of the world at large. The restoration is not to be seen, in either case, as a return to some primaeval perfection but rather to a wholeness which makes further development possible.

The Bible portrays God as continuing to make his will known to human beings even in their state of alienation and hostility to him. A God who communicates is central to the Bible's presentation of the *missio dei*. This communication is itself Trinitarian in form. Rublev's marvellous icon has made us familiar with the beautiful story of God communicating his promise to Abraham and Sarah (Genesis 18). But it is not simply in stories such as this that God reveals himself in a Trinitarian way. The

Old Testament's understanding of divine revelation has to do with the Word of God being conveyed by the Spirit of God. The experience of the Spirit is one of the most primitive elements in the prophetic aspect of Hebrew religion. Old Testament reflection on it is based on a view of humanity which does *not* regard human beings as monads impervious to outside influence. Rather, it regards the human condition as open to a variety of spiritual influences. The "invasive" power of the Holy Spirit as it is depicted in the earliest parts of the Old Testament has to be understood in terms of such a psychology.[7]

Prophecy in the Bible has to be understood, of course, against a background of "inspired utterance" found in both ancient cultures and in many contemporary cultures. In some cases, as in much of Shamanism, such utterance has to do with sooth-saying and divination. In other cases, it may have to do with the work of poets and musicians, especially in sacral contexts. In many cases the oracles are used to reinforce and to strengthen the established social, political and religious structures of the group. There is some evidence in the Bible of the Hebrew prophets being pressurised to conform to such a stereotype, and many undoubtedly did (Jeremiah 6:14 and *passim*). There were others, however, like Jeremiah and Amos, who refused to be stereotyped in this way and were not willing to be merely chaplains to the Royal Court (Amos 7:10–17). It is characteristic of biblical prophecy that there *is* an element of challenge and judgement in it, not only against the nations roundabout but also against the very nation to which the prophets belonged. This ability to be critical of one's own tradition is essentially biblical and provides the wherewithal for the *ecclesia* to be *semper reformanda*.[8]

The inspiration of the Spirit leads to the conveyance of the divine Word. The Word is, like the Spirit, associated with the Creation (e.g. Psalm 33:6), but also with prophetic utterance (Isaiah 40:8). Already in the Old Testament, and later on in the period between the Testaments, there is a tendency to reify and to personalise the divine Word. This tendency reaches its climax in the Prologue to St John's Gospel, in the Epistle to the Hebrews and in the Epistle to the Collossians.

Not only does God call but he calls to save. The biblical paradigm for the divine call and election is the call and election of Israel. An oppressed, exploited and alienated ethnic minority is called out by God as a beacon of liberation. It is not just Israel that is liberated at the Exodus. A very mixed company – a rabble, no doubt of other exploited and enslaved peoples – joins them (Exodus 12:38; Numbers 11:4). The Pentateuch contains other accounts of contacts which Israel made with different groups of people during the wanderings in the wilderness. Some of those contacts were undoubtedly assimilative. The point which needs to be made here is that the Exodus proved to be liberating not only for the people of Israel but also for all those who joined them.[9] It is entirely understandable that groups of people such as dissenting Christians in Post-Reformation Europe, enslaved black people in the United States and now the poor in Latin America should seek to understand their situation and to organise their struggle for freedom in categories drawn from the biblical account of the Exodus of Israel. The Exodus trajectory will continue to illuminate and to be illuminated by the experience of subjugated peoples as they reflect on *their* reading of the Bible.

It is now being contended that the arrival and settlement of Israel in Canaan is to be regarded not only as a judgement on the corrupt Canaanite societies of that time but also as a catalyst for a social revolution within Canaan itself – a revolution which broke the established power of the temple-palace axis and replaced it with a community committed to equality and economic justice in the land. The theocracy of early Israel has been described, in this connection, as "the function of sociopolitical equality".[10] Goldingay remarks that the reverse could equally be true; that sociopolitical equality in Canaanite society could be seen as a result of the introduction of "mono-Yahwism" into it.[11] The situation as it is described in the books of Joshua and Judges is certainly complex. Different groups of people are treated differently for different reasons. Some are exterminated, others are allowed to survive (though under harsh conditions) and yet others seem to be incorporated into the covenant community. The tribes of Israel themselves do not emerge as paragons of virtue. It remains true, nevertheless, that the arrival of Israel in Canaan produced a most remarkable transformation in Canaanite society. As Chris Wright has said, "Israel, the people of God, not only thought of themselves as different – they *were* different."[12]

The seeming regression of Israel, later on, into monarchical patterns of government and cultic patterns of worship, which they had previously rejected under the influence of the covenant of Sinai; divine approval, albeit reluctant, of kingship; Israel's faithlessness and the subsequent judgement, exile, dispersion and return – these are all part of the complex pattern of Salvation-History. In the Bible's account of the History of Israel, the interplay between divine providence and human freedom is worked out in great detail. This is why biblical Salvation-History may correctly be taken as paradigmatic of all history. Nor is this to say that there are not other "salvation-histories". It is true that the call and election of Israel are unique. The circumstances of the call and the state of the tribes at the time of the Exodus, however, leave no room for pride. The election was, moreover, for witness; Israel was "to be a light to lighten the nations" (Isaiah 42:6; Luke 2:32). At different times and in different places, Israel responded to this task of witness in particular ways. Sometimes it was imagined that this task of witness had to do with bringing divine judgement on to peoples and nations. At other times, the peoples and nations are seen as streaming towards Mount Zion, the centre of the cult (e.g. Isaiah 2:2 – 4; Micah 4:1 – 4). At yet other times again, the fulfilment of biblical universalism comes at the end of the age, when the nations acknowledge Yahweh and are acknowledged by him.

There *are* passages in the Bible, however, where Yahweh is seen as working in the various histories of the peoples and nations roundabout Israel and Judah. Sometimes this divine activity is discerned only when its consequences impinge directly upon Israel or Judah. Such is the case with the prophetic perception that Cyrus is indeed the Lord's anointed, at least as far the termination of the exile in Babylon and the return to the Land are concerned (Isaiah 44:28 and 45:1 – 7). There are times, however, when it is perceived clearly that God has been active in the histories of peoples and nations from their very origins, just as he has been in the case of Israel (Amos 9:7). In at least some instances, we need to allow that this divine activity has led to a sincere response among the nations. God's call to Jonah to preach repentance to Nineveh and the subsequent repentance of the Ninevites must count as an example. The location of Job and his friends in the Land of Uz (in Arabia?) is another instance of a biblical writer discerning a response to God's activity outside Israel. The celebrated passage in Malachi (1:11 – 14) where the polluted sacrifices of an apostate people are compared to the sincere worship found among the nations is truly remarkable. Commentators sometimes try and get around the difficulty by claiming that the tense does not indicate the present but the immediate future and that there is, therefore, an eschatological element in the passage. Even if this is so, the immediate future often indicates an action so imminent that it may be deemed to have occurred already (2 Samuel 20:21). It is often remarked that if this passage were to be understood in its obvious sense, it would provide the only instance in the Bible where pagan sacrifices are regarded as offered to God. But is it necessary to go so far? Although sacrificial language *is* used in verse 11, it is used in a general sense and there is no reference to animal sacrifice. Indeed the word for "pure" in "a pure offering" is not the usual word for describing ritually clean animals fit for sacrifice, but instead has *moral* connotations. This gives us a clue, at least, that the intention of the prophet is not to approve the sacrificial cults of the nations but to recognise the possibility of a brokenness and repentance among the people of these nations which may be a sincere response to an apprehension of God, however obscure and distorted such an apprehension might be.[13] Nor is the prophet clear about the salvific value of such a response. It may be that it is a preparation for a further and more demanding disclosure (cf Acts 10).

An acknowledgement of the illumination of the divine Word in all human beings and of the work of the Holy Spirit in convincing the world of sin, righteousness and judgement, leads us to recognise that different groups of human beings around us may have salvation-histories of their own.[14] It is not necessary, moreover, that such salvation-histories should only, or even primarily, be discerned in the dominant religious traditions of these people. They might equally be discerned in counter-religious movements, such as the challenge of Buddhism or Sikhism to caste-conscious Hinduism. They may also be discerned in movements of reform within a religio-cultural tradition, such as the reform of Hinduism under the impact of Christianity. Or they may be discerned in secular movements which undertake to secure economic and social justice for the poor or to promote a respect for human rights in particular societies. The proclamation of the Gospel in contemporary contexts only comes alive when it resonates with an aspect of the salvation-history of a people.[15] The salvation-history of a particular people may rightly be regarded as *praeparatio evangelica* for them. The biblical Salvation-History would be the touchstone or the paradigm by which we could determine what is and what is not of salvific value in the history and culture of a particular people.

The *Heilsgeschichte* or Salvation-History way of discerning God's presence and work among a particular people is not the only way, of course. Even aspects of the biblical witness are not easily subsumed under this category. In the Bible itself devotional poetry, romance, saga and parable are all used for the self-communication of the divine.

God communicates. This much is common to all the theistic, revealed religions. God, the Creator of the world and of humanity, makes his will known to men and women. Their temporal well-being and eternal felicity lie in their obedience to God's will. Both Judaism and Islam hold that God has revealed his will primarily through his prophets, though the scriptures of both contain a number of theophanies as well. Where Islam is concerned, Kenneth Cragg has argued that the very fact of the divine communication implies divine involvement and vulnerability, for it invites possible rejection as well as acceptance. This involvement and vulnerability are seen especially in the qur'ānic affirmation that God helps the prophets with his Holy Spirit (Qur'ān 2:87, 253; 58:22). It is true that in Islam God is spoken of as being nearer to an individual than that person's own jugular vein (50:16). It is also true that on a number of occasions the Qur'ān speaks of supernatural help for the prophets and those faithful to their message. However, in Islam divine nearness often refers to omniscience or to God's readiness to hear prayer. It never means divine exposure to the vicissitudes of this world. Nor does divine help for humans compromise the omnipotence of God. Cragg argues (with some force) that divine nearness and divine help imply involvement and vulnerability. This may be a valid way of assessing the Islamic tradition. It must be remembered, however, that Islam itself has always refused to address it in this way.[16] It is possible to find perceptions of divine vulnerability among the prophets of the Old Testament (especially in Hosea, Joel and Amos). Even here, however, the tradition has developed in the direction of an emphasis of omnipotence and transcendence rather than on involvement and vulnerability.[17]

Divine theophanies, as they are found in the Old Testament or the Qur'ān (where they are sometimes, at least, a distinctive retelling of Old Testament accounts), *are* instances where divine distance appears to have been reduced in the experience of those to whom a revelation has been vouchsafed. The story of Moses' encounter with God, as he reveals himself in the burning bush, is recorded both in the Bible (Exodus 3) and in the

Qur'ān (20:9f). There is certainly a revelation of God himself here, rather than just his will or his commandments. And yet at the very climax of a theophany, both the Old Testament and the Qur'ān often emphasise the magnitude of divine transcendence (1 Kings 19:11 – 13 and Qur'ān 7:143).

The Hellenistic *milieu* of much early Christianity, while it provided the means for an articulation of Christian theology, was generally hostile to the Christian claim that the Logos, the rational principle of the Universe, had assumed humanity. This led to such Christian heresies as Gnosticism and Docetism in which, for one reason or another, the orthodox Christian doctrine of the Incarnation was denied. Much more seriously, the Hellenistic view of God, which held that he could not suffer (either in himself or with humanity) or change, began to infect the biblical view, inherited from the Old Testament, that God was compassionate and vulnerable. Even in as early and orthodox a writer as Ignatius (d. 108 AD) we find the confrontation between the biblical teaching and Greek thought so sharp that Christian doctrine can only be articulated in the form of a paradox: "There is one Physician, of flesh and of spirit, originate and unoriginate, God in man, true life in death, Son of Mary and Son of God, first passible and then impassible, Jesus Christ our Lord."[18]

What was new, disturbing and vitalising about Christianity then (and is still) was the claim that in the Person and work of Jesus Christ, divine distance had been finally, comprehensively and definitively overcome. Scripture and Christian tradition are full of clear testimony that it is God himself who addresses us in Jesus:

> In many and various ways God spoke of old to our fathers by the prophets; but in these last days he has spoken to us by a Son, whom he has appointed the heir of all things, through whom he also created the world. He reflects the glory of God and bears the very stamp of his nature, upholding the universe by this Word of power (Hebrews 1:1 – 3a).
>
> In the beginning was the Word, and the Word was with God, and the Word was God . . . . And the Word became flesh and dwelt among us full of grace and truth (John 1:1, 14a).
>
> That which was from the beginning, which we have heard, which we have seen with our eyes, which we have looked upon and touched

with our hands, concerning the Word of life – the life was made manifest, and we saw it, and testify to it, and proclaim to you the eternal life which was with the Father and was made manifest to us (1 John 1:1–2).

Repeatedly, in the letters he wrote on the way to martyrdom, Ignatius emphasises that it is belief in the Incarnation which is the touchstone or orthodoxy (Smyrnaeans, I:1, V:2, VI:I; Trallians IX:1, etc.). This is how he describes his doctrine of the Incarnation: "There is one God who manifested himself through Jesus Christ his Son, who is his Word, coming forth from silence, who in all things did the good pleasure of him that sent him" (Magnesians VIII:2). Again, "For our God, Jesus Christ, was conceived by Mary according to a divine purpose, of the seed of David, and yet of the Holy Spirit" (Ephesians XVIII:2).

Some two hundred years later Athanasius maintained this apostolic teaching, resisting the powerful Arianising influences in both the Empire and the Church: "For this purpose (i.e. the renewal of Creation), then, the incorporeal and incorruptible and immaterial Word of God entered our world. In one sense, indeed, he was not far from it before, for no part of Creation had ever been without him who, while ever abiding in union with the Father, yet fills all things that are. But now he entered the world in a new way, stooping to our level in his love and self-revealing to us" *(De Incarnatione 8)*.

Both Ignatius and Athanasius associate the incarnate Word with the Mind, Reason or Wisdom of God and thus imply the eternity of the Word. Also, both refer to Jesus as God in several places seemingly without qualification. This, then, is the climax (though not, of course, the end) of the *missio dei*. God has himself come to rescue human beings from the corruption which their transgression has brought about, both for themselves and for the world. This is no mere revelation of God's will *through* a prophet. It is not even a theophany which should terrify us by its *mysterium tremendum*. This is divine risk-taking, exposure and vulnerability in its most breath-taking yet entirely typical manifestation. God reveals himself to us as the mighty redeemer in circumstances of extreme weakness and helplessness. Gerard Manley Hopkins expresses it in his inimitable way:

The heaven-flung, heart-fleshed, maiden-furled
Miracle-in-Mary-of-flame,
Mid-numbered He in three of the thunder-throne![19]

Both Ignatius and Athanasius relate the "taking of flesh" of the eternal Word with the suffering and death of Jesus Christ. Combatting the docetism of those who denied that Christ really suffered in the flesh because they did not believe he really came in the flesh, Ignatius is at pains to emphasise the full humanity of Christ, "who is of the race of David, the child of Mary, who was truly born, and ate and drank, was truly persecuted under Pontius Pilate, was truly crucified and died, before the eyes of those in heaven and those on earth and those under the earth".[20] For Athanasius too the Cross of Christ is a special focus of God's revelation in him. But it is more than that: "The Word, being himself incapable of death, assumed a mortal body, that he might offer it as his own in place of all, and suffering for the sake of all through his union with it, 'might bring to nought him that had the power of death'."[21]

In the writings of both Ignatius and Athanasius there is a clear recognition that Christ "died for us", to put an end to death, to deal with sin and to inaugurate a new humanity through his Resurrection from the dead. Too often the Incarnation and the Atonement have been artificially separated from each other, and this has had inevitable repercussions on Christian mission. We have to insist, therefore, that both doctrines are integrally related and that the one does not make sense without the other. God reveals himself in Jesus Christ to deal with human sin and so to make peace with all human beings. In an important sense, every aspect of Christ's work – his ministry of healing, his teaching, his forgiveness of sin – has atoning significance. The Cross is the crown of this work of at-one-ment, not the only instance of it. The whole life of Christ typifies the new Adam who, by his life of perfect obedience and openness to the will of God, undoes the effects of the sin of the old Adam and brings a new humanity into existence.

So not only is Christ God's definitive revelation of himself, but this revelation is also to be seen as God's provision for the beginnings of a new humanity. In this sense, Christ may rightly be understood as the representative of all humanity. He takes on himself the task of fidelity abandoned by Adam and his race. In doing this he brings upon himself the hate and rejection of a sinful humanity, yet at the same time sets forth for humanity a new way of obedience and righteousness. There is, therefore, an *objectivity* about the Atonement. God has set forth Jesus as the beginning of a new or renewed humanity. Jesus has brought this new humanity to perfection by his suffering and death (Hebrews 5:8–9). But there is a *subjective* element as well. God, who is Love, calls us to *follow* Jesus, to be his disciples (Matthew 16:25). In following Jesus, who is the Way, we become identified with and incorporated into the new humanity which he has perfected and which God has approved by raising him from the dead (Romans 6:3–11). God in his wisdom and sovereignty has chosen (elected) Jesus Christ from all eternity. We, by our personal or corporate decision, turn away from our solidarity with the old, sinful humanity to being disciples of Christ and being incorporated into him (Ephesians 1:4–10).[22]

Solidarity with the new humanity in Christ brings us to the Church. It is often said, "Jesus came preaching the Kingdom of God and the Church came into being!" Is the Church simply a by-product of a delayed *Parousia* or is it possible to think of it as an eschatological community, brought into being by Jesus himself, as the herald and the embodiment of the new age, however near or far that new age might be? We have already considered the "invasive" power of the Holy Spirit in relation to prophecy in the Old Testament. The community which Jesus formed around him to preach and to live the coming Kingdom of God, a community nearly destroyed by the traumatic events of Good Friday, was recreated and empowered by the Holy Spirit after the Resurrection of Christ.

It is well known that in St John's Gospel there is no account of the Ascension of the Lord, and the Holy Spirit seems to have been given to the disciples more or less immediately after the Resurrection (John 20:19–23). In Luke/Acts, on the other hand, the Holy Spirit seems to have been given *after* the Ascension had taken place and some considerable time after the Resurrection (Acts 1:8, 2:1–4). In both accounts the giving of the Spirit is spoken of in initiatory terms and, in both, the giving of the Spirit is to empower the disciples for mission. Are there two completely different accounts here of how the Church received the Spirit? Is it completely impossible to harmonise them?[23] It is difficult to believe that there could be two such divergent traditions about such a constitutive matter. Not only were the events of Pentecost a public matter, but the early Church became used to similar experiences at different times and in many places. The Johannine account is of a more private event – an appearance of the Risen Lord to his disciples. The Ascension which John expects to take place (v. 17) is not described as having taken place in the meantime. Can it be that the account in John is proleptic – that is, it is an enactment of Pentecost for the disciples before Pentecost, just as there had been an enactment of the Passion before the Passion? Perhaps Barrett is right after all in claiming that every appearance of the Risen Lord was Spirit-bearing in one way or another and that it was only later that different traditions began to emphasise different occasions as initiatory.[24] Pentecost itself was not, of course, an appearance of the Risen Lord and it may be that the process which came to fulfilment in the baptism with the Spirit had begun somewhat earlier – at the time of an appearance, perhaps? The important point, in both John and Acts is that the gift of the Spirit is constitutive (or reconstitutive, to be exact) of the community, and that this community is a missionary community. From this point on, the life of this community (or these communities, as they rapidly come to be) is life in the Spirit. The Acts of these communities and of their members are acts of the Holy Spirit and their words are words of the Holy Spirit. Their evangelism is Spirit-filled, their healing ministry is a gift of the Spirit, their instruction to the churches is from the Spirit, and even their apologetic is the result of the Spirit's indwelling! The Holy Spirit is the common medium of all their activity and fellowship. At critical times in the life of the Church there is a special manifestation of the Spirit, but he is there all the time, the bond of love which creates and sustains the missionary community. Bishop John V. Taylor describes the work of the Spirit as a medium of communication in this way: "The Holy Spirit brings us into more vivid contact with one another and with God while remaining imperceptible himself."[25]

The same Holy Spirit who drove Jesus into the wilderness (Mark 1:12 and parallels), now drives the Church into wider and wider spheres of presence and mission (Acts 10:19–20, 44–48; 16:6–10). In the New Testament there is abundant evidence that the Church grows by breaking down the barriers of race, religion, gender and class (Ephesians 2:11–22; Colossians 3:11; Galatians 3:28). In general, we do not find the Church growing within "homogeneous" units, and where there is a tendency to withdraw into groups of common racial or religious origin, it is vigorously resisted (Galatians 2:11–21). From the very beginning there is evidence of heterogeneity in the Church, even though this caused serious problems, leading to some special provision for certain "homogeneous" groups (Acts 6:1–6). The rules set out by the Holy Spirit and the apostles at the Council of Jerusalem were formulated precisely to prevent the emergency of "homogeneous" groups of believers and to make continued table-fellowship possible (Acts 15:1–35). From the earliest times Christians as well as pagans referred to Christians as "the third race" or "the new race".[26]

A new kind of *genos,* neither Jew nor gentile, neither slave nor free, neither male nor female, but encompassing all of these, had come into being. The Gospel is universal not simply because the Church is extended through time and space, but also because the preaching and the reception of the Gospel breaks down barriers between people in particular places, thus creating the unity of the local church out of apparent sheer diversity. Such a unity should not destroy all diversity, of course. Differences of language, of culture, of ethnic origin may all be affirmed and celebrated within the local community of believers, but never at the expense of the unity which Christ wills for his Church.[27]

CHAPTER TWO

Universal, Translatable and Accessible

We have seen how the proclamation of the Gospel was already becoming universal in the apostolic age. The Christian Faith spread rapidly throughout the Roman Empire, and great centres of Christianity such as Jerusalem, Antioch, Ephesus, Corinth and Rome came to be established and recognised. It is important to note that although the *Pax Romana* made communication easier and provided some kind of unity for the peoples under its protection, nevertheless there always was a great diversity of races, cultures and languages *within* the Roman Empire. The fact that Christianity was particularly strong, in its early years, in cosmopolitan cities, with their very mixed populations, is good evidence of the Gospel's capacity to break down barriers and also of its universality. The overwhelmingly urban character of early Christianity (in contrast, perhaps, to the Galilean ministry of Jesus) is shown, for example, by the fact that most of the letters in the New Testament, and indeed in the sub-apostolic age, are addressed to churches in cities or towns. The early organisation of the Church was based on the city, and Christian ministers from the country (*chorepiscopoi*, for example) were subordinated to their urban counterparts. When Christianity became the official religion of the Empire, the very word for a person who was not a Jew or a Christian came to be *paganus* or "villager"! This usage also survives in the modern word "heathen"—that is, one from the heath or the country.[1]

It was not, however, only in the cosmopolitan cities of the Roman Empire that the Christian Faith was spreading. It spread also on the borders of the Empire and well beyond its confines. From very early times there has been a tendency among Church historians to present the movement of the Gospel, in the primitive period, as having been from Jerusalem to Rome. Indeed, this tendency may be discerned within Scripture itself, the book of the Acts of the Apostles being a clear example of it.[2] Before the emancipation of the Church, there were good apologetic reasons for this stylisation. Christians wanted to demonstrate that they were a legitimate religious group, a *religio licita,* within the Empire and that they were loyal citizens. At other times, however, the motives were not quite so worthy. For example, there was a desire to see Christianity acquire social and wordly power in the Empire (it is possible to read Eusebius in this way[3]). Even in modern times, an influential writer like Henry Chadwick can entitle the introductory chapter of his best-known work "From Jerusalem to Rome"! He goes on to say, "the main stream of missionary work flowed westwards and the fact that St Paul's eye had been towards Italy and Spain was fateful for the future identification of Christianity with European culture".[4] Christian traditions which speak of the spread of Christianity into Persia and India during the apostolic age are dismissed as legends on a par with the association of St James the Apostle with Compostella or Joseph of Arimathea with Glastonbury! This view is modified somewhat later on in the work, where it is admitted that the stories provide evidence for the existence of Christianity in these parts, at least in the third century.[5] Where the identification of Christianity with European culture is concerned, much depends on what is meant by the term "European". If it is to mean what in fact it does in current usage, then this identification, in its fullest sense, cannot be dated much before the reign of Charlemagne and the advent of mediaeval Western Christendom in its most typical form. By this time, of course, there were well-established "Christendoms" in Armenia (the first nation to become Christian) and in Ethiopia. There is ample testimony of the strength of the latter from Muslim sources, the Ethiopian Empire having had a great deal to do with the rise of Islām both positively and negatively.[6]

Bishop William Young has traced the origins of Persian Christianity at least to the sub-apostolic age and has also shown its distinctive character.[7] There is strong documentary evidence of the existence of Christians in the Parthian Empire (i.e. up to 225 AD). At this time there seems to have been little systematic persecution, though there were cases of harassment. From very early times, Christians in this part of the world read their Bibles in Syriac – a language very similar to the Aramaic spoken by Jesus and his disciples. It is true that Syriac or Aramaic does not seem to be the original language of the New Testament as we have it today and that the New Testament in Syriac is a translation from the Greek. This translation is, nevertheless, considerably older than many of the manuscripts of the Greek New Testament which have survived and is, therefore, very valuable for biblical scholars. It seems also to be the case that there is a Semitic basis to much in the New Testament and that the Syriac translations sometimes resonate with this in a way the Greek does not.[8] The worship of the Church of the East (as it came to be called) is focussed around the very ancient Liturgy of St Addai and St Mari (though other *anaphorae* are also used). The Liturgy, because of its development outside the Roman Empire, escaped Byzantine influence and retains very primitive elements.[9]

The fall of the Parthian dynasty and the accession of the Sassanids set the stage for a confrontation with the State, since the Sassanids emphasised the importance of Zoroastrianism as the State Religion. When, in addition to this, Shapur II (309–379) initiated fresh hostilities with the newly-Christian Roman Empire, the Christians inevitably came to be seen as a fifth column within the Persian Empire. They were seen as being loyal to Constantinople, and the actions of some of the Roman Emperors did nothing to assuage such fears. The result was a period of sustained persecution for the Church of the East. A fifth-century martyrology records that the persecution began with the imposition of penal taxation on the Christians.[10] When even this did not work, the clergy (including the Patriarch) were arrested and condemned to death. The churches were demolished and their sacred vessels were confiscated. Sozomen, a fifth-century Greek historian, was able to count sixteen thousand martyrs among the Persian Christians at this time. Even so, he admits that there must have been many others who could not be counted.[11] The Roman Martyrology too contains the names of Persian martyrs, such as Marius, Martha, Audifax and Abachum (whose feast day is 19th January), showing that not all Persian martyrs were martyred within the Persian Empire.

What the so-called Edict of Milan had been to the Church in the Roman Empire, the Edict of Yazdigard became for the Church in Persia. The Emperor Yazdigard (399–420) issued an edict of recognition and toleration for the Church of the East which resulted in relative peace, and even expansion, for the Church for two hundred years or so.[12] The arrival of Islām changed the situation markedly for this Church, and its history since then is a long tale of courage, boldness and determination in the face of circumstances that were, at times, very adverse indeed.[13]

The ancient Christians of South India have long had a relationship both with the "Nestorian" Church of the East *and* with their opponents in Christological matters, the Jacobites of Syria. In this connection, it is perhaps worth pointing out that at Nicaea it was Bishop John the Persian who signed on behalf of the whole of Persia and of the Great India. Records of attendance at synods of the Church of the East regularly show that bishops from India were present and that from the seventh century onwards, a metropolitan would attend such synods.[14]

Whatever its relationship with Western Asia, the Indian Church has always regarded itself as having been founded by the Apostle Thomas himself. There is evidence of trade between the Malabar Coast of India and the Middle East in those days. There seem also to have been Jewish settlements along the coast of India at that time (as indeed there are even today). There is, therefore, nothing improbable in the story that St Thomas came to South India, even though there is no firm historical evidence of such a visit. The Christians of St Thomas (as they call themselves) have very strong and ancient traditions of a visit by him, of his establishing seven churches all along the Malabar coast and of his subsequent martyrdom and burial at Mylapore near Madras. In this connection a very learned Metropolitan of the Mar Thoma Church has commented:

> The History of the Christian Church in the first century does not depend entirely on historical documents. Tradition is often more true and more compelling than plain historical proof. In this sense St Peter's founding of the Roman Church and St Thomas' founding of the Malabar Church may be said to stand on the same footing. Both are supported by traditions which are sufficiently early and sufficiently strong.[15]

There were, additionally, migrations of Christians from Persia and Syria in the fourth and eighth centuries. India has often been a haven for refugees fleeing persecution (such as the Zoroastrians from Iran), and the Christians would have been no exception. There is further evidence of the existence of the Christian Church in South India and Sri Lanka in the writings of Cosmas Indicopleustes ("the Indian Navigator") who lived in the sixth century.

There is another, completely different, tradition of St Thomas' visit to India which locates the place of his arrival in North-West India (what is now Pakistan). The apocryphal *Acts of Thomas* dates from the third century and was probably written originally in Syriac in an area within the influence of Christians from the Persian Empire. It is probably of Gnostic origin, though scholars believe that most of the Gnostic influence has been removed to make the work tolerable to orthodox readers. The work consists of thirteen "Acts" and a number of poems, including the famous "Hymn of the Soul", usually ascribed to the second-century oriental, Bardaisan. The work is a highly dramatised account of how the Apostle Thomas came to India at the time of a certain King Gundaphorus. He preached the Gospel, converted Gundaphorus and many others, and was eventually martyred there. This in itself is a strong indication that the tradition about Thomas and India had already taken root in the earlier part of the third century.[16]

Despite its Gnostic origins and the dramatised way in which the material is presented, there are elements in the *Acts* which ring true. Until the nineteenth century, the *Acts* was regarded, more or less, as a romance with little or no historical basis to it. In the nineteenth century, however, coins began to be discovered all over North-West India with the names of Gundaphorus in Greek and Gandharan on them. The coins refer to Gundaphorus as a king *(Basileus-Maharaja)* and appear to date from the first sixty years of the Christian era! A tablet called the Takht-i-Bāhī Stone, also discovered in the nineteenth century, seems to confirm this as the period of Gundaphorus' reign. It is now believed that Gundaphorus was a king of the Indo-Parthian dynasty which ruled over a vast territory stretching from the Punjāb to Afghānistān in the first century AD.[17] Bishop Young puts the question at its sharpest when he says, "until archaeologists found insciptions on the (North-West) Frontier, the very existence of this King . . . had been forgotten by historians – how then did the author of the *Acts of Thomas* writing in what is now south-west Turkey two centuries after Gandaphoros (sic), get the king's name right?"[18]

The so-called Taxila Cross was discovered in a field near Taxila and is now in the custody of Lahore Cathedral. It is thought to date from the first century also, though its Christian provenance has not been established beyond doubt. Rooney makes the important point that not enough account has been taken of the relation of this cross to other ancient Indian crosses. One characteristic which they all have in common is that they are all equilateral. Still, Rooney is undoubtedly correct in saying that the evidence of the Taxila Cross on its own is of little value if it is considered apart from the other documentary and historical evidence.[19]

North-West India, and Gandhara in particular, had been under the influence of the Hellenistic-Syrian Seleucids, who ceded the area to Indian control in the fourth century BC. Gandhara was, therefore, subject to both Greek and Syrian cultural influence. Apparently, this influence continued to be felt even during the Buddhist Period. It created a milieu which would have made it possible for Thomas to communicate the Gospel to at least some of the inhabitants of this area, even if this was in a limited way.

On grounds of cultural influence, linguistic affinity and geographical proximity, the "Northern" Theory has much to commend it. On the other hand, we must remember that it is in the South that there has been a continuous Christian community for centuries. They are the living bearers of an ancient Christian tradition, an important part of which is the claim that St Thomas himself founded these communities.

Egypt was, of course, part of the Roman Empire and at least some parts of it had come under considerable Greek influence. Alexandria was a major centre of Hellenistic learning and culture. The ancient language of Egypt, which came to be called Coptic, was influenced by Greek but retained, nevertheless, its ancient structure.

The Church in Egypt, called the Coptic Church, also claims apostolic origin. It is said that Egypt was evangelised by St Mark the evangelist, the disciple of St Peter. Certainly, during the persecution under Diocletian in the third century, the Church was strong enough to withstand ten years of ferocious oppression, which produced hundreds of thousands of martyrs. Coptic tradition is so rich in its martyrology that it is perhaps no exaggeration to say that the Coptic Church is a church of martyrs.[20] The Copts count twenty-one major persecutions between 202 and 642 AD, Diocletian's being counted as the seventh. In 642 AD the Muslim Arabs conquered Egypt and brought Roman-Byzantinian rule to an end. This was not, however, the end of trials and tribulations for the Egyptian Church, but only a shift in the direction from which they came. The irony of it is that many non-chalcedonian Christians, such as the Syrians and Egyptians, had thought that the Muslim invasion would deliver them from the hegemony of the Byzantines!

It is perhaps appropriate to note at this point that the origins of the Christian monastic tradition lie in the deserts of Syria and Egypt. The early hermits were Christians who had become alarmed at the direction the Church was taking after its emancipation. Christian eremiticism and its successor, monasticism, both have their roots, therefore, in a form of Christian dissidence which was specifically a protest against the Romanising worldliness of the Post-Constantinian Church. In the monastic tradition, a martyrdom of intention replaced the bloody martyrdom of the days of the persecution. It enabled the Coptic Church to survive when persecution returned.[21] It may well be that the ascetical movement, as it arose in Egypt, was an assertion of the essential Coptic character against the Graeco-Roman form of Christianity which had been imposed on the Egyptian people.[22]

Although the Coptic Church retained its language and read the Bible in it and also used it for liturgical purposes, it produced very great theologians and scholars, such as Clement, Origen, Athanasius and Cyril, who wrote and taught in Greek. Their influence was very considerable and the latter two have substantially influenced the development of credal formulations in the wider Church. After the Arab conquest, when Arabic became more and more the *lingua franca*, Coptic and other Middle-Eastern Christians (as well as Jews) began to write in Arabic. Professor Kenneth Bailey, formerly of the Near East School of Theology in Beirut and now at the Tantur Institute in Bethlehem, has remarked that after Latin and Greek, Arabic, of all ancient and mediaeval languages, has perhaps the greatest wealth of Christian theological manuscripts! A great deal of this material remains unresearched.[23]

Among the Copts, learning and the monastic tradition have always gone hand in hand with missionary ardour. Pantaenus, the first known head of the celebrated Catechetical School of Alexandria and the revered teacher of St Clement himself, is reported by Eusebius to have been a missionary in India. Saint Athanasius spent his time in exile as a missionary in Europe. Numerous other Copts – soldiers, merchants and artisans – carried the faith with them wherever they went. Coptic Christianity spread from Egypt towards the south and all along the Nile, right up to Nubia and the Sudan. Today, there is still a sizable Coptic community in the Sudan.[24]

But the greatest area of Coptic missionary enterprise is undoubtedly

Ethiopia. The Book of Acts records the conversion of the minister of the queen of the Ethiopians (Acts 8:26–39). It may be, however, that he came not from Ethiopia proper but from what is now modern Sudan.[25] There is also a tradition that St Matthew was sent to Ethiopia, but it is not accompanied by any historical evidence.

As far as history is concerned, Christianity really comes to Ethiopia in the fourth century through two youths, Frumentius and Aedesius, who were shipwrecked there. Gradually, they achieved recognition and power at the Court, which Frumentius, at least, used to promote the Gospel. He was later consecrated first bishop of the Ethiopian Church by Athanasius himself and took the title *Abuna* or "our Father". Since then every head of the Church of Ethiopia has had this title. The Coptic Church continued to supply the bishops for the Ethiopian Church well into this century. The Church is now autocephalous, with its own Patriarch. In the fifth century, scholars from Syria came to help in the mission of the Ethiopian Church by translating the Bible into Ge'ez the main literary language of Ethiopia. They translated some of the writings of the Fathers as well.[26] Throughout the years, and particularly in this century, missionaries from other oriental orthodox churches in Egypt, Syria and India have worked in the fields of medicine, theological education and pastoral work side by side with Ethiopians.

The Ethiopian Church itself has a very long missionary history. It is interesting, in this connection, to observe that the evangelisation of certain areas in the Ethiopian Empire followed upon military conquest and was an element in the imperial efforts at pacification. The similarities with the Christianisation of Western Europe are striking.

In the nineteenth century too there was a tremendous attempt to evangelise among people who followed traditional religions and also among Muslims. This attempt was greatly encouraged by the State, which expected that the Church would also propagate the culture of the dominant ruling group, the Amhara. Once again, it is very instructive to compare the missionary methods of the Ethiopian Church with those of Western Christian missionaries working in (say) East Africa at that time.

Monasticism has for a long time served as a missionary arm of the Church, both in the East and the West, and Ethiopia is no exception. Most of the missionary work was carried out by the monks, and the secular clergy were only marginally involved. Gradually, however, the monasteries became very wealthy and the monks became introverted and interested in theological controversy. Their interest in evangelisation waned. This interest revived periodically, usually at the behest of the Emperor.

Ethiopian Christianity is distinctive because of its early and deep inculturation into the Semitic and African culture of the people. Indigenous Jewish influence has also been an element in the formation of the Ethiopian Christian tradition. Christians from other parts of the world sometimes feel uncomfortable when they encounter these aspects of Ethiopian Christianity, yet it may be that these very elements are its strength.

Close identification with the State has been another feature of the history of the Ethiopian Church. It is undoubtedly the case that on many occasions the Church has been a tool in the hands of the State and has furthered its interests. Its special relationship with the State has sometimes brought about its alienation from minority ethnic or religious groups. At the same time, it has to be admitted that the Church's success in Christianising vast areas has only been possible because of State encouragement and help.[27]

It will become clear that there is no single missionary history of the Church. Different families of churches, different geographical areas and particular clusters of cultures may each have their own missionary history. A proper appreciation of the most recent missionary history of the Western family of churches will only be possible when it is seen as merely an episode (albeit a very important episode) in the missionary history of merely one family (albeit a very important family) of Christian churches.

The Church of the East too has a glorious history of mission. From the beginning, they were persecuted for attempting to evangelise among Zoroastrians. Zoroastrianism was at that time the State Religion, and any attempt at proselytising among its followers was punishable by death. Apostasy too, on the part of adherents of the State Religion, was punishable by death, preceded, at times, by torture. Yet the Church continued to witness faithfully in this early period of its history, and there are records which suggest that, despite persecution, some Zoroastrians *were* baptised and often paid the ultimate penalty.[28]

After the coming of Islām, all the churches in the countries which came to constitute the Islāmic world were severely restricted in their task of mission within their localities. Not only was it strictly forbidden to evangelise Muslims (the punishment for apostasy was, once again, death), but also it was often difficult to evangelise people from other non-Muslim communities, though some instances of this are recorded.[29]

The response to this situation quite often was to concentrate on *overseas mission*. The Coptic Church, a church claiming to be genuinely indigenous to Africa, continued its work in the Southern Sudan, in Ethiopia and in other parts of Africa. The Church of the East renewed its interest in India and China. Work among the Mongol tribes was also initiated. In 635 AD Alo-Pen reached China; he was the first Christian missionary to work in that country. By 638 Christianity had been accepted as a tolerated religion within the Chinese Empire. The famous Nestorian Tablet, erected in perhaps the year 781, celebrates a century and a half of Christianity in China. Christianity seems to have died out in China in the tenth century, as a result of the withdrawal of Imperial favour and the fragmentation of the empire into several fiefdoms. Work among the Mongols continued, however, and there were individual conversions of sometimes quite influential people as well as occasional mass movements. We know of a Metropolitan in China right up to the ninth century, and the tablet itself mentions a bishop and many priests or monks. There is evidence too of a hierarchy for the Mongol tribes which were becoming Christian. Right up to the time of the invasion of Baghdād in 1258 by the Mongols, they remained sympathetic to the Church of the East. The Crusaders in the Middle East, however, actually cooperated with the Muslims in the conflict with the Mongols, and we know that, later on, the Mongols became very hostile to all kinds of Christians and persecuted them ruthlessly. The eventual conversion of the Mongols to Islām must rank among the tragic failures of Mission history. The tribes, and even the Great Khans, repeatedly asked for Christian missionaries. Neither the East nor the West could supply them in adequate numbers (even the Pope could make only a token response). It is sobering to reflect that the whole history of Central and West Asia might have been so different if there had been a greater Christian response to an emergent people. It is even more tragic that Western and Eastern Christians were rivals in the mission to the Mongols and that they were able to observe Christian disunity at close quarters. This is not unique in the history of Christian Mission, and on many other occasions Christians were to be rivals in taking the Christian Faith to a particular group of people.[30]

The Church in India continued to have regular contacts with the Church in Western Asia. It obtained its bishops from both the Jacobites and the Nestorians without being troubled too much by scruples about doctrines! It was only after the arrival of Western missionaries, and the divisions caused by them, that Christians in India began to become conscious of doctrinal differences among Christians in other lands. When the Portuguese arrived, they tried to compel the Indian Christians to submit to Roman jurisdiction. The so-called Synod of Diamper (1599) did, in fact, initiate moves to Romanise the Indian Church. In 1653, however, there was a great rebellion against Roman jurisdiction and thousands of Indian Christians took the so-called Oath of the Coonan Cross, pledging loyalty to their ancient Church and vowing never to accept Roman supremacy. The result of the rebellion was the division of the Indian Christians into two factions – those who still had connections with the Patriarchate of Antioch or with the Church of the East and those who formed the Syro-Malabar Church, an Eastern-rite Uniat church, in communion with Rome. In the twentieth century there was another accession *en masse* to Rome, resulting in the emergence of another rite known as the Syro-Malankara.

The presence of missionaries from the Church Missionary Society among the ancient Indian Christians caused a reforming party to emerge in their church. Some of the members of this party eventually became Anglicans but the majority, having secured episcopal succession from Antioch, formed the Mar Thoma Syrian Church. They describe themselves as a reformed church in the oriental tradition and they are in communion with the See of Canterbury and the rest of the Anglican Communion.

Some of the Indian Christians came under the influence of non-episcopal evangelical missionaries. This gave rise to the Evangelical Church of St Thomas. There is also a small independent church known as Thozhiyoor Church and a small (Nestorian) Church of the East with a metropolitan at Trichur,

A large number of the ancient Indian Christian communities continue in the Antiochene tradition and, until recently, all members of the Indian Orthodox Church owed allegiance to the Jacobite Patriarch at Antioch. In recent years, however, there has been a division among them. Some have created their own Catholicos and have declared themselves independent of Antioch as far as jurisdiction is concerned, while others continue to recognise the link with Antioch.

The Orthodox are active in missionary work in many parts of Asia and Africa. The Mar Thoma Church too has a tremendous amount of missionary and evangelistic zeal, and is working in many different places in India, and also overseas. They have carried out pioneering work in places such as Nepal and on the borders of Tibet. Their evangelistic work, together with their ministries of care for the poor and the needy, may also be found in South-East Asia and even in more distant parts of the world. Huge evangelistic conventions, such as the one held annually at Maramon, are a feature of the life of the Mar Thoma Church. Well-run youth camps ensure that the young people are not alienated from the life of the church, and even in the *diaspora* it has managed not to lose the second or the third generation.[31]

One reason why the ancient Indian churches do not easily lose their members, even in the *diaspora,* is that there is a strongly communal character to these churches. They are cohesive and integrated communities where all the social and economic, as well as spiritual, needs of the individual and of families are met. From ancient times, several Christian communities have been given certain privileges by the Hindu rulers. These have given them an honourable place in a society that has been caste-ridden. On the other hand, as Alexander Mar Thoma recognises, this has also isolated them from the poor and the disadvantaged.[32] The Mar Thoma Church, in particular, has made a considerable effort to overcome these barriers. Several scores of congregations have been established among poor and disadvantaged communities. Problems of integration have, however, existed and are only now being overcome. In areas where the Mar Thoma are not traditionally strong, newly-evangelised groups are handed over for nurture to dioceses or congregations of the Church of North India or the Church of South India. The Mar Thoma are in full communion with these churches, which are not ethnically or linguistically homogeneous as the Mar Thoma themselves are.

The difficulties experienced by the Christians of St Thomas, in all their denominational manifestations, in evangelising people not of their own background and in planting new congregations among such people, raise questions of very wide importance for Christian Mission generally. Our claim has been that from the very beginning the appeal of the Gospel has been universal and that it has spread in all directions among people of very diverse cultures. An important reason for this is undoubtedly the capacity of Gospel to "make sense" in a wide range of cultures and contexts.[33] Professor Sanneh of Yale Divinity School calls this the "translatability" of the Gospel. In many cultures, such as those of Armenia, Ethiopia, the Christians of St Thomas and much of Western Europe, the Gospel has not only been rendered into the language, the symbolism and the idiom of these cultures, it has not only transformed these cultures in significant ways, but it has also been assimilated and "owned" in a way which has made it "at home" in these cultures. This is precisely the aim of inculturation or contextualisation, and these cultures can justifiably be held up as examples to others.

There is, unfortunately, a darker side to the matter. The very rendering of the Gospel so completely in the language, the symbolism and the thought-forms of particular cultures alienates other cultures. "If it is for them, it cannot be for us!" sums up the attitude. Many communities in modern Iran and Turkey believe that Christianity cannot possibly be for them because it is the Armenians and the Assyrians who are Christians! At the same time, traditionally Christian communities sometimes have attitudes which give the impression that they believe that somehow the Gospel is their special "possession" and that they almost resent sharing this "possession" with others. The book of Jonah in the Old Testament is a homily on this kind of attitude. The people of God are warned not to regard God's revelation as something exclusively for them. Rather, they are to share it with others, making repentance and faith possible for them also. The struggle in the early Church about the extension of the Gospel to the Gentiles is another example of this tendency to "domesticate" the Gospel into one culture, thus making it difficult for other cultures to have access to it.

It will have become apparent by now that there is an almost irreducible tension between universality on the one hand and translatability on the other. In order to be universal, the Gospel must be translatable. This translation, this rendering of the Gospel into the idiom of a particular culture, however, cannot be at the expense of the very universality it is supposed to promote. No one culture can be allowed to "own" the Gospel in such a way that other cultures are denied access to it. No one culture, no one age, may claim that the rendering of the Gospel in terms of *its* intellectual or cultural traditions is binding on other cultures and other ages. The Church's recognition of the most primitive testimonies to God's decisive saving acts in Christ as "canonical" or authoritative for the Church is also to be understood within this context. The relevation to which the books of the Bible are an immediate and reliable witness was given in particular historical and cultural *milieux*, and the careful study of these is very important indeed if we are serious in our desire to apprehend the divine reality and to comprehend, however inadaquately, God's will for us. But it is not enough. Together with our study of the original *sitz im leben* of the Bible, we must also be prepared to relate its "horizon" or "horizons" to our own "horizon", our own cultural and historical situation. It is only in relating these horizons to one another that we will be able to discern God's revelation as revelation *for us.*[34]

In recent years there has been a fresh awareness that *all* of us read the Bible in terms of our particular context and that each context, because of its historical and cultural formation, is equipped to engage specially with certain "trajectories" in the Bible. They may have to do with God's rescue of an oppressed people (the Exodus trajectory) or with the prophets' concern for justice and mercy. These may have to do with the announcement of judgement on oppressors or with *motifs* of salvation understood variously in corporate or individual terms. The distinctive witness of each group (or even individual) as to how it reads the Bible is extremely important not only for the group itself but for the whole Church. But precisely because the witness of *each* is important for the *whole,* complementarity becomes necessary. Each group, while maintaining its distinctiveness, must listen, as much as possible, to the testimonies of others. These must be allowed to modify, qualify or even correct its own testimony. The Reformers of the sixteenth century were surely right in their insistence on the possibility of *private judgement.* That is to say, on the right of individuals and groups to read the Bible in their own distinctive way, so that it comes "alive" for them in their specific situation. At the same time, such a way of reading the Scriptures cannot be regarded as final or ultimate (2 Peter 1:20–21; 3:16)[35]. It needs the witness of other individuals and other groups of Christians as to how the Bible has come "alive" for them in *their* situation. It is by engaging with others in this way that a particular "tradition" can become whole. *Both* private judgement and the corrective and encouraging rôle of the Church are important in an authentic and mature reading of Scripture.[36]

The whole matter has eccesiological implications as well. It will have become clear by now that particular groups of Christians need other groups of Christians if their understanding of the Christian Faith and of God's will for them is to be whole. That is why it is important to insist on the importance both of the local church and of the world-wide fellowship (or communion) of churches. It is becoming increasingly common now to speak of Christian unity as a unity-in-diversity and to speak of the Universal or Catholic Church as a communion of churches. Such a communion of churches maintains fidelity to the Apostolic Faith while, at the same time, it encourages inculturation and exploration of that Faith. Provided, of course, that such inculturation and exploration remain open to the requirements of complementarity.[37]

What is true of local churches in communion with each other, is also true of individuals within the fellowship (or communion) of the local church. The ways in which a particular believer reads the Bible and appropriates the Christian Tradition have to be balanced by the ways in which other Christians in a particular fellowship do these things. Once again, we are faced with unity-in-diversity or, to be more exact, unity-in-*reconciled*-diversity. The principle of complementarity, when it is applied to the local church, requires that such a church should, as far as possible, consist of a wide range of humanity – young and old, male and female, rich and poor, black and white and so on. It is true, of course, that such heterogeneity is not always possible, particularly in remote situations. Reconciled diversity remains, nevertheless, the ideal for the local church as well as for the world Church. Churches may be more or less homogeneous because of their geographical location or the nature of their society. In Christian terms, however, such homogeneity must always be understood as incidental and cannot be elevated to the status of an ecclesial or missiological principle. The Gospel is about the breaking down of barriers, and this needs to be seen first of all at the local level (Acts 6:1–6; Galatians 2:11–14; 3:27–29; Colossians 3:11).[38]

While the local church cannot aim to be homogeneous, it may be right, in plural situations, to encourage Christians with certain affinities – professional, cultural or linguistic – to meet together for the purpose of mutual encouragement, for the more complete expression of the Christian Faith in their own idiom and for the reaching of those who are not Christians but who share in the common affinity. By definition, however, such groups are not churches, though they are part both of the local church and of the world-wide Church. While it is recognised that in their common life they will seek to render the Gospel into a particular idiom and that in their outreach they will utilise this idiom so that the Gospel "makes sense" to those of their kind, this cannot be at the expense of prophetic witness. It is part of that witness that the Gospel breaks down the barriers between human beings which are the result of corporate and individual sin. Mutual accountability between Christians of different backgrounds within the fellowship of the local church and between local churches within the fellowship of the Universal or Catholic Church is also an element in that transformation of individuals and communities which is brought about by the proclamation and the presence of the Gospel. It is also recognised that when the Gospel is *first* rendered into a particular idiom, a more or less homogeneous group may emerge from the response which is made to the Gospel in a particular situation. This homogeneity must be regarded as provisional and cannot, in any case, be regarded as final. Every group of Christians has to be challenged about the implications of the Gospel for them, and these include the implication that Christians are called to live together in reconciled diversity.

CHAPTER THREE

Restriction, Reformation and Counter-Reformation

The gradual "Christianisation" of Europe and the establishment of the Holy Roman Empire (which, according to Voltaire, was neither holy, nor Roman, nor an empire!) and of various "Christian" kingdoms brought about, in Europe, the emergence of what is often termed Western Christendom. In spiritual terms, the unity of this entity was to be found in a common (though often uneasy) relationship with the Papacy. Internally, there was a great deal of conflict between and within the independent kingdoms and, sometimes, with the Papacy. There was, however, a kind of unity against external enemies. At first, there were the barbarian tribes of one kind or another. But even as they were being subdued and made to submit to the Christianity of their conquerors, Islām arose as a new danger in the South and East. In both its Arab and Turkish forms it was to remain a significant threat to Europe until well into modern times, even though a great deal of the European territory which fell under Islām's sway was eventually recovered, some of it even in mediaeval times (in this respect, Europe's example is paralleled only by India). The identity of Western Christendom was forged, to a large extent, over and against the rival system to the South and the East.

While Islām provided the foil for the emergence of a European identity, it also effectively isolated Europe from contact with a very great part of the world. This was because the Arab navies were dominant throughout the middle ages and also because Muslim powers controlled the overland trade-routes to the further Orient. Apart from the physical obstacles, there were other forces at work. Christianity had become an important element in the emerging consciousness of various European peoples, shaping their identity and their cultural, political and spiritual destiny. This European identity was often seen, and sometimes still is seen, as being essentially opposed to the value systems and expectations of other peoples and cultures. In other words, the very success of inculturation in Europe jeopardised the Gospel's universality and the possibilities of it being commended to other cultures. We have seen how this has happened with other "Christianised" peoples at other times and in other places. Europe was no exception. The Crusades are only one instance of how European contacts with the outside world were to take place largely in an atmosphere of mistrust, suspicion and, often, downright hostility for a very long time.

At the same time, it has to be admitted that there *were* individuals and groups in the mediaeval Western Church who remained concerned about mission. Mention must be made here of St Francis of Assisi and of the several attempts he made to preach to Muslims in Syria, Spain and Morocco. In the end, he was able to preach in the presence of the Sulṭān Al-Malik Al-Kāmil at Damietta. The Sultān was not converted but was very impressed by Francis' sincerity and dedication. The Franciscans became noted for their willingness to cross cultural and political boundaries in order to preach the Gospel. Many were martyred and many more were tortured and abused. It needs to be said, however, that at least on certain occasions these Franciscans invited persecution by insulting leading figures among people of other faiths. Whatever individuals may have done in particular cases, the order itself had quite a sophisticated theology of mission. Preaching meant presenting Christ positively, and this was meant to result in Baptism. Martyrdom was not the aim of the missionary's life, but risks had to be taken if the Word of God was to be proclaimed. There were two "modes of presence" – first, the witness of life which did not entail verbal proclamation, and, secondly, preaching. The latter was meant to await "discernment" about the rightness of the occasion. It could be intermittent, varying in nature according to situations and people. From actual accounts of Franciscan missionary work in this very early period, it becomes clear that sometimes there was a large gap between theory and practice.

The Dominicans, an order created specifically for preaching, were also active in sending missionaries to the Muslim world. These missionaries too suffered great hardships and persecution. Among them was Raymond Martin (1230-1284). He became a well-known scholar of Islām, showing familiarity with the work of Muslim theologians such as Al-Ghazzālī and refuting the work of certain so-called Islamic philosphers who were, at that time, becoming popular in Western Europe (it is now known that these philosophers were regarded as heterodox by many Muslims).

Perhaps the most well-known figure from this period is the Spanish layman, Raymond (or Ramón) Lull (1233-1315). He had a dramatic conversion at the age of thirty, having seen a vision of Christ crucified. He was convinced that he had been called to mission among Muslims (it is worth noting that the part of Spain from which he came had only recently been recovered by the Christians after three centuries of Muslim rule). The rest of his life was spent in making personal preparation for the fulfilment of his vocation, in trying to convince the Western Church generally of the vital need for peaceful mission to Islām, and in carrying out his own missionary work in Tunis, Cyprus and Algeria. He was attacked, arrested and expelled many times. His last preaching tour took him to Sicily and Tunis, and on this occasion too he was beaten and expelled. He later succumbed to the injuries which he had sustained during this last mission.

Mention must be made here of John Wycliffe (1320-1384), the Oxford theologian and reformer. Wycliffe refused to limit God's saving power to the ministrations of the Church. He claimed that it was possible for people to respond to Christ outside the visible Church. He believed that Muslims and others would be vouchsafed a vision of Christ at the point of death. Their subsequent fate would be determined by their response to this vision. He advocated a return to evangelical poverty for the leaders of the Church. This would prepare the Church for Mission and make it more credible in the eyes of those who were not Christians.[1]

Despite these instances, the Western Church in the late middle ages cannot be called a missionary church, though some parts of it *were* mission-minded. It was the opening of the sea-routes both to the East and to the further West early in the sixteenth century which gave a new impetus to Mission. The Pope, in successive bulls, had divided the newly reached lands between the Spanish and the Portugese. Along with ecclesiastical sanction for colonisation went the mandate for missionary work in the colonised lands. This came to be known as the *Padroado*. In brief, it meant that the Spanish and Portugese colonial authorities were responsible not only for the pastoral care of settlers in these lands but also for the evangelisation of the indigenous populations. The *Padroado* was the chief means for Roman Catholic missions until it was replaced by the Roman congregation, *De Propaganda Fide* (which is now known as the Sacred Congregation for the Evangelisation of the Nations or of the Propagation of the Faith).

The Counter-Reformation gave rise to new religious orders such as the Jesuits, who pledged complete obedience to the Pope and were not beholden to other powers, whether ecclesiastical or civil. From the beginning the Jesuits were active not only in the recovery of Protestant "heretics" and "schismatics" but in missionary work in colonised lands and even beyond (in Mughul India and in Japan, for example). From the beginning there were tensions, sometimes to the point of conflict, between the *Padroado* and one or more of the orders. There was rivalry too between the different orders. Sometimes this conflict and rivalry were clearly to the detriment of Mission. Such was the case with the city of Thatta on the Indus. The Carmelites had established a presence there in the seventeenth century, but the Augustinians arrived a few years later armed with *Padroado* authority, and tried to dislodge the Carmelites from Thatta. The result was that each order tried to obstruct the work of the other and, eventually, the missions of both orders failed.[2]

Stephen Neill has said that the principal obstacle to the evangelisation of the indigenous people of the Americas was the cruelty with which they were treated by the colonists.[3] Joachim Kahl, in his passionate denunciation of the Christian Church in his book *The Misery of Christianity,* enumerates the cruelties the Indians had to suffer at the hands of the Christians.[4] Yet it was often members of religious orders who had the courage to resist the civil and ecclesiastical authorities and to champion the cause of the Indians.[5] Therefore rivalry between the *Padroado* and the orders or between the orders themselves sometimes allowed a prophetic ministry to take place.

With all its defects, and they were many, the period of the Counter-Reformation has to be viewed as a time of great vitality where Roman Catholic missionary work is concerned. Nearly every Portugese and Spanish expedition carried its own clergy. New churches were established in many different parts of the globe. The religious orders, in particular, were exploring at the very frontiers of the then known world and were quite often adding to the sum total of human knowledge through the discoveries they were making and through bringing different peoples into contact with one another. The West was also encountering Christians belonging to traditions wholly unknown to it, though it cannot be said that these Christians were treated with the respect and sensitivity they deserved. In some cases there were bold experiments in the inculturation of the Liturgy, and the Bible was being translated or retranslated into a host of languages.

The Reformation was clearly a series of the most dramatic events that Europe had witnessed for generations, perhaps even for centuries. A great deal was accomplished on both sides of the divide because of it. Corruption was challenged and, in many cases, eliminated. The Bible was restored to its rightful place in the Church and serious study of it was revived on all sides. The Liturgy was purged of superstitious accretions and revised in accordance with the needs of the time and what was then known of the practice of the Primitive Church. There was renewed emphasis on prayer and the Christian life.

It is all the more sad, therefore, to have to record that the Reformation and the Reformed churches seem to have had little awareness of the need for World Mission. Indeed, this was an accusation often made against Protestants by the polemicists of the Counter-Reformation. They could "pervert" Christians but they could not convert Jews, Turks or pagans to the Faith.[6] The charge was all the more telling because it was made in the sixteenth century, a time when Europe had burst its bonds and when European political, economic and cultural interests were in the ascendancy all over the world. Moreover, the *Padroado* and the Counter-Reformation were vigorously, if not always wisely, engaged in missionary enterprise. Why were the churches of the Reformation silent on this matter? The reasons which are given for this extraordinary phenomenon may be divided into three main categories: geographical, political and theological.

It is often said that the countries and churches involved in the Reformation had no *access* to the newly reached lands, as the sea-routes were controlled by Spain and Portugal, both Roman Catholic powers.[7] It is also said that until the Peace of Westphalia in 1648 the Protestants were literally fighting for their survival. There could be no thought of Mission until this was secured. The dissensions and quarrelling among the Protestants also sapped their strength and left little energy for missionary activity. Historically all this is unanswerable, and yet Warneck points out that "no lament was raised over the practical impossibility of discharging the missionary obligation, which was brought so near by the opening of the world". He comes to the depressing conclusion that "this strange silence can be accounted for satisfactorily only by the fact that the recognition of the missionary obligation was itself absent". "We miss in the Reformers," he goes on to say, "not only missionary action, but even the idea of missions. . ."[8]

In their doctrine of the Church, the churches of the Reformation generally emphasised the pole of locality over and against the pole of catholicity. Locality, furthermore, was usually identified with a region, a ruler and a specific people. *Cuius regio, eius religio* had the effect of producing national churches which were closely identified with the apparatus of the State which, in turn, was seen as their protector. Neill remarks rightly that it was hardly possible for such churches to become missionary in the real sense of the term.[9] They were limited not only to geographical boundaries but often to specific ethnicity and to the limited vision of local rulers. "Translatability" of a sort had been achieved, but only at the cost of sacrificing universality.

The theological underpinning for this abandonment of responsibility for the world was provided by a curious kind of dispensationalism which limited World Mission to the times of the apostles! The apostles had proclaimed the offer of salvation to all the nations, it was held, and there was no need to make a second offer to those who had refused the first![10] Closely allied to this view was the doctrine, taught by Calvin among others, that the Kingdom of God could not be advanced by human industry but was the work of God alone. Even those who believed that God used means in the exercise of his sovereign will believed that the absence of means for a particular people and their presence for another was a sign of that sovereign will, to which Christians must submit. It was not until much later that the view which regarded Mission as one of the means used by God came into prominence. It is not too much of a caricature to say that at the time of Reformation it was widely believed that if God wanted the heathen to be saved, *he* would provide the means for their salvation. There was little reflection on the vocation of churches and individuals to bring this about.[11] It was not until well into the eighteenth century that such views began to be challenged in a systematic way. However, there were a few figures, such as the Dutchman Adrianus Saravia, who did not accept the usual Protestant view of Mission. Saravia, who was a refugee in England, eventually became Dean of Westminster in 1613. He argued that the missionary mandate found in the Great Commission must be for every generation because it was accompanied by our Lord's promise that he would be with the Church until the close of the age (Matthew 28:19-20). This promise had never been understood to mean that he would be with the apostles only. In the same way, the command, to which the promise was attached, could not be understood as being limited to the apostolic band. Saravia went on to point out that the apostles themselves chose fellow-workers and successors to continue their work and that, as a matter of fact, the Church's missionary work had continued down the ages as more and more people had been challenged by the Gospel and had responded to it. For holding these views, Saravia was strongly attacked on the continent of Europe by both Reformed and Lutheran theologians.[12] It is quite astonishing for us in the twentieth century to see quite how much energy was expended in arguing *against* Mission. As we have noted earlier, the situation did not change materially until the Dutch and the British acquired access to the new sea-routes. Sustained exposure to different sorts of people who had never encountered the Gospel made a theological re-evaluation of Mission more and more necessary for the churches of the Reformation. That, however, is a different and later story.

So far in this book, we have had occasion to comment on the Mission-history of the ancient, non-Chalcedonian churches and we have also begun our consideration of the Mission-history of Western Christianity. There is however, a large family of churches which we have scarcely touched upon – that is, the Eastern or Chalcedonian Orthodox churches. Their Mission-history is very long and impressive. These churches, whose heartlands have been, at various times, in Asia Minor, the Middle East and Eastern Europe, have an honourable history of missionary involvement in Central and Eastern Asia and, more recently, in Sub-Saharan Africa.[13] Once again, as with the Oriental Orthodox, we see that Mission is closely related to the life and witness of monastic communities and, indeed, of individual monks. At the same time, one has to acknowledge the fact that sometimes Orthodox lay people have been very effective agents of mission.[14]

In theory, at any rate, Orthodoxy is commtitted to inculturation, and in the past the translation of the Bible and of the Liturgy into the vernacular has made a profound contribution to the penetration of the Church into a number of very different cultures. There is also a healthy emphasis on the importance of the local church, but this is balanced by Orthodox teaching on the necessity of maintaining communion between local churches. In practice, however, in some cases the experiment in inculturation has been allowed to petrify, so that the Bible and the Liturgy are not in the modern vernacular but in an older form which is not so easily understood by the people. There are signs, however, of renewal in this area, and both the Bible and the Liturgy are beginning to be heard in fresh and challenging ways.

The emphasis in Orthodoxy on the translation of the Gospel into the idiom of each culture has sometimes led to the emergence of a "communal" kind of Christianity in which local or national cultures have become closely identified with the Faith. As we have seen, this can lead to an experience of alienation from the Gospel for *other* cultures, and also to a stultification of Christianity in cultures where it has acquired this communal character. In this context, we need to note Orthodoxy's insistence that the process of inculturation needs to be guided throughout by specifically Gospel values and that the ultimate aim is not merely identification with the culture but the transformation of it. Presumably this transformation is partly, at least, for the sake of Mission.[15]

CHAPTER FOUR

"Non Angeli, sed Anglicani" [1]

If the Reformation churches were not interested in World Mission, how is it that the kinds of Christian tradition which received their definition at the time of the Reformation eventually became world-wide families of churches?

The answer lies in a mixture of commercial, political and theological developments which took place in the seventeenth and eighteenth centuries. The accession of the Dutch and British, often in rivalry with each other, to sea power is obviously an important factor in the gradual spread of the churches of the Reformation throughout the world. We have to note, however, that these churches were primarily "expatriate" in character and that their members regarded the evangelisation of the indigenous populations as, at best, a secondary activity. Ministers and missionaries, moreover, were often civil servants on the payroll of the secular power and could not, even if they wanted to, be independent of the wishes of the trading companies and the colonial powers. In this respect, there is a similarity between the *Padroado* and the arrangements for spiritual work made by the Dutch and the British. It is not surprising, therefore, to observe in this context that the exercise of Mission was extremely superficial and that the quality of converts was not high.[2]

The churches of the Reformation were, on the whole, churches in which the Bible was eagerly and avidly read and where it was easily available in the venacular. It was inevitable, therefore, that sooner or later the Bible would challenge the torpor regarding Mission which had been induced in these churches by a false doctrine of dispensationalism and by an over-identification with the specifics of state interests or of ethnicity.

Change, however, came about slowly, and although there *were* instances of the Bible being translated into particular languages and of apologies for the Christian Faith being written in the seventeenth century, basically a theology of Mission did not begin to be developed until the eighteenth century. In that century it began to be held that while God was sovereign in his election, he used means of grace to bring about the salvation of the elect. Bebbington points out that the word "means" became the key term in the promotion of the view that God uses human beings in the fulfilment of his purpose.[3] It was this doctrine of "means" which allowed people like Jonathan Edwards to remain basically Calvinistic in their orientation and yet to develop an interest in Mission to those who had not already been reached by the Gospel. The Baptist, William Carey, not only argued that it was obligatory for Christians to use means for the conversion of unbelievers but demonstrated his commitment to this view by personally pioneering Mission work in India. It was now held that the Great Commission found in Matthew chapter 28 was binding on Christians of all ages and could not be restricted to the time and the work of the apostolic band. "Mission", Bebbington says "was now held to be essential to Christianity".[4] Adrianus Saravia had at last been vindicated.

The *Ecclesia Anglicana,* which almost from the beginning has not been just the Church of England, acquired many of its present characteristics from the time of the Reformation, although it has also retained some of the characteristics of the mediaeval church. It is true to say, therefore, that it is a church of the Reformation, albeit with a certain continuity with the pre-Reformation church. Despite the fact the Saravia was an Anglican (eventually becoming Dean of Westminster) and expressly related his work on Mission to an Anglican understanding of episcopacy, Anglicanism exhibited the same lack of interest in Mission as the other churches of the Reformation.[5] Neill records the sobering fact that in the seventeenth century only one Indian was baptised according to the rites of the Anglican Church.[6] This was despite the fact that there was a British Ambassador at the Mughal court from early in the seventeenth century and there were chaplains attached to the East India Company from that time onwards.

Both the Society for the Promotion of Christian Knowledge (SPCK, founded 1698) and the Society for the Propagation of the Gospel (now USPG, founded 1701) had among their aims the pastoral care of settlers in colonised lands *as well as* the evangelisation and teaching of non-Christian people in those lands. In the early years both societies were very ecumenically minded. For example, they cooperated with the

Lutherans in such matters as the translation of the Bible and the provision of pastoral care for settlers, troops and indigenous converts. Neill remarks, in this connection, that Anglicans in India, of all kinds of churchmanship, found no difficulty in accepting, for over one hundred years, the pastoral and even sacramental ministry of German and Danish missionaries who had not received episcopal ordination.[7]

It remains true, however, that the spread of Anglicanism throughout the seventeenth century, and through much of the eighteenth, was predominantly *coincidental.* That is to say, it coincided with the spread of English-speaking people throughout the world. These people, naturally, took their church with them and usually took great care to see that it resembled the church at home as much as possible. All over the world one finds Anglican churches founded by these early settlers, and it is obvious that they took great pride in belonging to the English Church and in establishing its worship and doctrine in the colonies.[8]

The eighteenth century in Britain was a time of great turmoil for Christianity. But it was also a time for exciting new beginnings. The preaching of both Wesley and Whitefield had warmed the hearts of many and, more importantly perhaps, had raised questions about personal faith, the experience of salvation and the necessity of assurance. Evangelicalism was "in the air" and many in the Church of England were deeply influenced by it. It is true that some took a passive attitude to political involvement, limiting it to respect for authority and the payment of taxes. There was, however, another aspect of the matter, which is symbolised by the close relationship between the conversion of John Newton and his conviction that slavery was morally indefensible. Along with spiritual awareness there was a commitment to social change. Newton helped Wilberforce in the latter's campaign against the slave trade. The campaign for the abolition of slavery itself was carried forward by members of the Clapham sect. This informal group of influential Evangelical Anglicans was also responsible for many efforts to improve the condition of the poor both in the United Kingdom and overseas.

In the nineteenth century the witness of the Clapham sect continued and was strengthened by the campaigns of the seventh Earl of Shaftesbury. Shaftesbury campaigned tirelessley for the amelioration of the conditions for workers in factories. He secured legislation to limit the hours of work which could be required of them. He was also instrumental in securing the restriction on the employment of women and children in mines and collieries. He pioneered attempts at bringing education to the working classes and was closely involved with the Young Men's Christian Association. It may be worth noting at this point that both Wilberforce and Shaftesbury supported the emancipation of Roman Catholics. In this they stood within an Evangelical tradition which advocated the extension of civil liberties, particularly the freedom of religion.[9]

It will be obvious to the reader that many of the concerns of those who belonged to the Clapham sect and, later on, of Shaftesbury, were profoundly related to issues of mission. The concern for *World Mission,* which was undoubtedly central to Evangelical thinking from the end of the eighteenth century, arose then out of a nexus of views and commitments which sought to understand the claims of the Gospel on the individual and on society in a holistic way. The formation of the Church Missionary Society in 1799 can be said to herald a new era in the world-wide expansion of Anglicanism. If colonial expansion was largely *coincidental,* this new king of expansion may well be termed *Evangelical.* This is not to deny that there were evangelical aspects to the colonial expansion, nor can it be denied that there were "colonial" aspects to this new kind of expansion. The CMS has often been described as "the first effective organ" of the Anglican Church where World Mission is concerned. Many other bodies, some of them older than the CMS, have emulated it.

Previously, agencies to promote the mission of the Anglican Church had been established with ecclesiastical approval and with the sanction of a Royal Charter. Evangelical activity, however, whether evangelistic or social, was based on the principle of voluntary association. The CMS too, while seeking the goodwill of Church authorities, saw itself as an independent organisation which could take initiatives in mission without waiting for opinion to change in the Church's hierarchy.

Since the founding of the CMS the emphasis on independence has been gradually replaced by a recognition of interdependence and of the need for partnership with churches, at least some of which owe their existence to CMS-supported mission. At a time, however, when churches everywhere are tempted to produce structures and models of leadership which reflect the values of the world around them, whether these values are tribal, feudal or entrepreneurial, it is all the more important to reaffirm the abiding validity of the voluntary principle.[10] It is the vocation of Church leaders and of mission agencies to encourage and to enable individuals and groups of Christians to exercise their apostolate in appropriate ways. The official structures of the Church – congregational, diocesan or other – do not have a monopoly on mission. Indeed, in certain situations, new forms of Christian expression come to the fore *precisely* when traditional structures are under threat. This is clearly the case in Latin America, where the strains caused in the Roman Catholic Church by the paucity of priests has led to the rapid growth of basic communities. These have come about as a result of lay initiative and are usually led by lay people. They lead the community in worship (even quasi-sacramental worship), in Bible study, in evangelism and in social concern.

No amount of reiteration that the "basic" structures of the Church are the parish or the diocese can obscure the fact that it is these new forms of Christian expression which are at the cutting edge of mission.[11] The voluntary principle is also useful in situations where there are political, economic or ideological restrictions on the work of the Church. Groups of Christians can, in such circumstances, take bold initiatives, even risks, which the institutional Church cannot be expected to take. In many local situations, Christian commitment is made credible by the organised involvement of groups of Christians in addressing matters which are of concern to the local community. It is the task of the institutional church not only to encourage and to support such involvement but also to become involved itself, in a serving role, if it is appropriate for it to do so.[12]

If there is to be another truly exponential growth in all aspects of Christian Mission, it is vital that the voluntary principle be encouraged in all parts of the Church, and that the leadership of the Church should see the rooting of mission in Christian communities, at all levels, as one of their primary duties.

It has often been said that Anglicanism, because of its formation at the time of the Reformation, is instinctively establishmentarian and has a tendency to support the existing order.[13] It is certainly true that the members of the Clapham sect belonged largely to the ruling classes and that their campaigns were designed not so much to create an awareness of their condition among the poor and so to bring about change, as to address those with political and economic power in the land. It is correct, therefore, to say that in most cases their approach to social problems was conservative and ameliorative rather than radical and revolutionary, though there *were* some areas where they approached radicalism.[14]

Paradoxically, it was Anglicanism's attachment to the doctrine of the divine right of kings which led to a significant movement of dissent within it. To be sure, there had been dissent before, such as the attempts of the Puritans in the sixteenth and seventeenth centuries to reform the Church of England according to their Calvinistic programmes. This was a remarkable and sustained movement, but it seems not to have emphasised the universality of the Church and, Richard Baxter apart, seems not to have been interested in World Mission.[15] The Non-Jurors were those members of the Church of England who refused to take William and Mary's oaths of allegiance and supremacy on the grounds that this would break their previous oath to James II and his successors. The bishops and the clergy among them were deprived of their sees and their livings by an act of Parliament without there having been canonical proceedings against them. They organised themselves into worshipping communities, though some continued to worship in their parish churches. The bishops ensured proper ministerial succession, and there was a great deal of discussion about the Liturgy. The latter resulted in a eucharistic rite which relied heavily on what was then known of primitive Christian worship and also on the more "Catholic" 1549 Book of Common Prayer. The Non-Jurors negotiated for union with the Eastern Orthodox Churches, and Eastern influence is discernible in their worship. The liturgical tradition of the Non-Jurors, with its emphasis on "primitivity" and "catholicity", was inherited by the Scottish Episcopal Church and survives both in the 1764 Prayer Book and in the 1982 Scottish Liturgy.[16] It is well known, of course, that the Scottish tradition itself was hugely influential in the formation of a particular kind of Anglican liturgical pattern which survives to this day in many parts of the Anglican Communion.[17]

Their loyalty to James II made it necessary for the Non-Jurors to challenge the established order in England as it came to be after the so-called Glorious Revolution. Their negotiations with the Eastern Churches show their awareness of the need for a world-wide communion of churches, and their revisions of the Liturgy in the light of primitive practice show their awareness of the need for a "catholicity" which extended not only through space but also through time. All of this led to a "high" doctrine of the Church, in which the Church was viewed as an autonomous, spiritual society with its own distinctive laws. The Church, while it owed obedience to the State, could not be expected to obey every whim or fancy of those in power, especially if these were contrary to the Church's laws. The foundations for dissent in Anglicanism had been laid on the bedrock of the establishment, the divine right of kings.

In the aetiology of the Oxford Movement, John Keble's assize sermon on National Apostasy, preached on 14th July 1833, is of crucial importance. It is generally regarded as the foundation event of the Catholic revival in Anglicanism. The issue was the suppression of ten Irish bishoprics, and the main point was not so much *whether* the bishoprics ought to be suppressed, but *who* had the right to suppress them. Fidelity to a high doctrine of divine revelation and a high doctrine of the Church led inevitably to conflict with the State on matters having to do with the State's pretensions about *spiritual* authority over the Church. It is true that some Catholic Anglicans, under the influence of F. D. Maurice, returned to somewhat Erastian tendencies. At the same time, however, another tradition developed the view that the proper relationship between Church and State could only exist where there was "a free Church in a free state". In the view of men like J. N. Figgis (1866-1919), society was an aggregate of voluntary associations and power was delegated to the State, as a unifying structure, to balance the claims and order the relations of those associations. While the State had a limiting function in society, it could not claim too much for itself and could not interfere with the autonomy of the associations. Not only was the Church one such institution, it was also an institution of divine origin and had to be especially vigilant so that it did not compromise the divine revelation of which it was a vessel and vehicle.[18]

It is interesting, in this connection, to compare the emerging awareness among Catholic Anglicans that the Church was a voluntary organisation with the growing realisation among Evangelical Anglicans, a generation or so earlier, that voluntary organisations could be constituent and loyal parts of the Church. What has been said of the Church *vis-à-vis* the State can also be said of the *ecclesiolae in ecclesia*, the basic communities, the mission societies and the development organisations, *vis-à-vis* the Church.

Catholic Anglicans were naturally committed to the "catholicity" of the Church. This emphasis not only covertly challenged the Reformation doctrine of *cuius regio, eius religio* and its usual corollary, the (merely) National Church, it also provided an impetus for the missionary movement. Catholicity was interpreted not simply in terms of the universal character of the existing Church but also as a vocation to make the Gospel known to all men and women. In other words, as well as an "already" aspect to Catholicity, there was also a "not yet" aspect. The Church was actually Catholic because it was a fellowship of Christians throughout the world, but it was potentially Catholic in that it sought to be more and more inclusive of men and women throughout the world.

To what we have called the *coincidental* and the *Evangelical* expansion of Anglicanism, we have now to add the *Catholic.* The Society for the Propagation of the Gospel preceded the Catholic revival but, along with the Universities Mission to Central Africa, it became, and remains, an important agency for the missionary work of the Church. Bishop John Davies, writing to mark the one hundred and fiftieth anniversary of the Oxford Movement, has this to say about the missionary aspect of Catholic Anglicanism: "The Catholic Movement found itself challenging and crossing boundaries, both of social order and of geographical demarcation. It became a movement concerned with social responsibility, and it shared powerfully in the total European venture of international church extension."[19] The Oxford Movement was born as a movement of protest. This protest was based on the recognition that the Church was a divinely founded and ordered society and that its first loyalty was to God. The Church's relations with the State, whatever their character, could not be allowed to obscure this fundamental truth.

The prophetic element in the Catholic revival, however, went far beyond questions of ecclesiastical polity. It led to a commitment to those who were disadvantaged in society and who had been neglected by the Church. It is no accident that many of the great men and women of the Catholic tradition in the Church of England are known for their ministry in poor urban areas. Many of the religious communities too, when they were revived, were located in areas of acute need. These communities have established a great tradition of commitment to the educational, medical and social needs of the poor. It is true that some were content to ameliorate the lot of the poor without challenging the basic structures of society which caused poverty. On the other hand, there were some who bore a prophetic witness in this respect too. On occasion they may have been naive and ill-informed, but their commitment was never in doubt. They played a significant rôle in the education of public opinion regarding the plight of the poor and in securing legal and social protection for them. They tended to be libertarian in their thinking, and this led them to a rejection not only of Erastianism in Church-State relations but also of hierarchical authoritarianism in the Church.[20]

It is sad to have to note that the prophetic element of Catholic Anglicanism is not greatly to the fore in contemporary Britain. Catholics seem to have withdrawn from sharp, and sometimes uncomfortable, encounter with a needy and sinful world into the cosiness of exaggerated concern with ecclesiatical polity, and sometimes politics. There is also perhaps too much investment of energy in matters of ritual and ceremonial concern. This is not a matter for discussion here, but the debate over the ordination of women to the priesthood and episcopate has also divided and weakened the Catholic movement in the United Kingdom and elsewhere. All is not darkness, however; religious communities of both men and women continue to be involved in addressing contemporary social issues. The Community of All Saints, for example, have remained faithful to their vocation and continue their apostolate of service and care for the elderly, the terminally ill (particularly children) and the homeless.[21] The Community of the Glorious Ascension continues with its vocation of encouraging the religious life in specifically secular contexts, especially in relation to the employment of its members. The Franciscans are active in evangelistic work in academic settings as well as in the inner-city. Lay and clerical Anglicans have sought to continue the radical tradition which arose out of the Catholic Movement in associations such as the Jubilee Group.

On the whole, however, the radical initiative has passed from Anglicans in the United Kingdom to Anglicans elsewhere. The missionary movement born of the Catholic Revival tried to establish churches which were entirely in accord with Catholic principles and practice. In the mission areas, the Catholics did not have to compromise with the largely unsympathetic leadership of a State Church. Catholicism, in such a context, was allowed to flower in its wholeness. The absence of conflict with the State and over matters of churchmanship, moreover, released the energies of Catholic Anglicans to fight for a just society and on behalf of the oppressed.[22] The prophetic rôle of the Church of the Province of

Southern Africa, symbolised in the person of Archbishop Desmond Tutu, is a direct result of the formation of that church according to Catholic principles which have their origins in the Tractarian revival. In the context of increasing reflection throughout the Anglican Communion on issues such as interdependence and partnership in mission, it is entirely right to expect that churches such as the CPSA, and their leaders, will be able to bring their witness of radical commitment to the Gospel and its values to the United Kingdom.

Recently, the centenary of that influential collection of essays in Anglican theology, *Lux Mundi,* has been celebrated. The work was subtitled "A Series of Studies in the Religion of the Incarnation" and was to determine the "incarnationalist" approach of much Anglican theology in the years that followed. This approach has enabled Anglicanism to develop a very strong commitment to a pastoral presence which is deeply rooted in the community it seeks to serve. It has also bread a dislike of "hit and run" efforts in mission, and there has been a tendency to think that the right to mission has to be bought in terms of a presence that is strongly committed to the context. Anglican incarnationalism has, however, been attacked on the grounds that it has a tendency to endorse the *status quo* and that it produces a Church which is content to be "influential" and "ameliorative" in its commitment rather than radical and revolutionary.[23]

We need to remember that Bishop Charles Gore, the editor of *Lux Mundi,* came to be closely associated with the development of a kenotic Christology in the later part of the nineteenth century. The origins of this doctrine can be traced to the Reformation, when some began to speak of Christ's "two states"; the state of humiliation and the state of exaltation. The main texts on which this doctrine was based were Philippians 2:5-11 and 2 Corinthians 8:9. The latter speaks of the "richness" of the pre-existent Christ which was given up for our sake at the Incarnation. The former speaks of his exaltation with God before the Incarnation, his "humiliation" at the Incarnation and his exaltation because of his obedience which led to the Cross. In other words, Christ's obedient "self-emptying" did not lead to an easy identification with the *status quo* of the society in which he was incarnate. Rather, it led to rejection by that society at every stage of his witness and ministry. Finally, it led to crucifixion. God's way of reconciliation, which he sets forth in

Christ, is, therefore, a very costly way. Costly for God in terms of vulnerability and rejection, but costly also for human beings, as it calls them to follow Christ in obedience and discipleship, even if this may lead to rejection and suffering.

It is true that kenotic Christology emerged to the fore in the nineteenth century largely as a response to the critical study of the Gospels, which tended to show that Jesus was truly a man of his times and that even though he could challenge many of the beliefs and practices of his contemporaries, he also shared with them a common view of the world and of human existence. Indeed, this had to be so if there was to be a common area of discourse between Jesus and his contemporaries which would make it possible for them to understand his proclamation. The New Testament itself portrays Jesus as being ignorant of some matters, such as the final consummation (e.g. Mark 13:32), and as being thoroughly rooted in the idiom of first-century Palestine. It also portrays him, it needs to be said, as *transcending* and *challenging* that culture and that idiom.

It is extremely important to understand these concerns of those who developed kenotic Christologies. From our point of view, however, it is perhaps more important to notice the insistence on *costly* identification and on the willingness to suffer humiliation and rejection. It is this which saves incarnationalism from being simply an endorsement of the *status quo* and creates the conditions which make it possible for it to be the means of prophetic witness and human transformation.

Kenotic Christology has led, quite understandably, to kenotic missiology. It has been felt that mere presence is not enough and that there must be first a thorough examination of one's cultural assumptions and then an identification with the context in which mission is to be exercised. There must also be a preparedness to suffer opposition and rejection for the sake of the Gospel and its values, which Christians preach and by which they should live. At the same time, it should be clear that we are *called* to suffer for the sake of the Gospel. If we suffer because of our political, economic or social prejudices, that cannot be the evangelical suffering to which Christians are called. This imposes a serious obligation on Christians to determine through study, prayer and reflection whether the particular opinion, attitude or action which they are inclined to adopt is truly evangelical or not.

Cranmer's Books of Common Prayer, as well as the 1662 BCP, follow the Western liturgical tradition in having a strong doctrine of the Cross. Anglicanism needs to recover that doctrine if it is to be an agent of reconciliation which is not manipulative but is based on a profound recognition of human sin, of the need for repentance, both individual and corporate, and of the costliness of discipleship in a fallen world. Jesus said, "If anyone wishes to be a follower of mine, he must renounce himself, take up his cross and follow me" (Matthew 16:24).

One other aspect of Anglican involvement in World Mission needs to be mentioned. From the beginning of the nineteenth century the Anglican Church has sent, from time to time, "missions of help" to several of the ancient oriental churches. These missions were often sent in response to requests from particular churches for assistance, and many took place at critical times for those churches. The intention of these missions was emphatically not to proselytise but to assist in the strengthening and the renewal of the local church. The earliest of these was the CMS' mission of help to the Indian Syrian Church of Malabar (1816). The early missionaries were very discreet and earned the respect of the church's bishops. They made it clear that they did not want a new denomination to come into being; rather, they wanted to see the renewal of the Indian Church. To this end they established themselves at the newly founded seminary in Kottayam and devoted themselves to the training of the clergy. They were also active in the translation and production of the Bible in the local vernacular. Later on, however, other missionaries were not so discreet and patient, and this led to friction between the missionaries and the church leadership. Eventually the mission was terminated, though not without much bitterness on both sides. A small number of the Indian Syrians left with the Anglicans, who continued their work among non-Christians. Ultimately the Anglican diocese of Travancore and Cochin was formed as a result of their labours.

There were, however, many in the Indian Church who wanted it to be reformed and renewed and who wished to stay in it. They secured the consecration of a new metropolitan from the Jacobite Patriarch at Antioch and attempted a reformation in the church. The result, sadly, was another split, and the Mar Thoma Syrian Church emerged as a reformed episcopal church of oriental origin. Another wing of the Indian Church continued with its allegiance to the Patriarch at Antioch. The Mar Thoma Church is today in full communion with the Anglican

Communion and with the Churches of North India, South India, Pakistan and Bangladesh (churches in which Anglicans have united with Christians of other traditions). There is even talk of organic union between the Mar Thoma, the Church of North India and the Church of South India, so that a united, episcopal Church of India, rooted in the ancient oriental Christian tradition, can come into being.

It is worth noting, perhaps, that influence has not been just in one direction – that is, from the Anglican Church to the Mar Thoma Church. It is true that Abraham Malpan and other early leaders of the Mar Thoma were deeply influenced by Anglican theology and liturgy and sought to make reforms, in their own theological and liturgical tradition, which were inspired by Anglican ideas.[24] At the same time, Anglicanism in India came to be deeply influenced by the oriental tradition. As early as the 1920s an Anglican liturgy was produced for the diocese of Bombay which exhibited certain oriental features. This liturgy was very influential in the production of the later *Liturgy for India* contained in the Prayer Book of the Church of India, Pakistan, Burma and Ceylon. It was also an influence on the *Ceylon Liturgy,* still in use in Sri Lanka. The CIPBC Prayer Book also restores the *Maranatha* to the Anglican rite and allows the use of the *Mangalasutra* (a kind of garland) in place of, or in addition to, the traditional ring at weddings.

The *Book of Common Worship* of the Church of South India has been, perhaps, the single most influential document on recent liturgical revision throughout the Anglican Communion. It may be worth noting, therefore, that the BCW, and other liturgies of united churches, display many oriental features. The *Trisagion* has been introduced, as well as an *epiclesis* in the Eastern form. The old Syrian response, "your death we commemorate..." was introduced by the CSI and is now common all over the world. The litany form of intercessions was adopted by Anglicans in India from the oriental tradition. It was retained by the CSI and is now almost universal in the Anglican Communion. Anglicans in India (and now those in the united churches) have also adopted certain postures and other practices relating to worship from the orientals. It is common, for example, for the ministers (and sometimes the people as well) to remove their shoes during the Eucharist. Attitudes of reverence such as prostration and kissing the Holy Table and the Bible are common. The Peace can take the form of a traditional *"namaste"* greeting. Incense and flowers are offered in the Indian way. Many of these features are, of course, common to all Indian religious devotion, Christian as well as non-Christian, but there are specific Christian adaptations which may be discerned. Many of these have been learned by churches of Western origin from the ancient oriental Christians.[25]

In 1842 the Church of England dispatched the Revd George Percy Badger on an investigative mission to the Assyrian (or Nestorian) Church of the East. Badger became a great friend of the Assyrians and assured them of the Church of England's desire to see the Assyrian Church restored to a flourishing condition. A year later the Society for the Propagation of the Gospel withdrew its support of the mission for financial reasons, preferring to concentrate on missions to colonial territories.

In 1868 the Assyrian Church requested the Archbishop of Canterbury for assistance with primary and secondary schools and also with theological education. Thus the Archbishop of Canterbury's Mission to the Assyrians was born in 1885. For many years this mission, which consisted mainly of clergy and the Sisters of Bethany, laboured among the Assyrians, running scores of schools and a seminary for young men. The missionaries brought about a renewal in the study of Syriac (the theological and liturgical language of the Assyrian Church) and made numerous discoveries of valuable theological and liturgical documents.

The Assyrian Church has faced many vicissitudes in its long history, not least in the twentieth century. In addition to persecution, it has also had to contend with the proselytising activities of both Roman Catholic and Protestant missions. In such a context, the Anglican mission may be commended for eschewing proselytism and working for the renewal of this ancient church.[26]

Because of the situation in South India, Anglican relations with the Syrian Orthodox Church (or the Jacobites) were more strained. Canterbury explicitly supported the claim to autonomy of the reformist party in the Indian Church and advocated the emergence of a relationship between Antioch and the Indians which was similar to the relationship between Canterbury and the bishops of the Anglican Communion who were outside England. Naturally, the Patriarch who still claimed jurisdiction over the Indian Church did not take kindly to this suggestion. A mission of help was, nevertheless, organised to help the Syrian Church establish its own school in Turkey. This mission became a model for

Anglican cooperation with oriental churches.[27]

In Ethiopia too, the Anglican Church has not made any attempt to proselytise among the members of the Orthodox Tewahedo ("One Nature") Church, even though many of the missionaries have been from Evangelical Anglican societies such as the Bible Churchmen's Missionary Society (BCMS) and the Church's Ministry Among the Jews (CMJ). Converts from the Jewish community (the Falashas) and from the animists have been baptised into the Orthodox Church. Since the Revolution the missionaries have had to leave, and the sole Anglican presence now is the chaplaincy at Addis Ababa, which continues to provide assistance to the Orthodox Church. Its pastoral work is focussed on a largely African, expatriate congregation, though it should be noted that the chaplains are mostly European![28]

More recently, considerable numbers of Anglicans have arrived in Ethiopia as refugees from the Sudan. Arrangements for their care are being worked out with the assistance of CMS, between the Episcopal Church in the Sudan and the Anglican diocese of Egypt (of which Ethiopia is a part).

We have seen how chaplaincies were established to care for the English-speaking expatriates as they spread all over the world in the course of trade, settlement or imperial administration. We have been able to note that although pastoral care was the primary function of the chaplains, they were also expected to evangelise the indigenous, non-Christian population. Generally speaking, this system did not work, though there were outstanding mission-minded chaplains. Provision had to be made for evangelists and other missionaries whose *primary* concern would be to engage seriously with the indigenous cultures, languages and religions. The chaplaincies survived, however, right through the colonial period to the present day. Their rôle continues to be the pastoring of expatriates, but their relationship to the local church is often ambivalent.

In Europe, both the Church of England and the Episcopal Church of the USA maintain *separate* ecclesiastical structures with overlapping episcopal jurisdictions (a practice which Anglicanism is said to abhor).[29] In the Church of England's diocese in Europe, many of the chaplains are supplied by voluntary societies. In some locations these chaplaincies are viewed with concern by local Anglican Churches, such as the Lusitanian Church in Portugal and the Reformed Episcopal Church in Spain.

Churches in communion with the Anglican Communion, such as the Old Catholic Church, also have ambivalent relationships with the chaplaincies.

In Asia, Africa and Latin America, chaplaincies can present the appearance of being in a time-warp. Many of the features of a dominant Western presence *vis-à-vis* the local church, which have almost disappeared from the scene elsewhere, can be perpetutated in certain chaplaincy structures. Many champlaincies now minister to multicultural and multilingual congregations. In some cases, moreover, they are important ecumenical centres. The amenities of a chaplaincy may be used by a wide range of Christians who are not Anglicans. Despite all this, the chaplaincies are still staffed predominantly by Anglicans from Western countries. World Mission is today in the process of being internationalised or reinternationalised. Anglican chaplaincies too need to be internationalised so that they may be able to minister more effectively to their increasingly diverse congregations. These congregations, in many cases, have great potential for mission – but that is another story.

Part Two

CHAPTER FIVE

Christ's Commission in Contemporary Contexts

The 1988 Lambeth Conference may well go down in history as the harbinger of a new mood. It may well be seen as the Conference which turned away from the traditional Anglican emphasis on matters of ecclesiology and preoccupation with moral questions to a renewed interest in Mission. Not only is the section on *"Mission and Ministry"* the longest in the Conference's Report, but also at least three of its *"Pastoral Letters"* bear directly on questions related to Mission, and several of its *"Resolutions"* are about urgent Mission-related concerns.

Regarding the past, the Conference quotes from a recent document: "Though there are notable exceptions, the dominant model of the Church within the Anglican Communion is a pastoral one. Emphasis in all aspects of the Church's life tends to be placed on care and nurture, rather than proclamation and service."[1] The Conference demands, however, "a massive shift to a mission orientation throughout the Communion".[2] The documents of the Conference reveal a holistic understanding of Mission but, at the same time, underscore the priority of evangelisation. A renewed commitment to evangelisation is seen as the foundation for a commitment to other aspects of Mission such as relief of those in need, development and transformation, and working for just structures in society. Indeed, a concern for evangelisation and these other concerns are seen to be closely interrelated, so that a concern for one will naturally lead to a concern for the others.[3]

The Conference recognises that the process of evangelisation will vary from time to time and from situation to situation. In the case of those of other faiths, for example, the communication of the Gospel can only take place in the context of sensitive listening and dialogue. The Conference commends the incarnational approach in evangelisation, believing that the evangelists must be deeply committed to the situation of the people they are seeking to evangelise. The Report relates with approval, for example, the practice of certain clergy and evangelists who attach themselves to nomadic peoples on the move and traverse the terrain with them. In this way, they are better able to reach them with the good news and also to nurture them in the faith once they have made a response of commitment. While stressing the need for primary evangelism among those who have never meaningfully encountered the Gospel, the Conference also recognises the necessity of evangelising the many baptised who are barely nominal in their adherence to the Christian Faith. Nor is the evangelist excluded from being "evangelised" by the very Gospel which he or she seeks to bring to others (see 1 Corinthians 9:23).[4]

The call for a *Decade of Evangelism* which is made both in the body of the Report and in the Resolutions, and which has gained world-wide attention, has to be understood in the context of the Conference's special concern for Mission. The call has certainly to do with an ecumenical consensus that it is appropriate to focus on the Church's evangelistic task during the closing years of the second millenium. The Conference was well aware that the Roman Catholic Church had already begun such preparations. Among the charismatics too, of all denominations, there are programmes emerging towards this end. Lambeth '88 has been followed by two major international and interdenominational conferences on Mission – one, sponsored by the World Council of Churches, at San Antonio and the other, sponsored by the Lausanne Movement, at Manila. At both there have been voices which have advocated the endorsement of the next decade as a decade for Mission in one form or another. At the time of writing, the official documents of neither conference are available, but reports indicate that Manila, at least, has called for a decade dedicated to evangelisation. Whatever emerges from San Antonio, it is clear that there is renewed interest in evangelism in World Council circles as well. The Evangelism desk of the Commission on World Mission and Evangelism, the body which organised the San Antonio Conference, was very active in the preparation for it. It even sponsored a dialogue on evangelism between radical "ecumenicals", Orthodox, conciliar evangelicals and non-conciliar evangelicals. In 1987 the so-called *Stuttgart Statement,* which emerged from this dialogue, affirmed the necessity of what is called "intentional" or "invitational" evangelism. It was to be a major resource for San Antonio. Preliminary documents from San Antonio indicate that there was a firm commitment to intentional evangelism there. To a very great extent, the bringing of evangelism to the agenda of the World Council has been the result of a relentless crusade conducted by one man – Raymond Fung of the Evangelism desk at Geneva. His regular newsletters have been extremely effective in identifying issues in evangelism. They have provoked not only thought but response as well, and are the beginnings of a conciliar theology of evangelism.

Why has the subject of mission and evangelism, which was nearly taboo and certainly unfashionable in some circles, now become a matter of universal concern in the World Church? Going back to Lambeth '88, as perhaps a microcosm of the World Church, we have to note that for the first time the largest single contingent of bishops was from Africa. In addition to this, there was a significant increase in the number of bishops attending from Asia and the Pacific region. Many of these bishops came from situations where the Church is growing very rapidly and where there is a need to review its structures to determine whether they are suitable for a rapidly developing missionary situation or not.[5]

Some dioceses in Kenya, for example, are reporting a rate of growth in excess of ten per cent per annum! Bishops, as a matter of course, confirm scores of candidates at one service, parishes are divided and sub-divided at a phenomenal rate and there is increased concern for the unreached. Bishop David Gitari of Mount Kenya East, in an address to the Lambeth Conference, identified both the positive features of the growth and some of the problems which attend it.[6] The Anglican Church in particular, but other "mainstream" churches as well, are faced with urgent questions about the appropriateness of many of their structures and practices in the light of this rapidly changing situation. Also, they have to take into consideration the astounding growth of the Independent churches and the ecumenical questions which this raises.[7]

The parochial system was organised in England by Archbishop Theodore of Tarsus (602-690), the only Asian ever to have been Archbishop of Canterbury. It is thought, however, that its roots go back into the pre-Christian past of England, when the feudal lord was supposed to supply a pagan priest who would provide the ritual necessary for the religion of the community. Whatever its ancestry, there can be little doubt that in the past the parochial system has been instrumental in creating a meaningful Christian presence in every local community in the land. It has localised Christian presence in an effective way and made the church approachable and familiar. The question now is whether the parochial system remains an effective vehicle of evangelisation and ministry in England. As Anglicanism, and indeed the Roman Catholic Church, spread throughout the world, the parochial system was exported, often lock, stock and barrel, to other parts of the globe. Under the pressure of new missionary situations, however, its validity is being questioned.

Bishop Gitari in his Lambeth address outlines the strategy of his diocese for the evangelisation and pastoral care of various nomadic or semi-nomadic peoples inhabiting the northern part of its territory. In such contexts a stationary parish priest or mission base can often be at a severe disadvantage. Contact is made with these groups only sporadically, making evangelisation and instruction difficult. Even after baptism, there are problems in providing teaching and in discipling new converts. The Diocese of Mount Kenya East has tried to overcome these problems by having itinerant evangelists *and* pastors who accompany the tribes as they move in search of water and pasture. Here is a new model of outreach and pastoral care which has emerged from the situation of one church. Interestingly, on the evening when Bishop Gitari gave his address, Bishop Bashir Jiwan from Pakistan also provided strong corroborative testimony that this was indeed an appropriate way to evangelise and to care for nomadic people.[8] Both bishops were emphatic that this was a necessary alternative to the parochial model in their situation.

In Latin America, the Base Ecclesial Communities have arisen because it has been impossible for the parochial structures and the ordained ministry in the Roman Catholic Church to evangelise and to minister among vast sections of the population. As Leonardo Boff points out, these communities emerged in response to a real danger that the Christian presence would disappear entirely from some of the poorer parts of society. However, liberation theologians are generally at great pains to emphasise that these communities are not simply a tactic in evangelism, nor are they surrogates for the institutional Church. They are a genuinely new way of being the Church which is, however, rooted in apostolic and primitive Christian practice. The liberation theologians are convinced that the thousands of base communities which exist around the world are a result of the Holy Spirit's work. They emphasise the fraternal and supportive nature of these communities, which is in contrast to the remote parochial structure. They underline also the informality of these groups and their worship. The immediate way in which the Scriptures are related to the group's social, economic and political context is also a distinctive aspect of these communities.[9]

In societies such as England, where the parochial system seems well established, there are pressures for change too. It is well known that large numbers of people from the working classes, in urban as well as in some rural settings, have been alientated from the life of the Church for a very long time. At least part of the reason for this alienation is the fairly well-defined cultural basis for the organisation of English parochial life. The assumptions here favour middle-class values and skills, and those with other values and skills find themselves on the periphery.[10] In addition to this fairly established situation, in recent years there has been a proliferation of groups centred around a common interest such as music, sport or lifestyle. The people involved in these groups have not felt at home in the parochial situation, and where the Church has succeeded in ministering to them, it has been in extra-parochial contexts.[11]

The emergence of a plural society, with a significant presence of people coming from many different cultures, is another challenge which the parochial system has had to face. It has not been notably successful in doing so. Again and again one hears stories of how Christians belonging to ethnic minorities have been unable to adapt to the parochial system and have either ceased going to church altogether or have joined black- or Asian-led churches. Where people of other faith-communities are concerned, it is true that many parochial clergy and church workers have done a very great deal in bridge-building and in community work. But in matters such as evangelisation the parochial system has proved singularly ill-adapted.

The reasons for this are very complex, but have to do with the communal origins of the system. The parish church is inevitably seen by all sides as being deeply rooted in the host community and its religious heritage. It has very high visibility in the locality, and if a member of another faith became too involved in the life of the parish church, his behaviour would be perceived as "treachery" by his own community.

Yet again, the solution has had to be extra-parochial. Evangelisation in this context is best carried out *away* from parochial structures, so that the enquirer's privacy and anonymity may be preserved. A public approach, which cannot be perceived as "targetting" any particular community, may be suitable; so too may private situations such as small groups, where the possibilities of communal conflict are reduced. In parochial situations where there has been successful integration of people from different ethnic backgrounds, including people from other faith-communities, it is often the case that there has first been a ministry to them which has been private and specialist.

The demand for specialisation is, indeed, another challenge to the parochial system – a system which is founded on the assumption, only too common in other areas of English life, that a good generalist, with a smattering of theological, sociological and psychological knowledge, is adequately equipped for the task of pastoral care. This is not to deny that many parish priests have specialist knowledge in these areas; it is simply to pinpoint an assumption about the pastoral ministry. In urban priority areas it is becoming increasingly clear that the need is rather for specialist teams which work to enable local congregations in their mission. These teams will consist of clergy with *different* gifts and full- and part-time people with skills in counselling, social work, medicine and education. Although the work of these teams may be based in and around a large(ish) congregation, they will increasingly be called upon to minister also to cells, house-groups and basic communities. In this connection, it has been well said that the establishment of the Church Urban Fund should not detract from the urgent need in urban priority areas for *people* committed to the city and with skills necessary for ministry in the city.

The emergence of Local Ecumenical Projects poses yet another challenge to the parochial system. Many of the churches involved in these LEPs have a strong theology of "the gathered Church". If the Church of England persists with an ecclesiology which sees the Church as not only incarnate in the local community, not only immanent in it, but actually identical with it, the other churches will have serious problems. How is a congregation to be strengthened for mission in the community if a distinction is not made between the congregation and the community? What does it mean when it is said that the work of the Church should be directed primarily at the community and not towards the congregation? If this results in weak, ill-taught and half-committed congregations, how is the community served? The result is that the clergy and their surrogates get more and more involved in the wider community and the congregation is neglected as a potential source of effective mission in the locality.

The emergence and growth of both ecumenism and cultural variety have given rise to the need for a local Christian presence which is both united and diverse: united in worship, especially eucharistic worship, and in commitment to mission; diverse in the way in which the Faith is expressed, celebrated and studied. Groups belonging to a particular culture or sub-culture or to a particular Christain tradition would be encouraged to meet together to strengthen and encourage each other. But they would also be encouraged to cross cultural and traditional barriers for the sake of fellowship with other Christians and for mission in the community. This "unity in reconciled diversity" would be a powerful sign to the world that the Gospel can be communicated and lived in numerous different ways. It would also be a sign that diversity amongst Christians does not mean division and disunity but is rather the expression of a profound unity.[12]

One particular question which arises in England but which may have relevance elsewhere is, "How may new churches be planted in a situation where the whole land is, in theory, already divided up into parishes and where there is always someone who has responsibility for pastoral care and for evangelism in any given area?" In reality the situation is very different, of course. A large parish may be hopelessly understaffed and the congregation may be ill-equipped to cope with the numbers of people living in the parish. This may be specially so if a significant proportion of these people belong to minority cultures or have lifestyles which are very different from that of the churchgoers. Property development and other factors may produce shifts in population which affect the ministry of a particular parish. There may be a tendency for people to move away from the parish or to move into it. The parish priest may lose heart in a difficult situation or burn himself out or, indeed, lose his faith altogether. In all these situations a large number of people are put out of the reach of the Church, and the traditional claims of the parochial system are shown to need reassessment.

In come cases, of course, there is church planting *within* the parish. For example, the parent congregation might provide the finance, human resources and administrative support for starting up a new congregation in a newly built housing estate in the parish. In another situation, a group of committed parishioners might begin meeting in an area which has been neglected in the past and which they feel has potential for a new congregation.

Church planting *has* taken place across parish, deanery and even diocesan boundaries, however. A parish under pressure, for example, may invite a team of missionaries from another parish to assist it in its mission of outreach to the local community. A group from a talented and numerous congregation may voluntarily decide to join up with a small, struggling congregation in a nearby parish – with the agreement of the latter, of course! Such ventures *have* taken place, sometimes with the support of episcopal and archidiaconal authority.

Much more difficult is the question of small cells for mission or extra-parochial communities in situations where the incumbent is not cooperative. Mission-minded houses of religious communities or centres run by mission agencies can become the focus of a growing Christian presence in situations where pastoral relationships are difficult and where little or no pastoral and evangelical work is being done. Despite the Pastoral Measure and the Vacation of Benefices Measure, the parson's freehold still means a great deal, and there are several instances of mission being blocked by hostile incumbents who are themselves unwilling or unable to reach out to their parishioners. Should otherwise loyal Anglicans simply leave these areas alone until there is a change of incumbent, or is it their duty to encourage some kind of outreach (perhaps in cooperation with Christians of other denominations) in the area?

Holy Trinity Church, Brompton, has organised several day conferences on this issue, at which there has been a great deal of creative thinking about church planting in Anglican contexts in England. It is clear that, as far as England is concerned, this will be a major issue in mission thinking and strategy over the next few years. [13]

East Asia is another area where there has been rapid growth in the size of the Christian churches. This is true not only of Singapore and Korea, the most dramatic cases, but of Indonesia and East Malaysia as well. In Singapore, according to a recent survey carried out by the National University there, the Christian population is now approximately 20% of the whole, with a higher percentage for professional groups such as teachers and doctors. Most of this growth has taken place in the last two decades or so. It is accompanied by a commensurate decrease in the number of those following traditional religious systems such as Buddhism and Confucianism, and an *increase* in those declaring that they have no religion. In South Korea too, the Christian population is above 25% and perhaps approaching 30%. A comparatively large number of people (over a quarter) profess no religion.[14]

Both Korea and Singapore are societies which are undergoing very rapid social change. Both are numbered now among the so-called Newly Industrialised Countries (NICs). The processes of industrialisation and increasing urbanisation have been very fast and massive. Old values and old cultures have been put under severe strain by them. Governments have actively promoted changes in value systems, sometimes in the belief that the old values retarded economic development. Industrialisation and urbanisation have both contributed to the destruction of the traditional material culture. The building of hotels and factories has often had priority over the preservation of temples, shrines, markets and even traditionally built homes. This deracination has produced a cultural and spiritual vacuum in Singaporean and Korean society. Christianity has often filled this vacuum, providing a spiritual orientation for people and giving them a system of values by which to live in the urban wilderness. To assess the social, economic and political basis for church growth is not to deny the spiritual and providential element in it. There can be no doubt that the disappearance of an old and often stultified order has been the Gospel's opportunity for taking root in receptive soil. As Christians become more and more aware of the implications of the Gospel, they are beginning to see that it affirms many aspects of their cultural background at a very profound level. Equally, the Gospel challenges many attitudes – both traditional and new – to wealth, the rights of all human beings and the place of women in society and opposes the supersititious practices associated with traditional cults.

Korea and Singapore are both societies to which Christianity is a relative newcomer. In Korea, for example, the Roman Catholic Church has a presence which is approximately two hundred years old, while the other churches, including the Anglican and Orthodox, have had a presence for barely a hundred years. Evangelisation in these contexts, moreover, has often been accompanied by the requirement that the baptizands should abjure many aspects of their traditional culture which were deemed to be superstitious or demonic. It is true that in many traditional societies there often are such elements, but sometimes the baby was thrown out with the bath water and much that was precious was lost. Industrialisation and urbanisation, as we have seen, have brought about the destruction of traditional culture. This has been compounded by the rejection of the culture by the Church and its agents. The result is a Christianity which is vigorous and expanding but at the same time rather shallow and excessively dependent on the West, not only for its theology but also for forms of worship, architecture and church government.[15]

The Gospel cannot be rooted in a people unless it is allowed to address the deepest concerns of their culture. It must be translated not only in to the language and idiom of a particular culture but into the ways in which the people think, pray and celebrate. In the East Asian context this means, first of all, a recovery of some of the traditional culture which has been lost either because of modernisation or because of the hostility of the Church. Is it possible to argue that just as the Chinese word *Tao* is used as a translation of the words "Gospel" and *"Logos"*, it may be possible to translate the *content* of the Gospel in categories derived from *Tao,* the ancient Chinese philosophical system? Again, Chinese art has very definite symbolism, and the symbols bear values which differ from the values of the symbols in Western art. If Christian themes were to be discussed and described in the Chinese tradition, it would be very important to respect the integrity of the tradition and not to seek to impose Western symbolic values on it.

When William Carey reached India at the end of the eighteenth century, his first priority was the translation of the Bible into both the classical and the popular languages of India. Astonishingly, he produced translations of the complete Bible into Sanskrit, Bengali and Marathi! When he began his work, however, he was faced with a problem: how should he translate the word "God"? He had before him the entire Hindu pantheon. In the end he chose the word *Ishwar,* which was used by Hindus to refer to God as the supreme personal being. Henry Martyn too, in his translations into Persian and Urdu, did not hesitate to use Islamic religious terminology to convey Christian truth.[16] Arab Christians have for centuries used the term *Allah* as their normal word for God. Indeed, already in the Septuagint and then in the New Testament, *theos,* the pagan word for a god (and, in a feminine form, for a goddess), was being used of the God of Israel.

The fact of the matter is that the Gospel has to be made incarnate in the culture, the idiom, the thought and the art of the people to whom it is brought if it is to become intelligible to them and if it is to take root among them. The rapidly growing churches of East Asia have a prophetic ministry in discerning what is God-given and good in their respective cultures. Perhaps the churches can be leaders here in enabling their societies to see that it is not necessary to destroy all that is traditional for the sake of modernisation. This process of conscientisation, of Christians and of others, has to be accompanied by a serious attempt at contextualisation in the Liturgy, in mission, in church government and in theological education. It is a matter of great encouragement that the churches of East Asia are beginning to regard the relation of the Gospel to their cultures as an urgent task waiting to be done.[17]

The disappearance of the old order in East Asia is one of the reasons for the growth of the Church in these lands. But cultic Christianity is part of the old order which is disappearing in Europe. It is right for European Christians to be aware of their Christian heritage, in both its positive and negative aspects. At the same time, however, they need to be conscious of the fact that the amalgam of Gospel and culture which produced "Christendom" and was, in turn, modified by it, is no longer credible and is disappearing just as surely as the traditional ethical, religious and philosophical systems of East Asia. European societies, because of their awareness of history, have produced a certain kind of conservation-mindedness and a widespread antiquarian interest. This, perhaps, gives an exaggerated impression of the extent to which the ideology of Christendom is intact. A recognition that the cults associated with Christendom are dead or dying would liberate the Church from captivity to the past and would allow the Gospel to engage in a variety of ways with contemporary European culture.

Secularisation is certainly an aspect of modern European society which needs to be taken seriously. Europeans generally live in a de-sacralised environment where the old assumptions about the reality of the supernatural are no longer in force. Perhaps more importantly, it is no longer thought necessary to account for the natural world and for human existence by positing a cause or causes beyond the natural world. It is almost impossible to exaggerate the pervasive influence of ideas such as these on the European mind. The emergence and strength of Logical Positivism in both continental and British philosophy in the middle years of this century is an indication of how far matters have gone. In its classical exposition, Logical Positivism allowed the validity only of purely logical statements, where conclusions were only explications of what was already contained in the premises, and of statements which depended on data obtained from the senses. The rest of intellectual endeavour, especially theology and metaphysics, was dismissed as "non-sense".[18]

The attack on religion was not just from the direction of philosophy. Sociology and anthropology too developed "explanations" of religion which tended to view it either as essentially a primitive view of the world or as a function of society which reinforced social taboos. In both cases the existence of a supernatural dimension of existence was overtly or covertly challenged.[19] Feuerbach's opinion that all religion is a projection of human concerns has been echoed not only by sociology and anthropology but also by a great deal of psychology. It has generally led to a grossly reductionist view of religion. Peter Berger has indeed shown that this need not be so and that the important question about the Feuerbachian position is whether ultimate reality corresponds to this or that human projection.[20] In fact, what Berger calls the "historical-psychological-sociological analysis" of religious phenomena has often led to scepticism. Historiography, as is has developed since the Enlightenment, has also often chosen arbitrary criteria for itself, such as the position that every event must be interpreted in terms of a closed system of finite causes. This has, by definition, excluded any consideration of the supernatural and its relation to human existence and the natural world. This "secularisation of consciousness" has gone so far that even Berger, who is concerned to recover a sense of the supernatural in modern society, can see no massive revival of popular, supernaturalist religion. The most he can see is the survival of "pockets" of supernatural religion organised more or less on sectarian lines and, one may add, occurring both within and without recognised "mainstream" religious bodies.[21]

In other words, the Church has to deal not so much with the remnants of religion but with societies, perhaps for the first time ever, based on a secular, naturalist view of reality. Science also, whilst confined, strictly speaking, to the observation, classification and evaluation of empirical data, has not been backward in offering cosmologies or ultimate explanations of the universe. These have varied from those tending to reduce the spiritual, moral and even mental to "epiphenomena" of the physical, to those which leave some room for "theistic hypotheses". The temptation generally has been to use the criteria of the empirical sciences, particularly the physical sciences, as paradigms for all meaningful human discourse. Because the sciences inevitably deal with antecedent causes and their effects, this has meant that it has become more and more difficult to use teleological language which emphasises neither antecedent causes leading up to an event or series of events, nor the analysis and reduction of an object to its constituent physical or chemical parts. Rather, such language emphasises the purpose or final cause for which a thing or a person exists and the place of an event or series of events in the achievement of an "end".[22]

It is true that in more recent years scientists, particularly in the field of astronomy, have become more open to the use of teleological language, especially in discussions about the universe's origin and evolution. The emergence of "the anthropic principle" as a postulate in such discussion is very significant. If I understand the matter correctly, it is being suggested that the evolution of the universe, with observers such as ourselves in it and with its many strange coincidences and its fine checks and balances, can only be adequately accounted for if it is postulated that such an evolution had the emergence of observers as its "end". In other words, the universe we observe must always have had the conditions which were necessary for the eventual evolution of intelligent life – that is, of observers. The existence of such observers demands a universe of this kind. The matter is very controversial, of course, and it is difficult for those outside the scientific community to comment on the discussion. It is fascinating, nevertheless, that such a discussion is going on at all.

Naturally, there are sceptics who maintain that human beings see themselves as the end or purpose of this cosmic process only because of their basic egocentricity – that is, because the process has produced *them*. It is true, of course, that there would have been no human beings if the process had not been, more or less, what it has been. We are entitled, however, to consider critically whether the attainment of consciousness and self-consciousness, of speech and thought and of moral and spiritual awareness is such as to permit human beings to be regarded as the acme of the cosmic process. Also, we need to remember that other ends have been attained which may not be final but are significant, nevertheless. The structure of the universe, the ecology of our world and the emergence and differentiation of life may all be regarded teleologically in terms of end or purpose, as well as empirically in terms of antecedent causes and analysis of constituent parts.[23]

It must not be easily assumed, of course, that the anthropic principle necessarily leads to theistic belief. It is quite possible to believe, for example, that this universe, which has in fact produced us, is only one of an infinite number of possible universes and that it is merely by chance that it is *this* universe which is actual rather than any other. On the other hand it is possible to interpret the principle theistically, and to hold that the universe is like it is because of divine providence.

In principle, it needs to be said that the Gospel must engage with modern, secular culture, as it has been formed by the influence of the Enlightenment, the development of the physical and life sciences and the critique of sociology and anthropology, as it engages with any and every culture. In this sense, the attempt to find "the secular meaning of the Gospel" is entirely valid.[24] Writers such as Van Buren and Harvey Cox, who wrote *The Secular City*,[25] are struggling to restate the Gospel in a world dominated by the paradigms of physical science and the scepticism created by the social sciences. The latter have often purported to demonstrate that religion has sanctioned and reinforced the existing social order, which has often been unjust. If this is the case, the Gospel cannot be identified with any religion; it must be religionless if it is to bring about human liberation. The dominance of the physical sciences, on the other hand, has tended to produce a world-view which is anti-metaphysical and which emphasises experience and experiment as the way to knowledge. It is understandable, therefore, that these theologians of the sixties stressed the "concreteness" of Jesus and of his ethics of love over and against metaphysical speculations about the existence and nature of God which could never be verified by appeal to experience or history.

It is arguable that some of the theologians in the "death of God" movement went too far. Instead of relating the Gospel to the secular age, they succumbed to the ideology of the age and were left with a vacuous if not self-contradictory message.[26] It is true that people in secular societies find it increasingly difficult to conceptualise the transcendent. The death of God theologians, however, may have been excessive in declaring that this dimension of human experience had ceased to exist altogether, at least in secular societies, and so had little relevance to the important concerns of these societies. Any engagement of the Gospel with the concerns of secular society will seek to discern the areas in which there is still a transcendent dimension to life which is irreducible. In a scientific age, the correspondence that there is between the order in the human mind and the order in the universe will, naturally, form an important part of the agenda for dialogue between Christians and others. Is it mere chance that the human mind can appropriate and classify the world, in such a satisfactory way, in terms of its own categories? Is the correspondence which makes technology possible simply fortuitous or does it reveal an order which is purposeful and in which ends are being achieved all the time by creatures which are themselves purposeful?

A leading theme in much contemporary literature is the significance (or insignificance) of human existence. The concern has to do with meaning and, therefore, with transcendence. Is human awareness and the search for meaning the ultimate joke or the ultimate tragedy in a random and meaningless universe, or is it possible to evaluate this search for meaning in a more positive way?[27] Transcendence experienced in listening to or playing music and in the production of works of art also deserves serious reflection in the context of Christian dialogue with the world. It is not that these are "gaps" in the secular world-view which may be filled at some time. Rather, either they are ways of seeing reality as a whole or they are aspects of human life which do not lose their significance even after scientific analysis has reduced them to their constituent parts. Their meaning lies beyond what they are in the merely physical sense.

Christian Mission must take the challenge of secularism seriously. The widespread belief among secularists that religions and religious people have blocked free enquiry in the past is not without foundation. Christians need here to return to their roots in the Gospel tradition, where the good news is announced unambiguously and unequivocally, but without an obligation to believe. Christians need also to be aware of the history of Christian thought. Again and again, what was at first perceived to be hostile to Christian belief was eventually found not to be so and, in come cases became a catalyst and even a vehicle for the restatement of Christian belief in a particular age or idiom.

There are some who believe that religious beliefs and systems simply provide sanction for the *status quo* and make change difficult. It needs to be said at the outset that not all change is for the better. It *is* true, however, that religion has often been used to buttress unjust and exploitative systems of government and economic activity. Christians will distinguish very carefully between the organisation and structures of institutional religion (even Christian religion) as they have developed in the course of history, and the Gospel itself, which will always be over and against merely human structures (even structures established in the name of the Gospel).[28] In Latin America it has become necessary to distinguish between the institutional Church, which has had a history of not only siding with the oppressors of the poor but of being an oppressor itself, and groups of Christians in the base communities and elsewhere who are bringing the Gospel to bear on issues of liberation, justice and freedom.[29]

A central concern of many of the so-called secularising theologians was that the Gospel should be so articulated and lived that secular men and women would begin to find it meaningful in terms of their own world-view and cultural assumptions. They were perhaps too sanguine in their belief that secular culture represented a signal advance in the evolution of human society. They were not aware of the environmental and social problems which the revolution in technology was to bring about. They were, possibly, too dismissive of the survival of folk-religion in allegedly secular societies. However, their insight that secular culture, like all other cultures, had arisen within the providence of God and therefore bore the image of God, has continuing validity. It needs also to be said, of course, that this culture, like others, is fallen and invariably distorts the image of God in human beings. It remains true, nevertheless, that there is, in the words of Emil Brunner, an *anknüpfungspunkt* or "attachment-point" between the Gospel and any culture (including secular culture) which makes it possible for the Gospel to address that culture.[30] It is crucial for the future of the Christian Faith that the dialogue between the Gospel and secular culture is continued. There is a need, therefore, to return to some of the concerns of the secularising theologians, without endorsing their optimism about secular culture and without going to the extremes of the death of God theology.

While the influence of secularism is steadily increasing, there remain many societies, especially in Africa, Asia and Latin America, which are characterised by a "sacramental" understanding of reality. In these cultures the preternatural is acknowledged as part of the continuing life of the community and its presence is often discerned through material objects or living persons. The need in such societies, however, is to allow the survival of a sacramental view of life which is consonant with technological development and which has experienced the challenge of World Religions such as Christianity or Islām. Paradoxically, the preaching of the Gospel has often been accompanied by a de-sacralisation of these cultures. This is partly because the sacral aspects of these cultures were judged to be superstitious and even demonic by those who brought the Gospel to them, and sometimes even by the early converts. Wherever there are human beings who remain open to spiritual influence, there is always the danger that such influence will *not* be good. The presence and influence of the demonic *is* a real possibility in many cultures.

At the same time, we must be alert to the possibilities of spiritual influence for the good in many situations. Ancestor-reverence is a case in point. In East Asia and in Africa there are ancient traditions which have to do with expressing respect for and solidarity with one's tribal and family ancestors. The effect of this is to provide a particular community with roots, to give its members a sense of history and of solidarity with the past and with each other. These are the positive aspects of ancestor-reverence which lead to a sense of community. Human sinfulness and supernatural evil are well able to turn something good in itself into a vehicle for superstition, magic and the demonic.

The Church has to be very discriminating in how it is to encourage the survival of a sense of the sacred in a particular culture without appearing to endorse that which is of dubious value and which may be downright evil. Some Balinese Christians do *not* believe that contact with the spirits of the dead is in itself evil. It is so much a part of the culture that it is difficult for them to see what is wrong with it.[31] Christians in Singapore, on the other hand, find it difficult even to live in a house where there is a shrine for ancestors. Whatever the possibilities of contact with the dead, the Church must remain ever alert to the danger that the practice will result in exposure to supernatural influence that is evil.

In Africa the tendency among theologians is to hold that it is the Divine Trinity which sacralises the whole world. The Father is identified in many African contexts with the High-God of traditional religion. Theologians such as Bediako have argued that Christ is the true Ancestor, both in the cosmic sense as being the principal agent of creation (Colossians 1:15-20) and in the sense of being the progenitor of the Christian community (Hebrews 12:2).[32] The Holy Spirit permeates the world and the Church and so sacralises them.

Questions, of course, continue to arise and answers must be sought. Given the continuity that there is between traditional African views of God and the Christian view of God, what are the discontinuities? If Christ is the Primal Ancestor of all, how is he related to the plurality of ancestral spirits of clans, tribes and nations? Is the patristic doctrine of "recapitulation" helpful in enabling us to see that Christ sums up in himself all that is believed about ancestral spirits, while at the same time affirming the continued veneration of one's ancestors? The Jesuits in China had come to the conclusion in the seventeenth century that honours paid to ancestors and to Confucius were "civil" in character and therefore permissible. On various occasions Rome agreed with them, but ultimately the so-called "Chinese Rite" was suppressed.[33] In the end, of course, the status of the ancestors will depend on whether the Church regards them as being, in some sense, *praeparatio evangelica* and as having had some opportunity to respond to the proclamation of the Gospel after their terrestrial lives (1 Peter 3:19-20). It needs to be emphasised that any honours paid to ancestors, whether of clan, tribe and nation, or to spiritual ancestors – that is, the saints – cannot be at the expense of the central Christian teaching that believers have immediate access to God in prayer, in the preaching of the Word and in the Sacraments. The importance of this last and of worship generally cannot be overstressed in the context of sacramental cultures. The contextualisation or inculturation of worship is perhaps the most important of the missionary tasks, after evangelisation itself. How sensitively this is done will determine to a very great extent the course of the Christian enterprise in a culture.

The use of appropriate symbols, meaningful posture, the right language and music and suitable forms of corporate expression will determine the effectiveness of sacramental worship in particular cultures. It is well known that in sacramental cultures objects (particularly those used in worship), food (again, especially that used in cultic ways), buildings and persons come to be seen as mediating transcendence. The cultures in which the different books of the Bible came to be written were also sacramental. It is crucial for inculturation that the "horizon" of this aspect of the Bible should be allowed to meet the "horizons" of sacramental cultures. Out of such a meeting will emerge an expression of the Christian Faith which is rich in symbols and which does not have a desacralising effect in the culture. Churches in sacramental cultures can give back a sense of the sacred to the World Church wherever it has been lost. Those engaged in cross-cultural mission, especially those from secularised cultures, need to learn the language of the sacred if they are to communicate the Gospel in specific cultural settings.

Another aspect of sacramental cultures, which is crucial for mission, is the fact that in such societies religious language belongs to the public domain. Religion has not yet been "privatised" and it is quite natural for religious topics to be discussed freely in community gatherings, both formal and informal. The mediation of the Gospel in these societies will have to reckon with this aspect of their culture. How the Gospel is mediated, what kind of language is used and how people respond to the Gospel will all be determined by this communal reality. So will hitherto sacrosanct attitudes to Christian *diakonia* and its frequent separation from the process of dialogue and evangelisation.[34]

Liberation theologians have often noted the effects that the formation of a basic community has on the people. These range from a greater concern for the poorest in the community, to a sense of belonging and the strength that comes from togetherness. The stronger help the weaker and the gifts of all are celebrated. These are welcome developments, but perhaps there ought to be a more sustained investigation of the *religious* background of these communities. They have arisen largely in contexts where religious awareness is very important and where different streams of religious traditions exist side by side. Christian traditions coexist with indigenous Ameri-Indian ones, for example, and even traditional African ones. There have been serious attempts at syncretisation and many new religious movements have come into existence. Even the faithful within the churches continue in their allegiance to other cults. In such a context what is the sacramental aspect of the basic community? Is it an attempt at inculturation? How may authentic forms of inculturation be distinguished from the inauthentic and merely syncretising?[35]

We have seen that the scope of the Gospel has been universal from the beginning. At different times and in different places, apostolic men and women have taken the Gospel to many different peoples and, gradually, the Church has taken root among them. The revolution in the technology of transport and of other kinds of communication in the last and present centuries has accelerated the process of mission and evangelisation throughout the world. The rôle of Western imperialism was ambivalent in this respect. The trading companies, which were often at the head of the imperial enterprise, discouraged Christian mission if it was perceived as damaging to their commercial interests.[36] Where the Crown was directly involved, mission was sometimes discouraged because it conflicted with the imperial authorities' strategic or political interests.[37] It is also true, however, that the imperial *pax* facilitated mission through the security and reliable transport which it ensured.

The emergence or re-emergence of nation-states in the post-colonial era has tended to limit the movement of Christian missionaries. At the same time, there are now strong churches in many of these states, and it can be argued that the need for cross-cultural, or to be more precise, cross-national missionaries is not so great. In countries where churches are experiencing strong numerical growth, however, there are vigorous new movements encouraging cross-cultural and cross-national mission once again. Political circumstances permitting, there can be little doubt that these movements will have a significant impact on the whole of Christian mission and on the world in the next few years.

Political circumstances, however, are precisely what compel us to introduce a note of caution. It seems likely that the boundaries of nation-states and of regional associations (such as the EEC) will be more and more tightly drawn for economic and cultural reasons. Global unity, which has become possible because of the revolution in communications, is gravely threatened by a resurgence of ethnocentricity and of economic protectionism. In such a situation, it remains the Church's task to encourage the exchange of partners between national churches so that the catholicity of the Church may be highlighted, but also so that expertise and fellowship may be provided where it is most needed. Ideally, this is what ought to be. In practice, of course, there are all kinds of restrictions on the free movement of people. This makes it necessary for the local church to recognise its responsibility as the primary agent of evangelisation in its area. It is true, of course, that the local church has to be enabled to fulfil this rôle, but its task cannot be usurped by others. If they come; it must be in partnership with the local church in its various manifestations.

This is so even if the local church is from an ethnic, caste or social background which is different to that of the majority of a locality's inhabitants. If such is the case, the local church needs to be encouraged and assisted in its mission, but never replaced.[38] Cross-cultural mission will have to be carried out more and more *within* national frontiers.

Having taken lessons of the past to heart, and having been forewarned of future dangers, it is possible to imagine the coming World Church which will truly reflect the universality of the Gospel. People of all nations, tribes and tongues belong to it already. The gifts which they bring need to be accepted and affirmed by the world-wide fellowship of believers, so that each member of this fellowship is enriched by all the other members, and all are enriched by each, however humble. As the American Episcopalian theologian, John Knox has said, "The Church is a fellowship in the love of God whose mission is to be an ever-widening sphere of an every-deepening reconciliation."

CHAPTER SIX

Renewal, Mission and Transformation

We have seen that the Church in the twentieth century has faced major challenges in nearly every area of its life. There has been the challenge of mass secularisation in many parts of the world. In other parts, the Church has had to deal with new or resurgent ideologies and religions. The encounter with the poor and their rights has also significantly affected the agenda of the World Church, as has rapid expansion in certain parts of the world. The ecumenical movement continues to challenge the different denominations to come together in the unity which Christ wills for his Church, and so to become a sign and an instrument for the human unity which is part of God's redeeming purpose (Ephesians 1:9-10; Colossians 1:20; Revelation 21:22-27). Our relationship with our environment and the proper stewardship of the earth's resources is also increasingly becoming a matter of urgent concern for Christians.

On the one hand are the challenges, and on the other, God is manifestly equipping and enabling his Church to meet these challenges. If this century is one of challenge to the Church, it is also one in which she is experiencing profound renewal in many areas of her life and witness. In his charge to bishops and others, assembled together in 1987 to draft the working papers for the Lambeth Conference, the Archbishop of Canterbury, Dr Robert Runcie, noted that renewal is a characteristic of the Church in our times and that authentic Christian reflection on mission and ministry must take full account of it. He outlined the different areas of the Church's life where renewal is being experienced. Acknowledging the Charismatic Movement as a significant force, he also noted renewal in liturgical worship, in reading the Bible in context and in communal living as important ways in which the Church is being revitalised.[1]

The Pentecostal revival seems to have begun in the early years of this century. Although its earliest manifestations were connected with the mainstream churches, it soon came to be organised on denominational lines. Until the late 1950s the Pentecostal denominations were a distinct family of churches characterised by the presence and use of such gifts of the Holy Spirit as prophecy, healing and *glossolalia* (or speaking in tongues).[2] In the sixties, however, congregations and Christians in the mainline churches began to be renewed by the Holy Spirit and to receive these gifts. The movement has since grown from strength to strength and numbers a great many clergy as well as laity among its adherents. The last two Lambeth Conferences (1978 and 1988) were each preceded by Charismatic Conferences attended by many of the bishops. Pope John XXIII's "opening of the windows" (the Italian word *aggiornamento* which was used by the Pope actually means "renewal") and the Second Vatican Council exposed the Roman Catholic Church to change on many fronts. One result of this new openness has been experience of the Holy Spirit among bishops, priests and faithful which has been discernibly Charismatic. The movement has mushroomed in the Roman Catholic Church and there are thousands of Bible study and prayer groups all over the world.[3] The Charismatic Movement is certain to be a most influential factor in the shaping of the Coming Church. A recent study of the renewal movement in the Church of England identified the Charismatics as the fastest growing constituency in that church, affecting everything from Liturgy to management.[4] Other churches are in similar situations.

The contemporary Charismatic Movement is obviously related to the earlier Pentecostal revival and the churches to which it gave rise. There are, however, important areas of difference as well, and theological language is one of them. The Pentecostals usually speak of a "baptism of the Spirit" but the mainline denominations, to which many Charismatics belong, usually regard all true Christians as baptised in the Spirit. Roman Catholics, Anglicans and some Lutherans, moreover, speak of sacramental baptism as the complete initiation which cannot be repeated. The experience of the Spirit in renewal may be spoken of as a "fullness of the Spirit" or as "a realisation of the meaning and power of the gift which was in baptism once bestowed" or as a manifestation of "what objectively took place during the rite of initiation", but it should not be spoken of as "baptism".[5] Michael Harper is correct in seeing sacramental baptism, in the early Church, as a total initiatory rite which included "water-baptism" but which also included other aspects of initiation, such as teaching and the laying-on of hands. It is all the more puzzling, therefore, that he continues to insist on the use of the term "baptism in the Spirit" to describe the Pentecostal experience and to claim that it is an aspect of initiation. He acknowledges, however, that evidence from Scriptures and from Tradition for this use is not easily obtained. He points out that one reason for the term's continued use is the fact that it is a good description of an initial experience of renewal. Once again, he admits that there is little theological basis for such terminology.[6] Whatever one may say of Harper's position, it is clear that in many mainline churches, especially those with a "catholic" understanding of the Sacraments, the term is either being dropped quietly or its use is becoming subject to heavy qualification.

The practice of speaking in tongues is perhaps another area of divergence. The Pentecostal churches are, on the whole, insistent that this gift is the first sign of baptism in the Spirit. Charismatics from the mainline churches do not, as a rule, insist on this and are prepared to consider other manifestations as signs of an experience of the Spirit. Ecclesiologically too there are differences. Pentecostal churches, *mutatis mutandis,* have congregational ecclesiologies, whereas Charismatics generally espouse the ecclesiology of their own denomination. They tend to be inclusive in their attitudes, particularly towards Catholic and Liberal Christians, whereas Pentecostals tend to be sectarian and exclusive.

While the origins and development of the Pentecostal churches were often related to mass movements and were, therefore, strongly rooted among the so-called working classes, the contemporary Charismatic movement in the mainline churches, in Restorationism (or the house-church movement) and in para-church organisations such as the Full Gospel Businessmen's Fellowship, is visibly and increasingly middle-class.[7] The leader of a strong house-church movement in the south of England confessed recently that the movement had failed to make an impact in the inner city and was strongest among the "lower middle classes". The strongly Charismatic element in many of the churches in Singapore is mainly professional, English-speaking and middle-class. The Chinese-speaking churches remain largely untouched by the phenomenon. Teaching about the relationship between faithfulness, especially in giving, and prosperity tends to reinforce the attraction that this movement has for businessmen and other professionals.

Bebbington investigates, in some detail, the sociological and psychological background to the movement and concludes that from one point of view it may be seen as a response to the libertarianism and anti-authoritarianism of much of contemporary culture (though it must be acknowledged that the movement itself has spawned some very authoritarian structures). The movement has also been concerned with the re-creation of community, with free expression (especially in worship) and with the resurgence of creativity, especially in the arts.[8] It is, perhaps, needless to say that investigations into the social or psychological conditions of an event or series of events do not exhaust all the possibilities of explanation which may exist. It is quite possible to give a meticulous account of the social and psychological conditions which lie behind the Charismatic Movement and still believe it to be the work of the Holy Spirit.

In recent years the Charismatic Movement has often been accused of neglecting social concern. In turn its leaders have labelled activists in this area "shrill" and bitter. It has been shown that early Pentecostalism, because of its origins among poor and marginalised groups, had a fairly well developed social critique as well as an awareness of the need for ministry in this area. This commitment was gradually eroded, at least in Northern Countries, because of increasing prosperity among Pentecostalists of Caucasian origin. Other factors were the advent of widespread secularisation, the recession of the hope of "reforming the world", and theological developments such as pre-millenarianism which put the return of Christ *before* the millenium, thus excluding the view that the millenium could be a time for "spreading righteousness on the earth". The social protest aspects of Pentecostalism in Northern countries, to be found in a particular use of Scripture and in hymns and choruses, are still part of the traditions where Pentecostalism has taken root among minorities such as American Blacks or the Afro-Caribbean communities in Britain.[9]

In the South, particularly in Latin America, classical Pentecostalism began largely among the poor and marginalised who were trying to liberate themselves from the oppression of a rigidly structured social order. The Pentecostal churches, in such a context, were firmly committed to social egalitarianism and to encouraging self-help projects within the community of the faithful. In relation to the world, however, they tended to remain "rejectionist", thus reducing the impact of their egalitarian and developmental policies on the wider community.[10] While some have claimed that the Charismatic Movement, at least in the South, is genuinely a movement of the poor and has close affinities with the base communities, others have pointed out that the movement, even in the South, is basically middle-class and lacks the holistic approach characteristic of the base communities.[11]

It seems, therefore, that the Charismatic Movement throughout the world is quietistic in its tendencies and emphasises "spiritual renewal with a strong emphasis on praise and the *charismata*".[12] There are groups, however, such as the Sojourners, which have sought to bring Charismatic renewal and a commitment to social action together.[13] Among Roman Catholic religious who have been influenced by the Charismatic Movement, too, there is a tendency towards a holistic ministry.[14] In this matter, perhaps the assessment of Norberto Saracco, General Secretary of the Fraternity of Latin American Pentecostals, is the most realistic as well as the most hopeful:

> The Charismatic Renewal is neither radical nor reactionary in itself, but this ambivalence makes it capable of creating contradictory effects. Strong social conditionings have made it appear on the margins of every social change process. But in situations of social conflict, to abstain from participating is also a political option. A global evaluation of what has happened in Latin America shows us that charismatic "neutrality" has been an obstacle to the social change process and in certain circumstances has represented obviously reactionary positions. On the other hand, it is also true that in sectors of the movement an awareness of social problems is growing. The Charismatic Renewal has, in its theology of the Kingdom, in its concept of the Lordship of Christ, and in its sense of community and mission, the possibility of being a tool for social liberation.[15]

It has often been noted that the Charismatic Movement can have a negative attitude to people of other faiths and so discourages dialogue. Such an attitude is sometimes accompanied by a radically negative orientation to culture. Other faiths are often dismissed as vehicles for the demonic or, at best, as human efforts to reach God.[16] Any spiritual values or experiences which may be discerned in people of other faiths are seen as counterfeits of Christian values and experience. The Gospel is seen as totally "other" both in relation to culture as a whole and in relation to religious tradition. The result is that the expression of the Gospel remains alien, couched indeed in specific cultural forms, but forms which are not recognised as such. Where a religious tradition is concerned, the emphasis is on the replacement of the tradition by Christianity rather than on seeing the Gospel as a fulfilment of its hopes and aspirations. The result is often a shallow spirituality borrowed from elsewhere and not deeply rooted in the collective tradition of a people. The fundamental problem is theological; the presence of the eternal Word and of the Holy Spirit is seen as limited to the Church, preferably a renewed Church, which is then regarded as the sole or, at least, primary agent of evangelisation.[17] But the primary agent of evangelisation is God, who continues to illumine all human beings (John 1:9) and whose Holy Spirit brings the world to a consciousness of sin, righteousness and judgement (John 16:8). Max Warren understood this to mean that the evangelist, when he or she encounters a person of another faith, encounters Christ himself, active in establishing his sovereignty over all that has come into being through him.[18] John V. Taylor, Warren's successor as General Secretary of CMS, has this to say about the work of the Holy Spirit:

> The Spirit's witness to the Lordship and love of Jesus Christ is, therefore, in itself a kind of dialogue. In the person of Jesus, and in his body, the Church, the Spirit calls all men to respond. And like a fifth column in the heart of every man the Spirit himself moves in response. This is what Jesus appealed to when he showed such extraordinary faith in simple men and women...It is this which gives us grounds for believing that in any dialogue between the Church and the world, or between Christians and men of other faiths, the Holy Spirit is speaking in both participants.[19]

It has to be recognised, of course, that men and women resist the work of the Holy Spirit and obscure, by their sin and rebellion, the illumination of the divine Word. The Gospel cannot, however, be preached in a vacuum; there must be that in human beings which impels them towards an apprehension of it. There must be something which enables them to recognise the truth revealed in Christ, and to see the possibility of experiencing brokenness and repentance before God, and reconciliation and friendshp with God. The World Church owes a very great debt to the Charismatic Movement, since it has made Christians aware, once again, of the Person and work of the Holy Spirit. However, perhaps many Charismatics need to learn that the activity of the Holy Spirit is not confined to the Church; rather the Spirit permeates the world of which he, with the Father and the Son, is both creator and sustainer. In this connection, the Universal Church needs to learn from the Orthodox tradition, which understands the economy of the Spirit as universal in scope as well as in fact. This allows the Orthodox to be confident that God is preparing all human beings for a revelation of himself. At the same time, it makes them expectant regarding the ultimate response of people to God's revelation in Christ. Both the revelation in Christ and the response to it have to be seen as final and definitive, but it also has to be understood that they cannot be realised without that vital, preparatory work of the Holy Spirit.[20]

There *are* signs, especially among younger people, that a commitment to the the *whole* Gospel is emerging. Such a commitment takes seriously the need for the *gifts* of the Spirit. These gifts are wisdom in speech, faith, healing, miracles, prophecy, spiritual discernment, tongues and their interpretation (1 Corinthians 12:7-11). The *fruit* of the Spirit is essential too, if our commitment is to be truly Christlike. The fruit of the Spirit includes love, joy, peace, patience, kindness, goodness, faithfulness, gentleness and self-control (Galatians 5:22-23). The gifts and fruit of the Spirit make Christian service to our fellow human beings truly Christlike.[21] The presence and work of the Holy Spirit in our lives leads inexorably to a commitment to righteousness and justice. It leads to Christian presence among and ministry to the poor, the ill, the exploited and the marginalised.

At festivals of the young such as Greenbelt, this wholeness of commitment seems to be emerging. The worship is Spirit-filled but not "ghettoised", the art and the music is discernibly Christian and yet clearly related to the contemporary world, and in the seminars there is a willingness to struggle with the difficult problems of the day. It is a moving experience to see twenty thousand young people join in eucharistic worship, singing songs such as this one by Garth Hewitt:

> *Teach us how to walk in your footsteps, Jesus*
> *Teach us how to walk in your way*
> *Teach us how to show your love to our neighbour*
> *Teach us how to do it today.*
> *And we will dance, dance, dance, dance on injustice,*
> *We will stand, stand, stand, stand with the poor*
> *And we will sing, sing, sing, sings songs of freedom*
> *With Jesus the servant whose love is over all.*

Events such as Greenbelt *are* attended by the dangers of cults, of domination by personalities and of eclecticism, but they do make visible, in a striking way, a commitment to the *wholeness* of renewal.

There is a debate within the Charismatic Movement and between it and the Church generally as to whether Charismatic renewal is *the* way of renewal or whether it is only *a* way. Michael Harper seems to allow that renewal in the Church will take different forms – sacramental, liturgical, ecumenical, evangelistic and Charismatic. According to him, therefore, Charismatic renewal is only a part of the total picture, but a *necessary* part. Without it the picture is incomplete.[22] Bishop Moses Tay, on the other hand, seems to be claiming that Charismatic renewal is *the* way of renewal.[23] There seems to be some confusion generally in the discussion about the renewing work of the Holy Spirit. It is indisputable that the Spirit is renewing the Church. All authentic renewal must be attributed to the work of the Spirit of God. We should be prepared to see, however, that the renewing work of the Spirit goes far beyond the boundaries of our own personal or even communal experience. In other words, we should not be too quick in saying that *our* experience of renewal, however dramatic it may be, is the only or the main way of renewal. Rather, with spiritual discernment and in the light of Scripture we should be able to recognise authentic renewal in even the most unfamiliar settings.

The Bible is not a single book. It is a collection of very diverse material of various literary forms, having origins in very different cultural and historical contexts, written in different languages and containing a constellation of different viewpoints. At the same time, it has to be acknowledged that underlying this diversity there is a profound and real unity. It is obvious, therefore, that there can be no "neutral" or "objective" reading of the Bible which produces a uniform response regardless of culture or context. People at different times, in particular contexts and in various cultures relate to aspects of the Bible in different ways. The economic, political and social conditions under which a people live will determine, to some extent, how they read their Bible and what they notice in it when they read it. Traditional historical and critical exegesis is a necessary instrument in contemporary hermeneutic – that is, in the interpretation of the biblical stories for our times. It is necessary for us to know the precise historical and cultural circumstances in which a biblical tradition arose. It is necessary also for us to know the process of collection and redaction that the traditions were put through as well as the purposes of the authors and readactors in presenting the material in the way it has come down to us. We need to be aware, of course, that the historical and critical study of the Bible is not an exact science, and we have to note the assumptions (or the pre-understanding) which scholars bring to their work, both in terms of establishing the original context and meaning and in their interpretation of it in contemporary contexts.

In recent years a strong hermenuetical tradition has developed under the influence of existentialism which, while taking account of historical and critical study, is preoccupied with the question, "What does the text mean to me today?" or "How does the text authenticate my own existence?" Here the perspective of the interpreting subject is regarded as crucial in the hermeneutical task. A true understanding of the text can only be reached through a true understanding of my own situation. The dialectic between the text and my own situation brings about an apprehension of divine disclosure which is appropriated by a personal response of trust and faith in God. This existentialist approach, in its desire to preserve the absoluteness of the divine and directness of the divine-human encounter, has sometimes been characterised by a radically negative attitude to the historicity of the biblical texts. It is concerned not so much with the Jesus of history (or "Christ after the flesh", in Bultmann's words) but with the Christ of faith, encounter with whom is not contingent on our knowledge (or lack of knowledge) of the Jesus of history.

Two questions, among many that arise, may be mentioned. If the Christ of faith can be encountered in this direct way, what is the importance of the text? Secondly, how can I know that an existential encounter of this sort is possible unless I have testimony that it has occurred and continues to occur? In other words, the apostolic testimony (including the testimony to the Jesus of history as well as to the Christ of-faith) and the testimony of the Church throughout the ages are both crucial in creating the conditions for my own encounter and the testimony which arises from it.[24]

Another approach which has been developed latterly has to do with discovering the social, political and economic background of a particular text and with investigating the ideological assumptions which underlie the tradition encapsulated in it. This approach itself, however, can be informed by ideological presuppositions such as the belief that significant events in the history of a people can be accounted for satisfactorily in terms of categories which are primarily social, political and economic. Needless to say, such an approach does not always do justice to texts which are mainly religious and has a tendency towards the reductionist.[25] At the same time, nevertheless, scholarship such as this can become the basis for a powerful critique of the contemporary community in which a text is held sacred. The theocracy and egalitarianism of early Israel, the separation of Church and State in the teaching of Jesus and the "communism" of the early Christians, for example, can all be used to criticise the erastianism or the class-consciousness or the sanction for highly differentiated ownership of property in the contemporary Church.[26]

It is arguable, of course, that accommodation to the structures of society is also part of the sacred text. Thus the Monarchy is ultimately established in Israel in emulation of the surrounding nations. Despite its dubious origins, however, God uses it to bless Israel and to prepare them for the coming of the Messiah. The New Testament writers not only urge Christians to obey the secular power (Romans 13:1-7, 1 Peter 2:13-18) but recognise the right to private property even in the case of slavery! (See the letter to Philemon, but also the "household codes" in Colossians and Ephesians). In God's acceptance of the Monarchy in Israel, Goldingay sees divine willingness to begin with people (even his redeemed and liberated people) as they are and to use the institutions which are the most appropriate for them at that stage in their history.[27] Chris Wright points out, moreover, that human institutions are often transformed in the light of Israel's covenant with Yahweh and that he uses them to bring about the fulfilment of his own purposes.[28] The danger with such an approach, of course, is that it can be used to develop an evolutionary hermeneutic which gives perhaps too much value to the *status quo* and the possibilities inherent in it. As Wright himself acknowledges, there is a continuing need for the prophetic element which exists as a critique of the compromise, whatever the benefits which result from it.[29]

The hermeneutical circle is broken by many – in Latin America, for example – through a commitment to social and political transformation. The question now is not so much what the authors or editors of a particular part of the Bible meant. Nor is it primarily about its meaning for me. It is not even about the social, political and economic background of the text. It is directly about the capacity of the text to bring about justice and equity in the present order. The other approaches are simply preliminaries in the task of letting the text play its role in the liberation of the oppressed and the bringing about of justice.

It is not surprising to discover that the notion of the "event" is highly significant here. God has revealed himself in archetypal events which may be described as salvific. The biblical text has come about as a result of reflection on these events. God's saving acts in history come to a climax in the "Christ-Event". This is God's definitive revelation of himself. Salvation-History, as it is found in the Bible, from Exodus to Christ, has a certain unity and character which enables us to say that the God who acted in a liberating way at the Exodus or in the ministry of Jesus must always act in a liberating way.

This brings us to the importance of our contemporary experience. How are we to discern God's action in today's world? The answer, from a Liberationist perspective, would be by discerning where liberation and justice are being promoted. There is complex interaction here between the text and the context. The text must conscientise us so that we can discern God's saving action now. On the other hand, the present situation and its demands must lead us to the text so that we may discover how the liberating God acts in history. Some have claimed that it is our present situation which provides the hermeneutical key and enables us to interpret the biblical material in the light of our contemporary experience. Liberation theologians claim warrant for this position in the Bible itself. In the development of the Old Testament, particularly in the writing

Prophets, and in the interpretation of the Old Testament in the New, this dynamic is said to be already at work. The present event, whether that is Israel's apostasy, the consequent exile or the post-exilic period, provides the context for reflection on the older material having to do with the Exodus, the covenant at Sinai and the settlement in Canaan. In particular, the event of the Incarnation reveals new levels of meaning in the original text. The messianic prophecies, for example, come to be interpreted in the light of the coming of Christ. So too, it is claimed, present reality enables us to interpret the biblical material in a fresh way.[30]

But which aspects of present reality are to be regarded as interpretive of the biblical material? It is problematic simply to "read off" the presence of God from certain contemporary events. In the first place, how are we to decide which events are suitable for such an exercise? Then there is the ambiguity and ambivalence in the events themselves, which make any simple identification of an historical action with the will of God difficult. We must already have an existing discernment of how God acts in history if we are to discern how he is active now. The Scriptures, as records of his definitive saving-acts in the past, contain themes, such as that of the Kingdom of God or the Coming of the Messiah, which have been developed through reflection on and response to God's acts in history. It is interaction between such themes and present reality which discloses God's presence for us today. Theologically then, the demands of the present event cannot be allowed absolute priority as we interpret the biblical texts and determine how God acts today. Practically, however, it is precisely our present context which leads us to read the Bible in a new way and which elicits our response of commitment.[31]

In the last twenty-five years or so there has been a tremendous renewal in Bible reading. Much of this has occurred in base communities or in Pentecostal groups within the mainline churches, especially the Roman Catholic Church. It cannot be denied that some of this activity is escapist – an attempt to find in the Bible what cannot be found in everyday existence. In other cases, efforts are made to erect imposing systems of dogma or to establish authoritarian ecclesial structures. A great deal of Bible reading today, however, takes seriously the context in which the readers are placed. There is certainly a prior commitment to the Bible as a source of renewal and strength. At the same time, the context is

D

allowed to provoke sharp questions relating to the biblical texts. The answers obtained, as a result of group and individual reflection and meditation, highlight aspects of the Bible which have hardly been noticed before. The place of the poor in God's scheme of salvation has become a major element in the Church's concern today because poor people reading the Bible together have noticed the passionate advocacy of the rights of the poor in the prophets and in the teaching and lifestyle of Jesus himself. It is arguable that such a theme could not have become so prominent if the Bible were not being read in contexts of poverty.

Similarly, the recognition that law is unable to bring about justice, not only because human beings cannot fulfil the law's demands but because it is used by those in power to maintain the *status quo* of oppression, is an insight gained by the oppressed when reading (say) the Letter to the Romans. In such contexts, such a misuse of the Law is best seen in the Crucifixion. Unjust human beings used the Law to crucify the one who was sinless. God's justice, however, transcends the Law and is seen in his vindication of Jesus Christ in the Resurrection. This then becomes the basis of a hope for all those labouring under the oppression of law that God's justice will be established at last. The way of Christ not only sets forth the righteousness of God but it progressively makes human beings righteous (and does not merely impute righteousness to them). These people then encounter the ingrained injustice and unrighteousness in the world, which is maintained by the manipulation of the law in favour of the rich and powerful. Such an encounter is potentially transformative, as it challenges the values and systems of fallen human societies.

Traditional exegetes may well protest that Scripture regards the Law as perfect and just and good. The point in the present context is that it has been unable to bring about justice in a fallen world. It has, rather, been used by unscrupulous people to maintain injustice and oppression. It is Christ who, by his teaching, his living, his dying and his living again, sets out the way of true righteousness and becomes the hope of all those who confront wickedness. Again, others may say that such an interpretation of Scripture does not adequately distinguish between God's Law and the laws of human beings. This is true, but if God's Law can be misused, as it clearly was in the case of Christ, how much more are human laws susceptible to manipulation and misuse? In the end, the interpretation hinges on the experience of the disadvantaged that law and laws always work against them, while Christ is experienced as "for" them, renewing and strengthening them for their witness in a society which despises and rejects them.

It is well known that the emphasis on *praxis* in Liberation Theology has often led to the question, "Whose *praxis*?" This, in turn, leads to reflection on the *praxis* of contemporary Christians and Christian communities and the *praxis* of Jesus himself. The struggles of Christians against the present world order are informed by Jesus' own struggle against the powers of *his* day. At the same time, these contemporary struggles lead Christians to notice particular aspects of Jesus' ministry. Such situations have led to a renewed interest in the historical Jesus among Liberation theologians. It is the historical Jesus who is the crucial clue to the cosmic Christ. A Christology which is developed without reference to the historical Jesus is apt to be abstract and dogmatic. It is open to manipulation by those with élitist and class interests. Precisely for this reason, it can become alienating for the oppressed masses.

In sharp contrast to the scepticism in much of Northern theology about quests for the historical Jesus, there is optimism among Liberation theologians about what can be known of Jesus of Nazareth. Certainly, there is a need for critical historical and exegetical investigation. One has also to be aware of the concerns and motives of the redactors of the dominical tradition. All this does not, however, result in pessimism about the possibilities of discovering the Jesus of history. In fact, such studies reveal a unique individual with an overwhelming sense of mission and a tremendous capacity for suffering in the way of God. Despite the development and redaction of the dominical tradition, Jesus of Nazareth continues to shine through in his originality, his commitment, his suffering and his love. It is this which makes discipleship possible. Christian discipleship is being immersed in the processes of history, as Jesus was. It is an acceptance that suffering is the way of redemption. It is hope for ultimate vindication without holding anything back. It is service in the power of the Gospel but powerlessness in terms of the world and its values. Such discipleship would not be possible if next-to-nothing was known of Jesus of Nazareth.[32]

One striking result of the reading of the Bible in context by thousands of groups of Christians all over the world has been a renewal of interest in "doing Christology from below". These Christians are no longer so interested in philosophical, indeed metaphysical, speculation about the nature of Christ and the character of this world. They do not emphasise the need for the elaboration of systems of doctrine nor do they prescribe minimum standards of belief. They are, rather, interested in Jesus among the crowds in Galilee, in the implications of his encounters with the temporal and religious powers and in his acceptance of rejection and suffering as an aspect of his calling. These do indeed lead to an estimation of his Person and work, but in a way that is concrete and historical rather than abstract and speculative.[33]

The contemporary division between those who wish to do theology from "above" and those who wish to do it from "below" is not new. It is found already in the tension between the Alexandrian and the Antiochene schools in the early Church. Then too the division was between those whose approach was allegorical (both demythologising and ahistorical), speculative and metaphysical and those who emphasised the exegetical and the historical. Theodore of Mopsuestia, who is revered as a saint in the (Assyrian) Church of the East, in his clear rejection of the allegorical method of Alexandria and in his critical approach to the Scriptures is an early example of this latter tendency.[34]

In Asia the tendency among Christians has been to relate to the so-called "High Religions" or "World Religions" – that is, Islam, Hinduism, Buddhism and the like. One result of this engagement has been the articulation of Christian theology in a polemical, or at least apologetic, style. This has often necessitated the use of methods and terminology which have been developed by these religions and the systems which they have spawned. As often as not, these systems have been scholastic, speculative and dogmatic. Theologians in Asia, as in Africa and Latin America, are now stressing the priority of history in the engagement of Christian theology with a particular people. Nor is this history that of the élite and the rulers. They are seeking, rather, to relate to the history of the ordinary people. This history is found embedded in folklore, in songs, in poetry and in folk-religion. It is always a history of suffering, of oppression and of endurance. To make sense of this, it is necessary to relate this *Minjung* (to use a Korean expression) or history of the suffering masses to history in the Bible. Once again, we are able to perceive God's saving action in the *Minjung*, in that its concerns resonate with the concerns of Salvation-History in the Bible. Again, we find that those theologians who take seriously the history of suffering people also take seriously history in the Bible and, particularly, the Jesus of history.[35] We have seen already that different trajectories and themes in the Bible resonate with different people in different ways. Particular social, political and economic circumstances illuminate and are illuminated by these trajectories and themes. Reading the Bible in context has made the Scriptures deeply meaningful to many thousands of Christians. This has brought about renewal in faith and commitment and has made these Christians effective agents of change in many difficult and challenging situations.

The Bible, however, is not given only to local contexts and to specific communities. It is a book that belongs to the whole Church and, in the end, it has to be read with the whole Church, past and present, in mind. This means, of course, that tradition can modify insights gained from reading the Bible, in context. It can also mean that tradition is modified by the contextual reading of the Bible. Where the contemporary Church is concerned, the insights gained by one local community through their reading of the Bible will challenge and be challenged by other local communities as *they* read the Bible in the light of *their* circumstances. In this way each local community will be enriched and corrected by the others. This is a necessary aspect of the *koinōnia* (fellowship or communion) which is the will of Christ for the churches. Thus, while insights and perceptions will arise in specific communities, they must be made available to the Universal Church so that they may be tested for authenticity, and also so that they may challenge and enrich other communities of Christians. Theologies of liberation, for example, have arisen in specific contexts, but their relevance for other contexts needs to be examined and their authenticity needs to be evaluated.

However, it needs to be said that they have already brought about a sea-change in the way in which theology is done all over the world by emphasising the concrete over and against the abstract. They have stressed the importance of the Church as local community and have allowed the contemporary situation in all its political, economic and social aspects to address the community of believers and the Scriptures which they read. They have produced a new hermeneutic, a new way of bringing the "horizons" of the Bible and the contemporary world together which is based on a commitment to the transformation of the present order and which reads the Bible in a way which promotes Liberation. At the same time, we have noticed that such a commitment, if it is to be authentically Christian, must not only resonate with the Scriptures but must recognise themes of justice and Liberation as integral to the Bible's major concerns. In other words, it should not just use the Bible to promote one ideology or another but should allow it to form the Christian conscience, while letting the context highlight aspects of the Bible which require personal and social transformation.

The community that reads the Bible together also worships together. Once again, we have to note a tremendous renewal in every aspect of corporate worship. No longer is worship confined to the rather formal gatherings in church buildings on Sundays; now Christians worship in small and large groups in homes, in factories, in offices, in restaurants and in other places of recreation. Such worship is always informal. It may include the Eucharist or Bible study or both. It may be Charismatic or meditative, though it is difficult to draw hard and fast distinctions here. A group may pattern its style of worship on that of a religious community such as Taizé or it may be more eclectic in approach. Music ranging from plain-chant to simple choruses may be used. There is often a strong intercessory element; there may be prayers for absent members of the group, for those in need, for justice and peace in the world and for the furtherance of World Mission. Some groups encourage periods of silent meditation, and there may be some guidance as to how such periods are to be used. Informal worship of this kind is a significant factor in the renewal of the Church today.

However, more formal worship, in church buildings and elsewhere, is also being renewed. The Liturgical Movement began in the Roman Catholic Church and, at first, was essentially a movement for the more scrupulous observance of the Tridentine rite and for the greater involvement of the laity in the celebration of the Liturgy.[36] The renewed interest in the existing rite led naturally to a study of its mediaeval origins and its primitive basis. Scholarship has now been able to recover a certain amount of the form and content of early Christian worship.[37] Knowledge of these has been a powerful impetus for reform, as, in many cases, the scholars intended it to be. The other aim of the movement—namely, the greater involvement of the laity—also led to pressure for reform. All this careful work came to a climax in the far-reaching changes to Roman Catholic Liturgy which were instituted by the Second Vatican Council's Constitution on the Sacred Liturgy.

Although the Liturgical Movement originated in the Roman Catholic Church, its impact has been felt in nearly every Christian tradition. The Book of Common Worship of the Church of South India is another landmark in liturgical renewal. It represents a conflation of the results of liturgical scholarship, oriental influences from the Mar Thoma and material from the Anglican and Protestant traditions.[38] In turn, it has influenced nearly every major liturgical revision in the last forty years or so, including Vatican II and many Anglican revisions.

There is tremendous ecumenical convergence in liturgical matters. The simplification of ceremonial, vestments and language is an aspect of this. The full participation of the laity in the readings, responses, music and prayers is another. Many churches have followed the Roman Catholic Church in the practice of the President adopting the westward position (that is, facing the congregation) at the celebration of the Eucharist. Perhaps the most striking feature of this convergence has been the commitment of the various churches to the use of the modern vernacular in the Liturgy. The most dramatic change in this respect has been in the Roman Catholic Church, where there was a switch from mediaeval Latin to a modern vernacular almost overnight as a result of Vatican II. Other churches have not been backward, however, and they have carried out significant revisions which have sought to embody the values of the Liturgical Movement in contemporary Liturgy, while remaining faithful to the doctrinal emphases of their traditions. In most of these, an attempt has been made to relate the Church's knowledge of primitive Christian worship, gained through scholarship, to the contemporary needs of Christians and the particular emphases found in specific traditions.

Corporate worship is increasingly being seen as an occasion which can symbolise the breaking down of barriers between Christians, whether these barriers are of race, class, nationality or gender (Galatians 3:28; Ephesians 2:11-22; James 2:1-7). There is a desire in all the churches to promote the use of inclusive language in the Liturgy. In recent years there has been a campaign for liturgies which do not appear to be exclusive in terms of gender. The matter is somewhat problematic; languages are changing very quickly and words may carry very different connotations in different contexts. For example until quite recently the words "man" and "mankind" were capable of bearing an inclusive meaning in Britain. In North America, on the other hand, this ceased to be the case a good many years ago.

Perhaps the more serious questions relate to the advocacy by some of inclusive language for the Godhead. The use of such language is opposed by others who claim that God is revealed as Father, Son and Holy Spirit and that we cannot tamper with the economy of divine revelation simply to satisfy our liturgical needs. It is perhaps true that the dominant metaphors and images for God in the Bible are masculine. This is understandable, since the books of the Bible were, after all, produced in strongly patriarchal cultures. What is remarkable, however, is the fact that there *are* other strands in the biblical tradition. These have been discovered by feminist exegesis and include, *inter alia*, passages which use maternal imagery to describe God's love and saving activity (Numbers 11: 11-12; Deuteronomy 32:18; Isaiah 42:14; 46:3-4; 66:7-9). Such exegetes have not failed to notice that the etymologies of the words for "womb" and "compassion" are closely related in Semitic languages (including the language of the Bible) and that in the Bible God's compassion is sometimes spoken of in terms of the womb (Isaiah 49:15; 63:15; Jeremiah 31:20; Hosea 2:23). Other passages, such as Isaiah 66:13, also use maternal metaphors to speak of God. It is also worth remembering that key words such as "Spirit" (*ruach*), "Wisdom" (*chokmah*) and "Presence" (*Shekinah*) which are used in relation to the divinity in Hebraic tradition are all feminine in form. In the New Testament, Jesus uses the imagery of the mother-bird to describe his feelings for Jerusalem (Matthew 23:37 and parallels). This is continuous with the Old Testament tradition which describes God's protection by the use of similar imagery (Deuteronomy 32:11).[39] All of this makes it safe enough to say that "whilst the paternal image of God remains dominant, the maternal image is a pervasive and significant strand in Scripture".[40] Expressions such as "the motherly Fatherhood of God" are used sometimes in an attempt to do justice to both strands in Scripture.

There is an issue here which needs to be debated. Should language about God be gender-free or should it be such that it includes both male and female imagery? Some inclusive revisions of the Liturgy, which speak of the Blessed Trinity as "Creator, Redeemer and Sanctifier" or which have recast the *Gloria Patri* so that we give glory to "God, Word and

Spirit", have already opted for gender-free language about God which is analogous to gender-free language about human beings. In the Christian devotional literature of India, on the other hand, there is a bold use of *both* paternal and maternal images, either separately or together in paradoxical form. So Krishna Pillai could write:

> *The God in whom the Three are One*
> *And who is One in Three*
> *Holy One in body, speech and mind*
> *In form the peerless Mother of all good deeds.*

N. V. Tilak of Western India, however, could bring both images together:

> *Lay me within thy lap to rest*
> *Around my head thine arm entwine*
> *Let me gaze up into thy face*
> *O Father-Mother mine!*[41]

Should inclusive Liturgy, where language about God is concerned, be an enrichment of metaphors so that additional, feminine metaphors are added to the existing masculine ones? The danger with gender-free language about God is that it tends towards abstraction and may produce sterility in worship. It is certainly true that feminist hermeneutics will attempt to get beyond the "incidental" androcentricity and patriarchy which many of the biblical texts reflect. It is said that this will enable it to recover divine revelation and redemption as they are seen to impinge on women:

This critical principle of feminist theology is the affirmation of and promotion of the full humanity of women. Whatever denies, diminishes, or distorts the full humanity of women is, therefore, to be appraised as not redemptive. Theologically speaking, this means that whatever diminishes or denies the full humanity of women must be presumed not to reflect the divine or authentic relation to the divine, or to reflect the authentic nature of things, or to be the message or work of an authentic redeemer or a community of redemption.

105

More positively:

> What does promote the full humanity of women is of the Holy, does
> reflect true relation to the divine, is the true nature of things, is the
> authentic message of redemption and the mission of redemptive
> community.[42]

It may be, of course, that such a critical principle is derived from the
Scriptures themselves and that this presupposes a prior commitment to
the Scriptures being interpreted. In such an approach culture is regarded
as incidental to the revelation which occurs in it, and it is deemed
necessary to make a clear distinction between culture and revelation.
Again, there is a danger of being left with a demythologised remnant.
Such a critical principle, if it is to be effective, has to be complemented,
therefore, with a celebration of maternal metaphors for God, of the
spiritual and other kinds of leadership of women in the Bible and of the
Church as a community where the barriers erected because of human
sinfulness are broken down.[43] Such a rounded approach will work
against an excessively abstract view of revelation and will "concretise"
it in ways which are meaningful and challenging for women. As a
consequence, inclusive liturgical language, instead of being impoverished,
will be greatly enriched.

The discussion about inclusive language is only a part of the wider
debate about the incultration of the Liturgy in particular and inculturation
in general. The use of inclusive language is, at least partly, a response
to developments in human societies which have led to a reappraisal of
the rôle of women in those societies. We have seen earlier that the Gospel
is translatable into each and every human culture. It has to be
communicated in such a way that it relates to the reason and values of
each society.[44]

Similarly, in worship it is necessary for Christians to read the Bible,
pray, break bread together and give thanks in ways that are appropriate
to each culture and in the language which is common to all in that culture.
Saint Paul taught the principle clearly enough in his instruction to the
Corinthian church about their worship (1 Corinthians 14:6-19). The
churches of the Anglican Communion are founded on the principle,
recovered at the Reformation but part of primitive ecclesiology, that each

local church is called to be and to become the Catholic Church in its own place.[45] The recovery of this principle led to the view that the local church is autonomous in the way in which it organises its discipline and worship, provided it remains faithful to the deposit of faith inherited from the apostles.[46] It is true that at the time of the Reformation political circumstances, such as the emergence of nationalism, led to the identification of the local church with the national church. This is not a necessary identification, however, and Anglicanism has flourished in many situations where there is no question of "establishment". Nor is it necessary for this principle to require autonomy only at a regional or national level. The principle is equally good at diocesan, parochial and basic levels.[47] This means, in effect that given the apostolic requirements of decency and good order (1 Corinthians 14:40) and also the maintenance and nurture of communion between the churches, each local community is free to organise its worship in accordance with its needs and the demands of its particular context.

In the Roman Catholic Church, Vatican II provided fresh impetus not only for the translation of liturgical rites into the vernacular but for a thorough revision of the rites. Much greater freedom was given to the national episcopal conferences and to religious communities to adapt the rites according to their own needs. This led to a period of tremendous creativity in the liturgical practice of the Roman Catholic Church in many lands. At the heart of inculturation in that Church is the perception, which we have already encountered in the fundamental documents of Anglicanism, that the local church is more than a territorial or administrative unit. It is nothing less than "an epiphany of the Universal Church, which in fact it endows with expression".[48] Vatican II taught that there were divinely instituted elements in the Liturgy which could not be changed, but there were other elements which were of human origin and which could vary from culture to culture and from place to place. Anything which is not bound up with superstition or error can, in principle, be used in the Liturgy.[49] This led to numerous local adaptations in terms of posture, music, dance, drama and vestments. In some cases, there were adaptations even of the eucharistic prayers and of the lectionary to suit the particular circumstances of the congregation. Vigorous hymn singing, lay participation as ministers of the Word, as leaders of intercessions and as extraordinary ministers of the Eucharist, led to a greater feeling of involvement among the faithful.

In more recent years, however, there seem to have been attempts made by the Roman Congregation for Divine Worship to control inculturation by issuing detailed instructions and by refusing to approve material forwarded to them by national episcopal conferences. At the same time, national liturgical commissions are now demanding that final approval for new liturgical texts and rites should rest with the local episcopal conferences, with the Congregation taking on a more advisory role. It is also being suggested that the Congregation should become a forum for the exchange of ideas between the local churches, thus encouraging "transcultural adaption".[50] The "indult" or concession of 1984 regarding the use of the Tridentine rite has been greeted with dismay by many episcopal conferences and liturgical commissions, as it is seen as a departure from Vatican II's commitment to the very basis of the Liturgical Movement – that is, the active involvement of the whole people of God in the eucharistic celebration. The establishment of a separate Congregation for the Sacraments is also seen as reflecting a pre-Vatican II understanding of the Sacraments. It is seen as a move which is likely to retard liturgical renewal in the Church.

There is a struggle going on between the local churches and the officials in the Vatican. The former have come to an understanding of the nature of the Church which emphasises the autonomy of the local churches and the communion which exists between them. For them, "soundness" in the Liturgy can only come from authentic inculturation which is in accord with this understanding. The Vatican is seen in this context as a focus for the communion between the churches and as a way of maintaining and enhancing that communion. It is increasingly *not* seen as the apex of a hierarchical church from which instruction is sent down to the local churches. The *magisterium* or teaching authority of the church is seen as subsisting in the bishops, who are united collegially with the Pope, not in the officialdom of the Vatican.[51] The outcome of the struggle will determine whether inculturation is to continue in a dynamic way in the Roman Catholic Church or whether it will lapse back into a state in which it is liturgically dormant. Once again, limitations on the ministry of lay women in the context of the Eucharist and on contextualisation in Africa give some cause for concern.

We have noted already the commitment of Orthodoxy to inculturation.

This is true of both the Chalcedonian and the non-Chalcedonian traditions. This commitment extends to inculturation in the Liturgy. Orthodox churches almost everywhere have, in the past, initiated the vernacularisation of both the Bible and the Liturgy. In some cases (as with the Armenians), the written language was virtually created by those who translated the Bible and the Liturgy into the vernacular. The problem in some cases is that inculturation was into the culture of a past age, which is often viewed as a golden age. The vernacular of that time is no longer the vernacular of today; indeed, it may be almost wholly incomprehensible. However, Orthodox mission theologians are well aware of the need to recover the commitment to inculturation, particularly in relation to the Scriptures and the Liturgy.[52] It would be interesting to see how the renewal of both Chalcedonian and non-Chalcedonian Orthodoxy will affect the Liturgy of these churches.

The Orthodox, of course, are not alone in having a constituency which values continuity and tradition to the point where, for some, these take precedence over pastoral requirements and mission. Such attitudes are common among churches which are said to exhibit features of what is called (mistakenly, in my opinion) "sociological catholicism"; churches, that is to say, which have reached a high degree of accommodation with the cultures in which they are found, sometimes going well beyond what is required for inculturation. In some churches, any move to revise the Liturgy or even to translate the Bible into a more contemporary idiom is regarded by those committed to continuity as a subversive act designed to undermine the "deep, unquestioned, implicit integration of life and faith, world and church, nature and spirit" which is exhibited by "indigenous and territorial churches with deep national roots".[53]

Other Christians, in the same situations, might well ask questions about the continued intelligibility of old rites, much as the Liturgical Movement began to question the appropriateness of mediaeval Latin in a modern and Univeral Church. We need also to ask how far archaic language is experienced as alienating by increasing numbers of those who attend church only occasionally. Can the Bible, in an archaic translation, be commended for personal reading or for group study? Much of the case made by traditionalists depends upon aesthetic criteria. So the language of the Prayer Book and the King James Bible is seen as beautiful and poetic, better able to evoke a sense of the numinous than the more prosaic modern services or translations. This, of course, depends on formation. Those who have a good background in the history, literature or music of a particular culture and of a particular period are more likely to be affected by such considerations than those who have not. Another ground for traditionalism in this area is the appeal to the "subliminal" value of the traditional Liturgy and the public reading of the older translations of the Bible. It is held that because of their familiarity, they have an impact on the subconscious mind which the newer liturgies and translations can scarcely have. Once again, this is questionable. If this really was the case, secularisation would hardly have made the inroads it has. Such a view fails to take into account the rapidly changing intellectual, scientific and social climate which makes it difficult for people to integrate the rest of their lives with their worship if that worship belongs to another age. Such worship can be preserved for antiquarian interest and for aesthetic value, but it must remain doubtful whether it can deliver where today's pastoral and evangelistic needs are concerned.

In a completely different context, the African Independent Churches are vigorously engaged in the contextualisation of the Christian Faith into traditional African culture. Some of these churches are experiencing rapid growth precisely because they are able to appeal to certain affinities, moods and rhythms which are to be found in many African societies. There is a strong sense in many of these churches that God should be perceived as revealing himself directly in the African situation, rather than through imported intermediaries, whether these are people, books or audio-visual media. This is one reason why there is such a strong emphasis on prophets and apostles in many of these churches. It is true, of course, that these churches *have* been influenced by other traditions, such as the Ethiopian, the Coptic, the Eastern Orthodox, the Roman Catholic and the Pentecostal. The main thrust, nevertheless, remains the expression of an authentically African Christianity. Some of these churches have now joined the conciliar movement. This gives us hope that they will enrich other churches everywhere, but particularly those in Africa, with their spirituality, their witness and their forms of worship.[54]

In any attempt at inculturation, there is always the danger that engagement might take place with aspects of a culture which are superstitious, unjust, exploitative or discriminatory. Ultimately, of course, the Scriptures remain the touchstone against which all developments are to be tested and, if necessary, reformed. Universal Christian Tradition also has a place, however, even if this simply means hearing about how Christians in past ages have coped with the problems raised by the engagement of faith with culture. The Gospel is universal, and therefore it is translatable into every culture. People of every culture, furthermore, can respond to the Gospel because it "makes sense" in terms of their values and their reason. Authentic inculturation, however, can never be an endorsement of *all* the values and *all* of the "reason" of any particular culture. Human beings of every society are fallen and sinful, and cultures exhibit this sinfulness just as much as they exhibit the image of God in which all human beings are created. The engagement of the Gospel with a culture will lead to inculturation, but it will also lead to a challenging of those aspects of a culture which particularly exhibit human fallenness. It is also perhaps worth noting that the doctrine of total depravity alerts us to the truth that *every* aspect of human behaviour and of human culture is affected by the Fall. This means that even those aspects of a culture which *are* suitable for inculturation have to be reviewed and purified in the light of the Gospel before they can be pressed into its service.[55]

From the very beginning, the Church has challenged Christians to share their material possessions with each other. The earliest Christian communities, at least in Jerusalem and its environs, held everything in common (Acts 2:44-45; 4:34-37), though it also seems clear that there was no compulsion to do this and that people could continue to hold on to their possessions if they wished to do so (Acts 5:4).[56] It may well be that the Gentile churches did not practice "communism" to the same extent as the Palestinian churches, though Tertullian is still claiming towards the end of the second century that "Christians hold everthing in common except the marriage-bed". However, this may have been the expression of an ideal rather than a description of the actual state of affairs, for Tertullian himself tells us that those coming to Christian worship first made a contribution to the common fund for the poor.[57]

Again, in the earliest times there arose the practice in the churches not only of looking after their own poor (Acts 6:1; Romans 12:8, 13; James 2:2-13), but of sending help to the poor in Jerusalem. This seems to have begun when the young church in Syrian Antioch responded to the famine in Judea by sending help through Barnabas and Paul (Acts

2:27-30). The agreement between Peter, James and John on the one hand and Paul and Barnabas on the other about their different spheres of mission had the relief of the poor in the Jerusalem church as one of the conditions of fellowship (Galatians 2:10). It is possible that the church leaders in Jerusalem regarded this as a kind of tribute, analogous to the contribution which Jews all over the world paid for the maintenance of the Temple and its ministry. Paul, however, saw it as a means of creating fellowship between churches of Jewish and Gentile origin and as an acknowledgement by the Gentile churches of the spiritual riches which they had received from Jerusalem.[58] By the time of the Corinthian correspondence (1 Corinthians 16:1-4; 2 Corinthians 8-9, cf. Romans 15:25-28), the church in Jerusalem appears to have fallen into a condition of extreme poverty. It has been suggested that one of the reasons for this may have been the "communism" of the church. It is said that the system of sharing all their goods and property had broken down. People had disposed of their assets and had become dependent on the distribution from the common fund. In time, as more and more converts were added to the church, this became insufficient for the needs of all, and there was great hardship because of this state of affairs.[59] This may be so, but it is worth remembering that Paul, in urging the Corinthians to give generously to the church in Jerusalem, assumes egalitarianism to be the basis of relations between Christians and churches. Giving is seen to be a kind of redistribution through which the needs of all are met and no one is left with excess (2 Corinthians 8:14-15, cf. Exodus 16:18). In any case, Paul has clearly established the principles of interdependence and interchange between the churches. Everyone has something to give, no matter how little or how much (2 Corinthians 8:12). Equally, everyone should be open to receiving both spiritually and materially, in accordance with their needs (8:14; 9:14).

Giving, sharing and caring is not, of course, limited to those within the fellowship of the Church. It is characteristic of the ministry of Jesus that he is forever reaching out to those outside the circle of orthodox belief and practice (Mark 2:13-17 and parallels, Luke 15 and John 8:1-11). He reaches out even to the Gentiles and finds faith in them (Mark 7:24-30; Matthew 8:5-13 and parallels). The parable of the Good Samaritan (Luke 10:29-37) clearly teaches that, where love for one's neighbour is concerned, there are no barriers of race, religion or class. We have to

112

care for those in need, however "distant" they may be in terms of culture, wealth or origin. Behind dominical practice is the Old Testament legislation about loving the stranger and providing for his needs (Leviticus, 19:9-10, 33-34 and passim in the Pentateuch). This legislation is based on the recognition that the Israelities were themselves strangers in the land of Egypt. The misfortune that befell them there should on no account be the lot of the stranger now in *their* midst. In the New Testament, Paul urges the Galatian Christians to do good to *all* (Galatians 6:10). The injunctions to generosity in giving in the Letter to the Romans and in the Pastoral Epistles are, at least by implication, about giving both within and outside the fellowship of the Church (Romans 12:8; 1 Timothy 6:17-19).

Among the Fathers too there is great concern for the poor which goes beyond the humanitarian ideals of the Graeco-Roman world. Some of the Fathers give a very broad definition of the poor, including in the term orphans, widows, refugees and lepers. Love of the poor is, moreover, related to love of poverty. Material possessions are held in trust and must be shared. Holding on to them and refusing to share is a kind of slavery. By serving the poor we are serving God himself, in whose image all human beings are made (cf. Matthew 25:31-46). God himself is concerned for justice for the poor (as the prophets of the Old Testament saw) and in Christ he has shown his compassion for them. Our concern for the poor, then, is an imitation of God's love for them.[60]

Throughout Christian history the institutional Church, religious communities and lay men and women have all in different ways contributed to the tradition of Christian concern for the poor, the ill and the stranger. Hospitals, for example, have their origins in the Christian East. There they served a variety of purposes, including the care of widows, orphans, the sick and the aged. In the West they came to be associated with the monastic communities, and particularly with traditions of hospitality. The Reformation resulted in some limitation of the work of these hospitals, but the lack was more than made up by institutions established by monarchs, city fathers and voluntary societies. Education is another area where Christians have contributed much. The academies in the East and, later on, the universities in the West, were centres of excellence in learning. The monastic communities, together with the universities, contributed to social mobility by making provision for people of humble origin to devote themselves to scholarship.

In more modern times the Sunday School movement has provided literacy skills to millions of men, women and children. Christians were also involved in providing schools for poor children.[61] The nineteenth century saw the revival of different diaconal ministries on the continent of Europe and in England. Perhaps the most significant and widespread movement for the restoration of such ministries in the Evangelical Church in Germany began at Kaiserwerth. The local pastor, Theodore Fliedner, commissioned deaconesses to work at first in his own parish and later on in other parishes throughout the land. At first they undertook to remain in the order for five years, but gradually membership became a life long commitment. The deaconesses were unmarried or widowed. The developments in Germany were a strong influence on the movement for deaconesses in the Church of England and in other parts of the Anglican Communion.

Interest in the diaconal ministry was not, however, confined to women. Johannes Wichern was responsible for the establishment of various diaconal brotherhoods. These concentrated on particular ministries such as education for the poor, prison work and the rehabilitation of those wounded in war.

While diaconal ministries exist in many churches in Europe, it has been primarily the influence of the German Evangelical Church which has led to the restoration of the order of deaconesses in England and, a century later, to the revival of the distinctive diaconate (open to married men as well as single ones) in the Roman Catholic Church.

The distinctive diaconate, often open to both men and women, has been restored in many Anglican provinces, and in churches where Anglicans have united with Christians of other traditions. However numbers vary greatly from province to province and, within provinces, from diocese to diocese. The Church of England's decision not to proceed with legislation on a distinctive diaconate at this time is related to the dilemma about the large numbers of women who have now been admitted to the order of deacon but who cannot yet be ordained priest. Many of these women have been trained in exactly the same way as their male colleagues who have proceeded to the priesthood. Also, the ministry which these women exercise is similar to the pattern of ministry exercised by their male priest-colleagues. Often there is little that is distinctively diaconal about their ministry. Their status needs to be understood and clarified before any further developments towards a distinctive diaconate can take place.[62]

A recent pan-Orthodox consultation, convened by the Ecumenical Patriarchate, called not only for the restoration on women deacons in Orthodox churches but for the extension of *diakonia* into the sphere of social service in response to contemporary need.[63]

There is generally a great deal of reflection on *diakonia* at the present time. This is, quite properly, the consequence of a great resurgence in diaconal ministries since the Second World War. This activity was focussed at first on the reconstruction of post-war Europe, but has, subsequently, also found expression in a great variety of development-related work in Asia, Africa and Latin America. Partnership between the generally richer churches of the North and the generally poorer churches of the South has concentrated on enabling the latter to establish and to develop diaconal ministries. These range from traditional involvements such as education and conventional medicine to new patterns of ministry in public health, literacy programmes, refugee relief and rehabilitation, community development, cooperatives, income-generation schemes and conscientisation programmes.

Inevitably, questions have arisen about the appropriateness of some models of development and also about ministries which are heavily involved with élite groups. It is alleged that churches in the South are often encouraged to continue with outdated models of mission which do not benefit the poor. Others allege, however, that the churches' involvement with the poor has become too radical and is hardly distinguishable from a political programme. Churches in the North, perhaps only semi-consciously, often act in concert with their governments (from whom they may receive financial support for diaconal ministries). However, the governments act primarily to further their geopolitical interests, and these are not always consonant with meeting the needs of the poor and oppressed. This has become clear in the history of the massive aid programmes for Afghān refugees. Such programmes have sometimes bypassed the local church and have included only token local involvement. Often they have been administered by expatriates and there has frequently been little accountability to the local church. And yet partner churches and agencies from the North always insist on mutual accountability as a condition of partnership. The most worrying aspect of the matter has been the heavy involvement in these programmes of governments which, at the same time, have chosen to support political and military factions which can hardly be described as progressive. Churches and diaconal agencies in the North will, at least, be implicated if a situation is produced where the rights of the Afghān people (including women) are further curtailed and their suffering is increased.

One issue which has been the cause of endless debate is that of resource sharing. Some years ago, there was a discernible desire among churches and agencies in the South to move away from *dependence* on the North. This resulted in calls for a moratorium in the receiving of both financial aid and personnel from Northern countries. The desire for *independence* is, however, gradually giving way to a realisation that churches as well as Christians are *interdependent* on one another. This recognition is leading to the view that the giving and receiving of resources cannot operate in one direction only. There has to be an *exchange* of resources and people for the enrichment of all. Churches have to identify the resources which they can give to the World Church and, at the same time, recognise their need to receive certain resources from the world-wide family of Christ. These resources may have to do with skills of a certain kind, such as those related to education or medical care, or they may have to do with evangelism, with the renewal of the Church and with the recovery of community.

A consciousness of interdepedence is leading to a recognition of mutual *accountability*. Particular churches and agencies may be stewards of certain resources, but these resources are God's gift to the *whole* Church for the work of the Kingdom. Churches have to be ready, therefore, in mutual charity and honesty, to submit their stewardship to the scrutiny of others. They should also allow their partners in the Gospel the freedom and the integrity to determine the areas in which they need assistance, and should not try to impose on them a programme which has been conceived elsewhere. Dialogue is necessary, of course, in determining priorities in resource sharing, but such dialogue must not lead to patronage, on the one hand, or dependence on the other.[64]

People of other faiths and, at times, secular humanists often accuse Christians of misusing *diakonia* for the purposes of proselytisation. They see the so-called "rice-Christians" or "milk-Christians" as the result of a programme of seduction by the churches. This issue is often a crucial one in the dialogue with people of other faiths.[65] It has resulted sometimes in long lists of complaints against the activities of the churches and, on occasion, these have been followed by new restrictions on the work of the churches in certain countries. It is true, of course, that some churches and Christians *have* misused *diakonia* in this way. Wherever this has happened, there needs to be repentance and a new beginning. However, at the same time, there is a need to be aware of the fact that *some* people of *all* faiths are liable to promote their beliefs in ways which damage their own integrity and the integrity of the people they encounter. We need to remember, moreover, that a great deal of Christian *diakonia* has been specifically directed to the needs of the poor and outcast. It should come as no surprise to anyone that such people have responded in large numbers to this recognition of their long-neglected humanity. Indeed, the prophetic character of certain kinds of Christian ministry, such as that directed against caste and racial discrimination or the oppression of women, for example, has led sometimes to the renewal of another faith tradition and even to the birth of a new kind of national consciousness.[66] Increasingly, people of other faiths are themselves getting involved in various kinds of service to the community. For example, a devout Muslim named Edhi has built up, from very simple beginnings, a marvellous welfare system in Karachi which provides many services, including hostels for the homeless and rehabilitation centres for drug addicts. He seems a man of complete integrity and attracts widespread support from all sections of the community. At the other end of the spectrum, many highly organised Hindu and Muslim Associations run medical and health programmes directed at the needy in society. From the Christian point of view many of these programmes deserve praise, and Christians should consider if cooperation is appropriate. In other cases, Christians may want to raise questions at least as sharp as the ones raised by those of other faiths in response to certain kinds of Christian activity.

The nineteenth century was a period of great revival for the religious communities. We have seen already that the Liturgical Movement began in a monastic environment. It is also true that it renewed the life of the Benedictines among whom it began. The Tractarian revival led to the restoration of religious communities for both men and women in the

Church of England. These were later to spread throughout the Anglican Communion. Many of these communities were deliberately situated in deprived areas and came to have a significant ministry among the poor and those in special need. The introduction of deaconesses and, in some cases, male deacons in the Reformed and Lutheran Churches on the continent also led to a renewal of disciplined, communal living. Orders such as the Evangelical Sisters of Mary at Darmstadt provided a model of community life for the non-Roman Catholic Churches.

These developments have continued and, in this century, we have seen the emergence of ecumenical communities such as Taizé. Another model which has re-emerged is that of Nicholas Ferrar's community at Little Gidding. This has been influential both within the Anglican Communion and outside it. In communities based on this model families, as well as single people, live together. They are bound by a simple rule, usually concerning prayer and lifestyle. The Archbishop of Canterbury's reference to the renewal in community life was not, however, restricted to the emergence and growth of religious communities, of whatever sort, important as this growth is. He was also concerned to point out that the *whole* Church, in its local, regional and universal manifestations, is experiencing a new emphasis on community as a way of being the Church.

The origins of the basic communities lie, undoubtedly, in the inability of the Roman Catholic Church in Latin America to provide an adequate system of pastoral support for local congregations. This failure is due to the chronic shortage of priests in that continent. Some priests, of necessity, began to delegate certain evangelistic, catechetical and pastoral tasks to the laity. Community coordinators were trained to provide instruction in the faith, to lead non-eucharistic worship and to take the initiative in the resolution of communal problems.[67] Once the laity had been enabled in this way, however, the movement began to acquire a life of its own. New or restored ministries began to appear among the laity. In addition to the ones already listed, ministries of caring for the sick, of teaching people to read and write, of helping the unemployed to find work, of advocacy of the rights of those even more under-privileged than themselves and of succour for the poor appeared and multiplied in these local communities. There was a new sense of solidarity and of celebration. People not only worshipped together but learnt together, worked together, ate together and played together.[68] In a curious kind of way the communities began to display the characteristics of work, prayer and carnival listed by W. H. Auden as necessary for human wholeness.

Canonically, it was not possible for them to celebrate the Eucharist without a priest, but they began to invest their eating and drinking together with sacramental significance. In time, a full-blown celebration of "the Lord's Supper" emerged which was eucharistic in form and at which the lay coordinator was the president. Liberation theologians are clear that, for many Christians, it is this "Lord's Supper", even though it is not canonically the Mass, which makes the Eucharist the centre and culmination of the whole life of the Christian community which Vatican II demands. Without it, thousands of Christians would only experience the Eucharist on those rare occasions when a priest could visit them. Boff remarks cuttingly: "The official *praxis* whereby a priest can celebrate the Eucharist without the community but the community cannot celebrate the Eucharist without the priest, continues to prevail in the Church".[69]

In view of these developments, it is not surprising that demands for the authorisation of members of the laity to preside at the Eucharist in the Anglican Communion have come from provinces and dioceses in Latin America.[70] Once again, the paucity of clergy is cited as a reason, and it is argued that there are lay leaders available in congregations which priests cannot often reach who would be suitable for authorisation. It is perhaps appropriate to point out that even the most ardent advocates of lay presidency among Roman Catholic Liberation theologians recognise that it is an anomaly made necessary by the existence of another anomaly – that is the requirement of celibacy for priests in the Latin Church. Boff, for example, agrees that "the normal thing for organized communities would be to have these community presidents receive the sacrament of order". He points out, however, that this is not possible because of ecclesiastical discipline. This discipline, which is acknowledged by all to be human in origin, is preventing the fulfilment of a divine command. He urges a return to the primitive practice of ordaining those who are married. Celibacy, he points out, is a gift which only a few have. Priesthood, however, is a necessary service for the Church. Such a service cannot be made to depend upon a "free charism" which may or may not exist in particular situations and at particular times.[71]

It is obvious that the churches of the Anglican Communion do not share the difficulty being experienced by parts of the Roman Catholic Church. It is part of the heritage which the Anglican Communion receives from the Reformation that priests can marry and that married people may be ordained. So if there are recognised leaders in a congregation who are deemed suitable to preside at the Eucharist, they should receive proper preparation and be ordained. The kind of preparation will vary from person to person and from context to context. Some will be able to benefit from the full range of theological education which is offered to those in more traditional training, though they may take longer to complete the course, especially if they are in full-time employment. Others will have more limited exposure to formal theological disciplines, but their gifts in leadership, pastoral care and evangelism, however, may more than compensate for their lack of conventional theological education. For some it will need to be made clear that though they are priests in the Church of God like other priests, the Church itself has recognised their vocation to be in a specific place. If the occasion arises for a wider ministry, further training may be necessary.

The emergence of theological education by extension as a way of ministerial formation provides a credible alternative to residential theological training, especially for those living off the beaten track.[72] Such a system of distance-learning, in which tutors visit remote areas and materials are oriented to self-learning, can be supplemented by occasional gatherings in local and regional centres where a greater variety of expertise can be offered and where people can learn from each other. Another model for non-residential formation is that of an ordination course. Here there is more frequent coming together, expertise is more often available and the reading and writing is directed to a greater extent.

The ordination of local leaders is sometimes regarded as a threat by the more traditional full-time clergy. This need not be so, as locally ordained ministries will need to be resourced, enabled and supervised. The *episcopē* of the full-time minister is therefore indispensible, if local ministeries are to survive and flourish. In turn, locally ordained ministers will enable the full-time clergy to fulfil their own ministry more effectively. In other words, we need to get away from a "clerical" understanding of the ministry and acknowledge that ordination is a God-given way of recognising certain ministries in the Church which have to do with leading worship (particularly sacramental worship), teaching and pastoral care.

Such ministries need supervision, and it is the task of the wider Church to make provision for such supervision. In episcopal churches, this is *ultimately* the bishop's responsibility, but he will delegate some of this to others. There is a place, in other words, both for a full-time ministry of enabling, encouraging and supervising and for local ministries having to do with leadership in the local community.

Liberation theologians are insistent that the base communities and their leadership are not simply a substitute for what cannot be provided by the official, hierarchical Church. They have become a new way of being the Church – or, rather, they have rediscovered the way in which the early Christian communities were the Church. Boff, therefore, refers to the base communities' "reinvention of the Church".[73] It is certainly true that the commitment, fellowship and enthusiasm characteristic of the early Church is largely to be found today in small communities of Christians gathering together for worship, evangelism or social action (sometimes all three), rather than in the traditional structures of the institutional Church. Whatever the protestations from official circles that the parish or the diocese is the basic unit of the Church, it is clear enough that these are often not the centres of dynamism and transformation which are required if the Christian Faith is to make an impact on the contemporary world. The strength and openness needed for this is very often to be found, quite paradoxically, in small communities of Christians, committed to each other and to the task of changing the world. If the Christian enterprise, in all its diversity, succeeds in the modern world, it will be because these communities have succeeded.

Also, hopes for renewal in the structures of the institutional Church must also, to a very large extent, depend on whether the "infectiousness" of these communities is allowed to come into contact with traditional ways of worship, study and organisation. There are signs that this is happening in Latin America, where, for example, the hierarchy of the Roman Catholic Church is to an increasing extent adopting the commitment of the base communities to renewal, advocacy and the struggle for justice. In other contexts a great deal is being done in official circles to shift the Church's concerns, so that there is a "bias to the poor". People are thinking and giving in ways which affirm the poor. A new commitment to being present, with local Christians, in situations of poverty is also becoming apparent in mission thinking.[74]

All this is very welcome, but the emergence of base communities is really about reversing the direction of mission, which until now has been from the affluent to the poor, from the North to the South, from technological societies to agrarian ones. Not only are the base communities about the capacity of the poor to evangelise themselves and those around them, they are also a significant element in the evangelisation of the affluent. The really important question now cannot be, "What can we do for the poor?" It must be, more and more, "What can the poor do for us?" We have seen already how the base communities have recovered the apostolic way of being the Church. The next phase must surely be their recovery of the apostolic way of mission – that is, mission from the poor and obscure to the affluent and well-known.

A recognition that the poor among the people of God have a mission to others in the Church as well as to the world at large should not cause us to romanticise the plight of the poor. Involuntary poverty, in which so many are trapped, has nothing to do with the evangelical counsel of poverty, which is a voluntary renunciation of property and wealth for the sake of the Gospel. It is part of the Church's task to seek the elimination of poverty both by developing its ministries among the poor and also by campaigning on matters of public policy which have a bearing on the situation of the poor. Poverty is often the result of exploitation by more powerful people and can result in chronic attitudes of mistrust towards the wider community and among the poor themselves. This can be a great hindrance to development, especially if it involves cooperation. The experience of exploitation by others can result in exploitation, within poor communities, by those who are more able, relatively wealthy or influential. Inertia, born out of despair, can also be a significant factor in many poor communities. If, in spite of this, we believe that poor Christians are the bearers of God's Word and will for us today, it is "not because the poor are good but because God is good".[75] It is divine providence which has brought the poor together and given them the strength to encourage one another and to face the world, not to destroy but to transform.

CHAPTER SEVEN

Fidelity, Freedom and Friendship: Christians in Plural Societies

In this last quarter of the twentieth century Christians have become increasingly conscious of the plural nature of many of the societies in which the Church is placed. In some cases, particularly in Asia and Africa, societies have been plural for centuries. In other cases, as in Western Europe, the immigration of people from other parts of the world has brought about a new plural situation.

Sometimes terms like "plural society" and "pluralistic society" cause confusion. People are not sure exactly what they mean. Is a plural society a society which is multiracial, multicultural or multireligious? It could be any one of these without being the other two, or it could be two of these without being the third, or it could be all three of these together. In the Middle East and in South Asia there are societies which are multiracial but not multicultural or multireligious. It is certainly possible for people of one racial stock to have cultural diversity which is not immediately related to religious belief, and it is possible for a society to have a variety of religious beliefs but to be homogeneous racially and culturally. Voltaire's remark that England had forty-two religions and only two sauces is illustrative of this last possibility!

Another point worth remembering is that even where two or more of the above-mentioned factors coexist, they may do so without being congruent. Singapore, for example, is multiracial, multicultural and multireligious, but at least some of its religions (such as Islam and Christianity) cannot be confined to one racial or cultural group. The relative homogeneity of many indigenous Western European societies and the significant immigration in recent years have together produced societies which are multicultural, multireligious and multiracial, *and* in which these diversities are often congruent. Such congruence, however, must be viewed as a special case and should not be allowed to become paradigmatic in reflection on pluralism in general.

Having determined that a society is pluralistic, one has then to consider whether it is pluralistic merely *de facto* or whether there is some *de jure* recognition of this plurality. In India, for example, there is constitutional recognition of the country's plural nature. Despite the efforts of militant Hindu fundamentalists, the country has succeeded in maintaining its "secular" character, at least as far as the official attitude to the followers of various religions is concerned. In certain Islamic states, on the other hand, even if there is a *de facto* plural situation, there may be a certain reluctance to recognise this state of affairs. The countries of Western Europe and North America are beginning to recognise the *de facto* plurality of their societies and are trying to give it *de jure* recognition too.

In view of the resurgence of religious fundamentalism which has occurred in many parts of the world, a secular polity, such as that of India, where no one religion or sect is regarded as "official" religion, offers perhaps the most scope for religious freedom. Such a separation of Religion and State does not, of course, exclude Christian or other religious *influence* on political, social and economic matters. David Nicholls has reminded us recently that "the attempt to Christianize or sanctify the secular order, breaking down any distinction between sacred and secular, has totalitarian implications, particularly in a situation of cultural and social pluralism".[1]

Some Christians in Western Europe, when they come to consider the plural nature of their particular society, tend to emphasise the plurality of *ideologies* rather than that of other, more visible, factors such as race, culture or religious belief. Is this because it is more possible to take an "absolutist" Christian position *vis-à-vis* these ideologies than it is in relation to rather amorphous matters like culture, religion and even race?

Where the Bible is concerned, stock texts are often used to buttress this or that position in relation to people of other faiths, for example, but the great variety of biblical evidence is not considered. The Scriptures were originally addressed to a number of different contexts. This variety has determined, to a greater or lesser extent, the theological emphases to be found in different portions of Scripture. Christians in the modern world also live in a variety of contexts. A reverent reading of the *whole* Bible will show the Christian community in a particular situation which emphasis in Scripture is specially appropriate for them when they come to consider an aspect of that situation.[2] In the matter of encounter with people of other faiths, is Elijah among the prophets of Baal a suitable paradigm for contemporary Christian attitudes, or are there other ways of looking at the situation? There is a worrying increase in the number of Christians who believe that only negative attitudes are appropriate in a Christian assessment of other religions. It is here that we need to relate the varying contexts in which the Scriptures were given to our own, once again varying, contexts. What importance, for example, does Melchizedek's encounter with Abraham (Genesis 14:18-20) have here? A Canaanite priest-king blesses Abraham, the father of the faithful, and Abraham makes an offering to him! Beginning with the Epistle to the Hebrews, Melchizedek has been a Christ-figure in Christian thought and his priesthood has been associated with the priesthood of Christ. At the same time, it is clear that he did not belong to the People of God as the term was understood in Old Testament times. Again, God used Balaam to confound the enemies of Israel (Numbers 22) and Cyrus to liberate his people from exile and oppression (Isaiah 44:28, 45:1). While Cyrus' significance may be assessed in purely political terms, this is much more difficult to do where Balaam is concerned, for his task was to prophesy *for* Israel (Numbers 23). Some years ago an evangelical society in the Church of England published a pamphlet which justified that Church's obligation to offer pastoral services to *all* the people of England (not just Church members) on the grounds that there is scriptural evidence that the prayers of non-believers are heard by God and that believers may pray for and with non-believers. In this connection, the pamphlet points out that Abimelech's prayer was heard by God and that Abraham also prayed for him (Genesis 20). The answered prayers of the crew of Jonah's ship are also mentioned (Jonah 1:14-16). New Testament evidence for non-Christians joining in Christian worship is cited too (1 Corinthians 14:23-25 and James 2).[3]

But is what is sauce for the goose also sauce for the gander? If one can not only pray with non-Christian English people but offer them the pastoral services of the Church as well, what about prayer with and for those who are followers of other religions? In religiously plural societies, there are many occasions where Christians are called to pray with those of other faiths. Civic occasions are perhaps the most common, but sometimes such prayer is required in evangelistic contexts as well. The present writer remembers going on an evangelistic visit with Joseph

Adetiloye, the Bishop of Lagos (now also the Archbishop of Nigeria), to the islands in the Bay of Lagos, where most of the inhabitants are nominally Muslim. The visits would always begin at the mosque, where some dialogue would take place, and would then go on to peoples' homes, coffee-houses and ultimately the village square. Here the Bishop would preach the Gospel and then there would be "dialogue-prayer". The Bishop would pray and the people would respond. This could go on for ten minutes or so. The visits always ended with a blessing by the Bishop. In my own experience, people of other faiths often ask the Christian to pray. This may be before a meal, at a wedding or a birthday or it may be at a funeral. Suitable prayer in such a context can be an important form of witness.

Many who have worked in hostile environments will know of people who have had a personal experience of Christ, yet continue in their previous religious allegiance. How is the Christian to regard such people? Then there are others who have experienced brokenness and repentance before God wholly within a non-Christian religious tradition. Where the latter are concerned, Sir Norman Anderson is prepared to say that such an experience must be evidence of the work of the Holy Spirit and that such repentance will result in salvation.[4] With regard to the former, we are to note that Elisha, the successor of Elijah no less, displays a curiously tolerant attitude towards Naaman's request for permission to continue going into the temple of Rimmon *after* he has been healed and has confessed the universal lordship of Israel's God (2 Kings 5:1-19).

Whatever may be said of individuals, in the New Testament, apart perhaps from Acts 17, it is hard to find a positive assessment of other religious *systems*. Saint John's Gospel teaches that the eternal Logos illuminates every human being (1:9). Romans 1 and 2 and Acts 14:17 allow for a vestigial knowledge of God among all people: the Fall has certainly corrupted and distorted knowledge of God, but something of it remains, nevertheless. It is part of the universalist (I use the term in the biblical sense) apologetic of the New Testament that we find in it great men and women of faith who stand outside the Jewish community. The Roman centurion (Matthew 8:5-13 and parallels) and the Syro-Phoenician woman (Mark 7:25-30 and parallels) are thus examples of faith which is possible for all if they respond to God's initiative in Christ. Cornelius (Acts 10) and the Ethiopian eunuch (Acts 8) are already

God-fearers, and find acceptance without formal conversion to cultic Judaism. At the same time, we have to note that little is said in the New Testament which might be construed as a favourable comment on the religious systems to which all such characters previously belonged. Among the Fathers too, there is a generally negative view of other religious *systems* while, at the same time, there is an acknowledgement that all men and women have been illumined by the eternal Logos and thus have a "sense of God" or an "attachment point" to God.[5] Justin Martyr and Clement of Alexandria, in particular, allow that knowledge of God is to be found among all human beings, especially in their philosophy and poetry, through the activity of the *Logos Spermatikos* or seminal Word (it should be remembered that certain kinds of poetry were equivalent to scripture in many of the cultures in which the Gospel was first preached).[6]

The missiological implications of this patristic doctrine are beginning to be discussed. Post-Vatican II Roman Catholic theology often uses it to argue for a real knowledge and experience of the divine mediated through other religions. Is this faithful to the patristic meaning and intention? The Fathers certainly saw the activity of the Logos in all human beings and in all human cultures, but they seem to have avoided saying explicitly that they saw it in other *religions*. Some scholars go further and claim that Justin, at least, uses the concept of *Logos Spermatikos* to account for the *criticism* of religion which is to be found in the ancient philosophers.[7] If this view is sustainable, the relation of *Logos Spermatikos* to other *religions* becomes a largely negative one. Kenneth Cracknell argues strongly for the view that Justin and Clement believed in the presence of the Word, before the coming of Christ, in both Judaism and in other cultures. Even he, however, is unable to establish that they taught the presence of the Word in other religions.[8] It might be argued, on the other hand, that the religion which was seen as being the object of the philosophers' attack was a debased form of folk or popular religion and that the philosophers themselves represented a higher or purer form of religion (there are certain similarities, in this connection, between the classical Hellenistic world and classical Hinduism). If this is so, could the Fathers' view that the seminal Word was present in certain kinds of philosophy and poetry in the Hellenistic world be used to develop a theology which sees the presence of the Word as a possibility in certain aspects of higher religion? Could such a presence be seen, for example, in the emergence of monotheism in certain cultures, or even in the belief in a "high god" found in many traditional religions? In other words, can this doctrine be developed to help Christians in their evaluation of inter-religious encounter as it takes place today in plural contexts? Also, if it is allowed that the eternal Word is present in the *world* and illuminates all human beings, where else, apart from religion, may the activity of the Word be seen? Could it be seen in counter-religious movements which challenge the *status quo* to which the official religion is party? At different times in the Indian context Buddhism, Sikhism and Christianity have all challenged the oppressive *status quo* created by the caste system (undergirded by Hindu social philosophy). Can such challenges, and the emergence of a new order, be regarded as the work of the eternal Word? In some parts of the world significant witness for human rights and economic justice is being carried out by individuals and groups committed to particular secular ideologies. Can we discern the activity of the Word in such witness? If truth found in ancient literature can be ascribed to the illumination of the divine Word, what about contemporary art, literature and music?

The development of biblical theology after the Second World War, with its particular emphasis on Salvation-History, raises all kinds of questions for Christians living in plural situations.[9] It is felt by some that Salvation-History, by emphasising the history of a particular people as the locus of God's activity, "tribalises" God and thus retards the emergence of a truly universalist theology. Against this, it is often said that the election of the people of God is to be understood as an election for witness and service, and leaves no room for pride.[10] The people of God are "a light to lighten the Gentiles" (Isaiah 42:6, Luke 2:32). Biblical universalism, as it is developed in the Prophets and also in the New Testament, is the belief that God's salvation is for all and that the people of God have been chosen as agents for the mediation of this good news to all. They are not the *only* agents, of course, for God is sovereign and he may work in any way he chooses, graciously revealing himself and bringing human beings to repentance and faith. In whatever way God chooses to reveal himself, the revelation is through Christ, the eternal Word, and those who respond to it are responding through Christ and in solidarity with him (whether consciously or, like the faithful of Old Testament times, unconsciously). Christ is the locus of the reconciliation which flows from God to human beings and from human beings to God. He personifies God's initiative of love, and at the same time is the new *anthrōpos* whose radical obedience cancels the effects of the sin of humankind, which is committed in solidarity with the old Adam and Eve.[11]

While the Salvation-History of Israel is central to an understanding of God's demands on us and his promises for us, it needs also to be related to God's work among the nations – that is, to *their* salvation-histories. Passages such as Isaiah 19:23-25 are often interpreted eschatologically, and this is correct. It is true that the final restoration and blessedness of Israel, Egypt and Assyria are placed in the context of the Day of the Lord. But such expectation has be be viewed in the light of other passages in Scripture which speak of God's activity among the nations in the past or in the present. Amos 9:7, for example, refers to the calling of the nations in relation to *the* determinative event in Israel's history, the Exodus. Jonah 3 and 4 clearly teach the possibility of repentance outside cultic Hebraic religion. In Malachi 1:11, this cult is compared to its disadvantage with the purity of offerings to God made by people of other nations (though not necessarily in the dominant cults of those nations). God's work among the nations is to be seen as a continuous whole and cannot be limited to the past, the present or the future. The history of Israel remains normative for us in our understanding of God's work, but that work cannot be confined to it.

Some Asian Christians, while not denying that God intervenes in the course of human affairs, find the *scheme* of Salvation-History too restrictive for cultures which do not have a linear view of history. Their emphasis would be not so much on a succession of "saving-acts" culminating in a final "day of salvation" but on a "cosmic Christ" who discloses himself to human beings in a variety of ways. Such a disclosure always results in widened horizons and increased awareness.[12] The Bible would then be seen as a record of the different ways in which God discloses himself. This would be as much in poetry, cosmology and "wisdom" as it would be in history. For the Church, God's disclosures in the Bible would be normative and all other claims about divine disclosure would be judged in the light of it, in terms of their consonance or dissonance with the biblical evidence. Such theologies, while they have much to commend them, find it difficult to deal adequately with the definitiveness and particularity of the disclosure in Jesus Christ, especially with the atoning significance of his death. In other words, they have a tendency towards the gnostic. They are valuable, nevertheless, in correcting the historicizing bent of much Christian theology by affirming the possibility of divine disclosure in thought, imagery and metaphor as well as in event.

How are Christians to relate to the State and to their fellow-citizens, who may or may not be Christians? Christians of different kinds often see the Sermon on the Mount as containing guidelines for their behaviour in society. There is little agreement, however, on *how* the Sermon should be interpreted so that it provides those guidelines. Conservative Christians sometimes point out that Jesus claimed to have come to fulfil the Law, not to destroy it (Matthew 5:17-20). This doctrine of fulfilment is then used to support the argument that "God's Law written in Scripture should act as a guide both for our personal lives and also for our efforts to influence society".[13] Others might say that an exegesis of the verses *following* the "fulfilment" verses would show Jesus' firm rejection of legalism and his emphasis, rather on "rightness of heart", on a change in disposition, on the "interior" rather than the merely external. The righteousness which exceeds that of the Scribes and Pharisees cannot be legalistic! It has to come about as a result of interiorising the meaning of the Law.

In situations where Muslim fundamentalists are campaigning for the strict enforcement of *Shari'ah* (Islāmic law) in all its aspects – financial, family, penal and political – many Christians use the Sermon on the Mount to show their Muslim friends that God requires rightness of heart more than rigid adherence to a legal code.

Jesus' own attitude to the Law of the Old Testament merits discussion here. While showing great reverance for the Old Testament, Jesus exercised complete sovereignty over it. He felt free to challenge the Mosaic law on divorce, for example, going back to God's intention for men and women at the time of the Creation (Mark 10:1-12). When we had a wedding in church in Pakistan, often many Muslim women would be present as guests. They never failed to be impressed by this teaching of Jesus regarding marriage. Again, he challenged the laws on the keeping of the Sabbath (Mark 3:1-6 and parallels), on ritual ablutions (Mark 7:1-8) and on pollution (Mark 3:1-6 and parallels; Mark 5:25-34).

The hermeneutical principle of "the canon within the canon" helps us to relate the New Testament, and particularly the teaching of Jesus, to the Old Testament. The emphasis of the Gospel on the interior over and against the external is an important part of the explanation for its accessibility to people of all cultures.

Given then that Jesus and his teaching are the ultimate arbiters for us of the demands which God's Law in Scripture makes on us, we need, furthermore, to reflect critically on the relation between God's Law as it is given in Scripture and the laws of a particular country at a particular time in its history. While God's work among the nations is to be taken seriously, the nations have also to be seen as participating in the general fallenness of humankind. In particular, what has been called the "collective egoism"[14] of the modern state, as expressed by its political, economic, social and legal structures, has to engage the attention of the Church in its task of prophetic witness *against* the world and *for* the values of the Kingdom of God. However influenced by Christianity a given tradition may be, the dangers of collective egoism cannot be excluded. The Bible has been used in the past to invoke racial supremacy, the divine right of kings, slavery and imperialism. For example, while Christians may approve of *some* of the Victorian values of nineteenth-century Europe, they have also to recognise that the countries of Europe were engaged in a massive imperial enterprise at that time. Whatever the benefits may have been, imperialism reduced people to dependence and subservience. Not only did this enterprise destroy cultures, but it also built the prosperity of sections of the European bourgeoisie on the exploitation of the people of Africa, Asia and Latin America. It is true that many of the people who came to be colonised were already oppressed by traditional social, economic and political systems. The replacement of one system of oppression by another cannot, however, be regarded as behaviour which arises out of subscription to Christian values.

The proletariat in European countries were also exploited. Men, women and children were made to work long hours in dark and cold factories and mines. At home they were not much better off, as large families were made to live in tiny tenements with the minimum of amenities. Many Christians were rightly in the forefront of the battle against these evils, but this was because they saw the discrepancy between the Law of God and the laws of their own time. *They* were not prey to romanticism about Victorian values. Talk about the "Christian heritage" of Europe needs to be treated with reserve. I am sometimes asked by people of other faiths, "If Europe has such a rich Christian heritage, how is it that it has given rise to such a permissive society?" As well as collective egoism we have also to take into account the pagan influence of the Renaissance and the secularising influence of the Enlightenment on the development of European polity.

There is certainly a very serious crisis in the moral awareness of people in Western countries. Sexual permissiveness, the breakdown of the family (not only the extended family but the nuclear family as well), epidemics of sexually transmitted diseases, alienation, depression and mental illness are just some of the features of this crisis. The relativisation and privatisation of values which have caused this crisis to occur are also part of the background which has allowed plural societies to emerge. Both the relativisation and privatisation of values and the emergence of plural societies are related, moreover, to one of the greatest achievements of modern Western civilisation – that is, the recognition of the value of the individual and of associations of individuals.

The recognition of the value of the individual is certainly rooted in the New Testament requirement of a personal response of faith to God's initiative in Christ. The Reformers in the sixteenth century recovered the insight that this faith is not merely belief in some dogma or other but is essentially trust in God – that is, it is about personal relationships. The Reformers, moreover, developed the doctrine of private judgement, which claimed that an individual could experience salvation through his or her own reading of the Scripture, without any mediation by the clergy. These were significant factors in the emergence of the idea of the value and freedom of the individual (of course, other factors were involved too). Christians in Western countries are faced, therefore, with a paradox: this recognition of individual value and freedom is seen as a gift of the Gospel, but it is also seen as having undesirable social consequences. Is this because the strongly corporate nature of much of New Testament thinking is today not allowed to balance its teaching on the individual? If the mediaeval Church was too corporate in its outlook, was the Protestant Reformation too individualistic? Does a synthesis need to be worked out between the two?

While the New Testament challenges Christians in the West to come to terms with its strong emphasis on the corporate, in other contexts it may challenge views of the corporate that are too oppressive. In such cases the value of the individual needs affirmation.

It is true that the West is characterised by relativism, but are *all* values regarded as relative? Surely respect for human rights, provision of adequate medical and educational facilities for all, concern for the less fortunate at home and abroad and respect for privacy are all values which have absolute or near-absolute status in most Western societies. It is true that collective egoism in the shape of a doctrinaire adherence to economic liberalism has recently challenged the absoluteness of some of these values. It may be, however, that this is precisely where the battle-lines will be drawn. An Orthodox Archbishop from the Middle East once said to me that the term "corruption" in the East generally refers to sexual immorality, whereas in the West it usually means dishonesty, especially in financial matters. Absolute values in the West today are clustered around this area: integrity in personal and social affairs, respect for the freedom of others, concern for the less fortunate and honesty in financial dealings. Any challenge to the excesses of entrenched privilege or of free-market capitalism will come because some or all of these values will be seen to have been violated.

Plural societies, of necessity, are societies where people from different cultural, religious and even legal backgrounds have come together. Many cultures and religions have a distinctive legal emphasis, and in some cases that emphasis becomes characteristic of the culture or religion. In such a situation it is vital for society to have a common law which is equally applicable to all its citizens but which also leaves room for different communities to preserve their own legal traditions, where these do not come into conflict with such a common law.

It is particularly important that all communities in a given society be governed by the same penal laws and the same laws on human rights, and the right to testify in court. Recent developments in some countries where Islamic fundamentalism has been ascendant have tended to compromise the position of non-Muslim minorities and of groups like women in this regard. Muslims should be able to order their personal lives according to Islamic law, but such a law cannot become the basis for inter-communal relations or for discrimination against women or religious minorities.

˙ With regard to penal law, Christians will want to agree with C.S. Lewis that retribution should be the basis for a proper view of punishment. In other words, the punishment must fit the crime. Deterrence is an effect produced by punishment, but it must not be allowed to become the only criterion for it. If it is, punishment will tend to become disproportionate to the crime. The concern will then be principally for what deters, not what a criminal deserves.[15]

At the same time, the principle of forgiveness, as much as that of retribution, must inform Christian theories of punishment. While Christians should be concerned to ensure that punishment fits the crime, they should also be concerned to ensure that there are possibilities of reform and rehabilitation for criminals. This means that punishments which mutilate the body or damage the mind cannot have the endorsement of Christians. Some Christians, at any rate, oppose the death penalty for similar reasons and also because of the terrible possibility of executing the wrong person. Because of the demoralising and dehumanising effects of prison, many Christians want society to examine seriously the possibility of non-custodial sentences involving service to the community and elements of restitution.

Whatever the variables in given situations, Christians will want to insist on the rule of law and the equality of all under a system which is equitable, just and merciful.

Christians will wish to maintain a prophetic stance within the society in which they live. This will involve them in opposing all forms of unjust coercion and restriction on human freedom. It will also involve them in witness against systems which are based on a degraded view of human nature and which seek to build the prosperity of a community on greed and selfishness. Christians will also want to witness strongly for the equality of all human beings in dignity and in the right to have access to opportunities. At the same time, it needs to be said that the witness of Christians will only be effective if they are in a living relationship with the society around them. The Church must remain part of the society in which it is set and must share that society's world of discourse if its mission is to be successful. A "ghettoised" Church cannot communicate the Gospel successfully, because it does not share a common language with the culture around it. Therefore, there is a sense in which Christians both belong and do not belong to the world in which they find themselves.

This tension must be maintained if, on the one hand, Christians are to retain a distinctive witness and, on the other, they are to *communicate* the Gospel to those around them. The Gospel must find a response in each culture while, at the same time, judging aspects of each culture.[16]

Some Christians living in plural situations are wont to respond in terms of models derived from the history of Israel, particularly the monarchy before the exile and the emerging hierarchy immediately after. These were periods when a pattern of homogeneity had already been imposed on the originally diverse origins of the people. Such diversity can be found recorded in the Book of Exodus (e.g. 12:38) and in the first chapters of the Book of Judges. An emerging consciousness of the need for national cohesion, however, produced a pattern of homogeneity for Israel. A response to pluralism which is derived from this period of Israel's history is likely to be "rejectionist" and reactionary. In a pluralistic situation, surely the New Testament communities with their acknowledged heterogeneity can serve as more appropriate models. Ethnic minorities would then not be regarded as "strangers and aliens" but as fellow-citizens with whom and to whom the Gospel must be preached.

Many plural contexts these days provide a marketplace for beliefs, ideas and ideologies. Christians have to recognise that their wares are not the only ones available, however passionately they may believe in their authenticity and in the urgency of the world's need for them. Further discussion is urgently needed about the relationship between tolerance and the mission of the Church. Recently I received a delegation of British Muslims who were experiencing difficulties in building mosques in this country and in obtaining proper facilities for the religious education of their children. They were especially concerned about the new Education Act and also that the law relating to blasphemy should protect all religious groups from scurrilous attacks on their beliefs. In expressing my sympathy for their situation, I was able to say that their position in the UK was a mirror image of my experiences in Pakistan. We too found it difficult to obtain permission to build new churches. Satisfactory provision for the religious education of our children was also an issue for us. We too felt helpless when aspects of Christian belief were attacked and ridiculed in the press and we had no right of reply. I promised my friends that I would do all I could to support their efforts to have places of worship in the UK and to have their children educated according to the tenets of Islam. I agreed with them that legal provision is needed to protect religious beliefs from scurrilous and *mala fide* attacks. At the same time, I made clear to them my commitment to freedom of inquiry, publication and speech, provided this freedom is not abused through the violation of privacy, the parodying of religious belief and the deliberate misrepresentation of situations. While it is right for Christians to promote the right of people of other faiths to worship freely and to be able to pass on their faith to their children, it is right also for Christians to ask their representatives whether such freedoms are enjoyed in countries where people belonging to these faiths are in the majority or where they have power. This principle of *reciprocity* is increasingly important in a world where many religions are resurgent and waking up to their missionary obligations. The future of Christian mission, as well as the wellbeing of people of other faiths, depends on the development of mutual toleration and respect, even in circumstances in which dialogue seems difficult and relationships are strained.

> *They say he only loves the righteous,*
> *I say he also loves the sinners,*
> *He accepts people of every sort,*
> *Be they Christians, Zoroastrians or Muslims!*

Part Three

CHAPTER EIGHT

Mission as Presence

We have seen already that the Franciscans developed a view of mission which distinguished between two "modes of Christian presence". First, it was held, there is the witness of life and worship, which does not entail verbal proclamation of the Gospel. Secondly, there is open preaching, which invites people to consider the claims of the Gospel, to repent and, ultimately, to be baptised. This approach was developed specifically in the context of mission to Islām in the middle ages, but it also has implications for other ages and other contexts, including contexts where one non-Christian religious tradition is dominant or where there is genuinely a multi-faith situation. It should be remembered that the second mode of presence is dependent upon discernment about the proper *kairos* for this kind of ministry. This does not mean that the second mode can be ignored for all practical purposes. Rather, the first mode is a way of careful preparation for the second.

Since the rise of Islām in the seventh century and its subsequent expansion, the ancient churches in Islāmic lands have been in a situation in which only the first mode of presence has been possible. Clearly, it has not been possible for them to evangelise openly. Even witness in the form of Christian symbols on buildings or of literature has been severely restricted.[1] In such a situation, Christians have had to develop distinctive views and practices in relation to mission. The ancient churches all emphasise the importance of the Liturgy in mission.[2] The Eucharist is a proclamation of the Lord's death until he comes (1 Corinthians 11:26). It is not, of course, simply *verbal* proclamation. The *taxis* or ordering of the Liturgy includes not only the ritual and the vestments required for the celebration, but even such fundamental aspects as the pattern of the church building! The use of icons, incense and candles ensures that all the senses are engaged in the celebration. The chanting, readings, homilies and prayers engage the mind and the spirit in the act of worship.

It is perhaps true to say that it is not only in the Islāmic milieu that the Orthodox instinct about the value of the Liturgy, not only as a cohesive force in times of adversity, but as a positive way of witness, has come to the fore. In the days before *glasnost* and *perestroika,* the Russian Orthodox Church was greatly restricted in its activites. It was not allowed to operate outside church buildings; children – even those of believers – could not be catechised; and the Church was not permitted to engage in any kind of diaconal ministry. It is reported that during the 1950s a Western clergyman once asked the then Patriarch, Alexi of Moscow, to describe the Russian Orthodox Church in a sentence. He replied, "It is the church which celebrates the divine liturgy."[3] In a sense this was true, because this was literally, nearly all that the Church could do legally. However, the Patriarch's words also evoked the Orthodox tradition of the centrality of eucharistic worship. That worship defines all areas of the Christian life, whether areas of faith or of witness. During this period of Soviet history, only a few churches were allowed to function as places of worship. Many others were turned into museums, libraries or even warehouses. Some were simply closed. However, the beauty of the celebration of the Liturgy and the silent witness of the devout continued to attract many – including intellectuals, artists and journalists – to the Faith of the Church. This, in turn, has enabled the Church to become a powerful symbol of the spiritual aspect of Russian culture, which is now being renewed.

A moving story from the pre-glasnost period is that of Valeri Barinov. He was a rather wayward soldier in the Soviet army, and was frequently stockaded for being drunk and disorderly. On one such occasion, he recounts, he was in a cell with only one rather narrow window to it. Out of this window all he could see was the top of the spire of a church with a cross on it. It was this cross which set Valeri thinking about spiritual matters, and this led to his conversion to Christianity. He became a leading jazz musician, but his work was regarded as suspect by the authorities because of its Christian content. He was at first confined to a psychiatric hospital (sharing his fate, of course, with a number of dissidents) and was finally expelled from the Soviet Union. Valeri's story shows vividly the value of presence, even when that presence seems very marginal indeed.[4] It may also lead some to a more positive evaluation of historic church buildings, which attract many tourists and other casual visitors. The mission potential of these buildings cannot be underestimated. Those charged with their care should make sure that they are not simply museums but lively centres of Christian worship and witness.

Although the Liturgy is central to Orthodox ideas about presence and witness, there are other aspects of the Christian life which are seen as important too. We have seen how in both the Chalcedonian and the non-Chalcedonian traditions, monasticism has played a vital role in mission. Whole monastic communities, smaller groups and even individual monks have often been the "forward movement" of the Church into areas where there was ignorance of and hostility to the Christian Faith. Missionary bishops, sent to labour in unchristianised areas, were drawn from monastic communities and other monks accompanied them.

In the Islamic milieu, however, another aspect of the witness of monasticism comes to the fore. The Prophet of Islam was deeply influenced by the piety and humility of the monks and hermits of the Syrian and Egyptian deserts. There are traditions that he had encountered in his youth, and the Qu'rān praises them for their humility and learning (5:85. It is also true, however, that the Qu'rān criticises the undue honour given to them at that time, 9:31).

Islamic mysticism or *Tasawwuf* (popularly known as Sūfism) emerged partly as a reaction to the increasing prosperity of the Empire under the Abbasid Caliphs and partly as a rejection of established legalistic and theological formalism. Its roots are certainly to be found in the Qu'rān itself as well as in Muhammad's religious consciousness. It was deeply influenced, however, by the living example of Christian monks, even to the point of adopting their robes of wool *(sūf)*, thus giving themselves and their movement a name *(Sūfī* and *Tasawwuf)*. Although Sūfīs hardly ever emulated the monks in their celibacy, they were influenced by a whole number of features such as vigils, meditation in lonely places, living in community *(khānqāh)*, fasting, hours of prayer and other ascetical practices common at the time. There was influence in terms of ideas too, particularly in the distinction made between asceticism as the human effort to discipline the body, the mind and the spirit *(maqāmāt)*, so that they are prepared for mystical experience *(hāl)*, and this experience itself, which was regarded as a divine gift. Christian metaphors and imagery, such as the soul's union with God being described in terms of a wedding, were also taken over, especially in poetry, which became a special vehicle for the dissemination of *Şūfī* ideas.[5]

In Şūfīsm Jesus is presented as the archetypal ascetic, whose cross is sometimes understood as symbolic of his life of self-denial. Although others are mentioned in connection with self-denying obedience which may lead even to death, Jesus is often the pattern for self-denial and sacrifice.[6] This picture of Jesus is obviously closely related to the Şūfīs' acquaintance with Christian ascetics.

The celibate life is one aspect of the witness of the Orthodox Church, and family life is another. This is particularly the case in Islamic societies. The sacramental character of Christian marriage and the lifelong monogamy which it entails are a powerful witness, especially among women, in societies where polygamy is permitted, divorce is common and marriage is seen as a contract which can be terminated by mutual agreement, by the decision of the husband or by judicial decree.

The contexts in which Orthodox Christians work, worship and witness are often characterised by suffering. In such contexts *marturia* or Christian testimony takes on a special significance. In this connection, it is instructive to be reminded that the Egyptian Church counts twenty-one persecutions in the "Roman" period between 202 and 642 AD. Some of these were at the hands of the pagan emperors but others, sadly, were at the hands of other Christians. The period from 642 to modern times is regarded as one of almost uninterrupted hardship and suffering.[7] To take another situation, in his novel *Christ Recrucified* the Greek writer Kazanzakis chronicles the way in which the traditions of Orthodoxy ensured the survival of his nation under Ottoman occupation.[8] Similarly, the presence of Armenians in so many parts of the world today, despite persecution, is profoundly related to the ministry of the Armenian Apostolic Church among the Armenian people. It is undoubtedly the case that the deep roots which Orthodoxy has in many cultures and in the hearts of their people have been responsible for the survival of those cultures, and often of their people too.

Survival and traditional understandings of mission are not enough, of course. It is encouraging to note that Orthodoxy is relating to contemporary contexts in ways which suggest renewal, if not newness. New-found freedoms in many communist dominated countries have led churches to review the whole spectrum of their work. Churches are increasingly permitted to engage in *diakonia*. They are once again able to offer help to the vulnerable, lonely, ill and poor. Catechesis of both the young and the grown-up is carried out openly. There are adult baptisms and many study groups which nurture the faith. Theological education is also being reviewed, and it is likely that these churches will need help in developing the curricula and faculties of their theological colleges. There is bound to be much greater interest in vocations, especially among artists and intellectuals, and the churches have to be equipped to meet this challenge.

Orthodox churches in Islamic lands too are experiencing renewal. This can be seen, for example, in a reawakened interest among *both* clergy and laity in preaching and teaching. Bishops and clergy, in a bold exercise of their teaching function, conduct large weekday meetings. Not all of those who attend are from the Christian community; others too are drawn by the openness and attractiveness of what is taught. Orthodox believers are becoming aware that the witness of the Liturgy has to be extended to the home, the neighbourhood and the workplace. They are learning how to bear witness to the eternal truths of the Gospel in a careful and sensitive way. Sometimes this can result in persecution, but then, Orthodox are well prepared for this.

The Franciscans have continued their modes of presence into modern times, and they can be found in many different parts of the world. In some cases only the first mode is possible for a considerable period. Friendship and sharing quite often lead to dialogue, and there is then something of the second mode as well. In Karachi, for example, the Franciscans have a centre called the *Darakhshān* (or "place of illumination"). The order has acquired a couple of flats in a large housing estate, and they are used for the formation of those with a vocation to the religious life, and also for hospitality and service. Anyone can go in at any time and expect a welcome. Members of the community offer free coaching to school children. There is a room for prayer and meditation which is widely used. The community's interface with the neighbourhood has raised important questions about human rights, freedom and justice. These in turn have led to the beginning of a dialogue on spiritual matters. The first mode of presence is gradually leading to the second.

Similarly, the White Fathers maintain a presence in another Islamic setting – that of North Africa. In a number of cities there are communities of priests and lay brothers ministering to mostly expatriate Christians and engaged in development and conscientisation. Their presence in this area, once a centre of Western Christianity, is deeply significant. It serves, among other things, to remind people that Christianity is a living faith. This reminder is perhaps even more necessary in a situation where one is surrounded by the ruins of a vanished Christian age. Members of the communities are drawn from many nations, some of them African ones. This is a demonstration of the universality of the Church.

The life and work of Charles de Foucauld (1858-1916) in the Sahara is yet another instance of effective Christian presence. De Foucauld led a hermit's life, first at the oasis of *Beni ^cAbbās,* and then in the Hoggar Mountains. His disciplined devotional life and his acts of love were universally admired, not only by the French but also by the Tuaregs and the other people in the area. There were no conversions, but he was deeply influential and made many friends. The Little Brothers and Sisters of Jesus are orders modelled on rules composed by de Foucauld, even though he did not actually establish any communities himself. These communities seek to combine the ideal of a contemplative life with deep involvement in the economic and social situation of their context. They are to be found in the poorest residential districts of cities, earning their living doing the most menial of tasks. They live in housing typical to the area and aim to have a standard of living which is similar to that of other residents. At the same time, they try to maintain their devotional and prayer life. In one city in Asia, I discovered a community of Little Sisters living on their own in a very deprived and volatile area. They were so loved and respected in the neighbourhood, however, that it was unthinkable that they could be harmed. In another city which is in a country in the grip of fundamentalist revolution, I came across a Little Brother who had so impressed the revolutionary guards that they had insisted on his staying in the country, despite the somewhat xenophobic tendencies of the revolution. The main aim of these communities is to establish a living Christian witness in the midst of deprived people.

Along with Samuel Zwemer, Bishop Thomas Valpy French (1825-1891), after his resignation of the See of Lahore, pioneered Christian work in the area around the Arabian or Persian Gulf. Although French died quite soon after the beginning of the work, Zwemer was able to continue it with the help of the Reformed Church in America. The co-operation between French (a senior Anglican from the Church

Missionary Society) and Zwemer (from the Reformed tradition) is characteristic of Christian presence and work in this very difficult part of the world.[9] Over a period of time, Anglican chaplaincies, ministering mainly to English-speaking people, came to be established in many of the countries of the Arabian Peninsula. The people to whom these chaplaincies ministered were either concerned with the administration and defence of the Trucial States (which were British protectorates) or were traders and businessmen. At various times the chaplaincies have been under the jurisdiction of the Bishop of Lahore, of the Archbishop in Jerusalem, and more recently, of the Bishop of Cyprus and the Gulf.

The rapid escalation in the price of petroleum in the 1970s created a boom economy in many of the states of the Gulf. This resulted in a great expansion of development projects, which attracted skilled and unskilled labour from many different parts of the world. Many of this new and very large workforce are Christians. They come from Korea, the Philippines, South India, Pakistan, Syria, Palestine and Egypt, and, of course, from a number of Western nations. They belong to many Christian traditions, ranging from Ancient Oriental to Pentecostal, and worship in many different languages and styles.

In many of these states it is government policy to regulate the number of church buildings quite strictly. It is because of this that the Anglican chaplaincies have assumed a new and quite unexpected significance. They are now centres which are truly international and ecumenical in scope. Not only are the chaplaincies' buildings used by Anglicans (and those in full sacramental communion with them) from all over the world, but also by people from a very wide range of other Christian communions. What was, only a few years ago, a rather anarchronistic Western presence, has very quickly become one which has large potential for witnessing to the universality of the Church in a missionary context. At St Andrew's Church in Abu Dhabi, for example, there are twenty-four worshipping Christian groups, ranging from Syrian Orthodox to Full Gospel! Anglican hospitality is generous, even to the point of providing some housing for the clergy of other churches. Facilities such as sacristies have to be shared by the different groups, some of whom may have been out of communion with each other for over fifteen hundred years! This discipline, in itself, promotes ecumenism. At the same time, it needs to be said that the structure of the diocese and of the chaplaincies does not adequately reflect the world-wide nature of the Anglican Communion. The Chaplains, as well as the diocesan staff, tend to be English, sometimes with very little multicultural or interfaith experience. Nor is this observation true only of the situation in the Gulf. Anglican chaplaincies everywhere are now ministering to Anglicans from all over the world. The international character of these chaplaincies will increase as travel becomes easier and there is more mobility. It is very important, therefore, that where appropriate, the ministry in these chaplaincies be drawn from Anglican provinces all over the world.

Christian presence in the Gulf is now very large and will be there, *mutatis mutandis,* for a long period of time. This is the first time since the rise of Islam that Christians have been permitted to live and worship in the Peninsula. There is great potential for Christian witness in terms of friendship, integrity in business dealings and hard work. Possibilities of sensitive dialogue also exist. Because of the climate, the way in which the working day is organised and the paucity in recreational facilities, lay Christians in particular often have more time than they have in their home countries. There is also a great deal of spiritual hunger and a desire for teaching among the Christian communities. This is an opportunity for churches not only in terms of catechesis but also in terms of preparing these Christians for ministry in multicultural and inter-faith contexts when they return to their countries of origin.

However, churches also need to be aware of the limitations to Christian work in this context. Overtly evangelistic work, especially among the indigenous population, is liable to result in prosecution. Even someone giving away Bibles may be punished by a fine, imprisonment or deportation. I have had occasion to visit in prison a Christian from Pakistan who was sentenced to several years in jail for giving a New Testament in Arabic to a non-indigenous Arab. Incidentally, his cheerful and courageous witness in prison was itself an image of Christian presence in that part of the world. Thankfully, he has now been released.

In Sacūdī Arabia there used to be only one Christian church building, and that has now been demolished. The large numbers of Christians there worship more or less clandestinely in embassies, in the premises of multinational firms and in their homes. Such meetings can, however, be broken up by the religious police. Copies of the Bible and other Christian literature cannot be taken into the country. Even objects of

Christian significance such as crucifixes, icons and medals are not allowed in and, if discovered, are liable to confiscation.

At a time when many Christians are rightly supporting the rights of Muslims to worship and to propagate their faith freely in situations where they are a minority, it is important that Muslims too should recognise their obligations in the creation of free and open societies in the countries where *they* have influence. Only in this way can understanding and co-operation be enchanced between Muslims and Christians. What is true of relationships between Muslims and Christians is true also of relationships between Christians and people of other faiths, whether these are Hindus, Sikhs, Buddhists or Jews.

In Afghānistān Christians have continued to provide badly needed medical care when even diplomats have left the country. The number of Afghān Christians is tiny, and many of the Christians working in Afghānistān come from other countries, some of them nearby and others further away. In Nepal the Christian Church is growing very rapidly among the people, and Nepalese Christians are evangelising their fellow countrymen. Both receiving baptism and baptising, however, have, until recently, been offences punishable by various terms of imprisonment. Several Nepalese were, until recently, in prison on this account. On the other hand, the Government welcome expatriate Christians from neighbouring countries and further away to work in the educational, medical and development fields. There is a great need for workers in primary health care, in the development of literacy programmes, in the prevention and cure of leprosy and in the rehabilitation of those cured. In all these areas, expatriate Christians are active in service. They have not been allowed, however, to take any part in evangelism. Their work and their way of life are the main ways in which they have witnessed for the Gospel. They are fortunate indeed that their presence and witness are so effectively complemented by the vigorous life of the local Christians, who through their suffering have witnessed powerfully to the power of the Gospel. The restoration of democracy in Nepal seems to be resulting in greater freedom of religion. It is to be hoped that soon the persecution of Christians will be a thing of the past.

Christian presence and work have to do with the willingness of Christians to remain, for the sake of Christ, in situations where the open commendation of the Faith is either not possible at all or is severely restricted. Christians hope that in such situations the quiet promotion of Gospel values in their living and working will act as salt in society, not easily visible but affecting for the good many areas of life. Christian worship, where this is permitted, is the light which is sometimes the only focus for witness in many societies. Christian presence cannot be passive, and there must be prayer and work for the emergence of more open societies where the Gospel can be freely commended in any number of ways.

CHAPTER NINE

Mission as Identification

Bishop John Robinson used to say that the origins of Paul's understanding of the Church as the Body of Christ lay in his conversion experience, in which the Risen Lord identified himself with his people (Acts 9:5; 22:8; 26:15). The other side of the Lord's identification with his people is his people's identification with him. It is only *en Christō* that believers can hope to find completeness and fulfilment. Baptism is seen, in the Pauline Epistles, as the point where solidarity with Christ, both in his death and in his resurrection, is most clearly expressed (Romans 6:3-11; Colossians 2:9-13). The metaphor of the Body recurs, however, throughout the New Testament and is a fundamental way of speaking about the Church (1 Corinthians 12:12-31; Ephesians 4:4-16).[1]

The language of incorporation into Christ has led to the perception that the doctrine of the Incarnation has a certain relevance for the life of the Church. We saw in Chapter 4 that the publication of *Lux Mundi* over a hundred years ago established a tradition in Anglican theology of thinking incarnationally about the Church. This tradition, moreover, is reflected in the provision for pastoral care which has developed in the Church of England. The requirement that the whole country be divided up into parishes and that the Church should have a presence in each parish is strongly incarnationalist in approach.[2] In recent years, the parochial system has come under considerable pressure because of greatly increased social mobility and the reduced number of clergy who are available to minister in parochial situations. In spite of this, however, the presence of the Church at the grassroots, even if in a severely weakened and marginalised form, has been of great value in helping the Church and the nation discern trends in public opinion, the results of economic and social policy at the local level, the special problems of minorities and many other matters of significance.

The incarnationalist approach has, however, come under strong criticism for its tendency to endorse the *status quo*.[3] It is seen as being "at home" in the Establishment and being, itself, a custodian of venerable tradition which, by nature, is inimical to change. It is criticised for being optimistic rather than realistic where the present order is concerned, and its approach to change is seen as gradualist and evolutionary rather than radical and revolutionary. It is seen as having an inadequate understanding of human sin and the way in which it pervades the structures of society. Because of this, it often has a weak doctrine of redemption, not perceiving that rescue from sin is a battle which involves both divine and human suffering. It fails to hold together the crib and the cross, incarnation and atonement, presence and reconciliation.[4]

Empirically speaking, where traditional Anglicanism is concerned, many of these strictures on the incarnationalist approach can hardly be gainsaid. We have seen, however, that many of its promoters went on to develop a kenotic Christology which emphasised the self-abasement, humiliation and rejection of the incarnate Christ. It is the willingness of Christ to bear humiliation and rejection rather than compromise the way set forth by the Father which makes his suffering the locus of reconciliation and the beginning of a renewed humanity. Any incarnationalist approach worth its salt, therefore, will hold together in tension identification and challenge, suffering and hope.

We have seen that the universality of the Gospel requires that it be rendered into the language, idiom and thought-form of each and every human culture. It is only then that the Gospel, which is the core of Christian tradition, and the cumulative tradition which has grown around it will be able to make an appeal to the values and reason of every culture. Throughout Christian history, and in particular in the last three or four centuries, we have witnessed this capacity of the Gospel to become incarnate in particular cultures. It is no exaggeration to say that the future of Christian Mission depends on Christians allowing—nay, encouraging—the Gospel to resonate with all that is God-given, true and good in every culture. It is only in this way that "the mind of Christ" for each culture will be discerned and lived. At the same time, we must allow the Gospel to challenge and even to judge those aspects of each culture which are not consonant with "the mind of Christ". In doing this, Christians need to be especially sensitive and to avoid hasty decisions which they may come to regret. The past is littered with examples of Christians pronouncing aspects of cultures to be fundamentally anti-

Christian, only to discover later on that such was not the case. There will, however, be situations in which greed, exploitation, oppression, genocide and injustice prevail. These things will be seen as contrary to God's will for human beings and will be condemned. In time Christians may come to see that social structures such as those based on caste and class and economic structures such as feudalism, *laissez-faire* capitalism and centralised planning of a kind which deprives people of personal liberty are fundamentally flawed and cannot merit Christian endorsement.

Such discernment, however, will only come out of sustained profound and sacrificial involvement and identification. Presence, if it is aloof and élitist, is not enough. For presence to be effective and transforming, it must involve identification. Contextualisation or inculturation involve not merely the discovery of linguistic and cultural forms into which the Good News can be translated. The whole context is to be engaged in the articulation and the formation of the Christian Faith in that context.[5] Both the Gospel and the bearers of the Gospel must be allowed to become incarnate in the context to which the Good News is being brought. This means that there can be no "hit and run" mission, no mission from a distance, whether that is geographical, cultural or intellectual. Admittedly, there are contexts where it is not possible for Christians to be present and identified in an incarnational way. In some of these contexts only very limited presence may be possible; in others, no presence may be possible at all. It has to be said, however, that such contexts are comparatively rare. Where they occur, it may be necessary to maintain some sort of witness through radio, television or literature. These media can also be extremely useful in focussing and strengthening Christian witness in other contexts where some kind of presence *is* possible. They can never, however, be substitutes for mission as identification.

The story is told of an Indian seminarian who was participating in what is called "theological education by immersion". Many theological colleges in India require students to immerse themselves in particular contexts, such as the cult of another faith, or communal tension, or poverty. Their initiation into theological education or their continuation in it then takes place against the background of such immersion and is in the form of disciplined reflection on their experience during it.[6] This gives theological education a certain "rootedness" in the context from the very beginning, and the aim is to sustain this throughout the process of formation. This particular student was sent to immerse himself in the poverty of a slum on the outskirts of a large city. He was required during his period of immersion to live, like everyone else, in a *jhugee*, which is a shack made of bamboo and corrugated iron. He wore the kind of clothes his neighbours wore and ate what they ate. However, he felt that despite all this the distance between them had somehow not been overcome. He was "educated" while many of them were illiterate; he had a future, whereas many of them had none. Although his lifestyle at theological college had been quite simple, it was beyond the reach of his new neighbours, and they knew it. They also knew that in time he would return to it. But then he got cholera by drinking contaminated water. While he was ill and fighting for his life in a nearby hospital, his neighbours protected his shack from vandalism, brought him little comforts and helped the hospital staff to look after him. It was when he had returned to convalesce in his shack that he realised that the barriers had finally come down. He was acceptable now because he had shared even a life-threatening illness with his neighbours. They knew that his sense of solidarity with them was serious, whatever the remaining differences might be.

Traditionally, Christian engagement in India has often been with the beliefs and practices of those of other faiths. In many cases, moreover, it has been with the highly sophisticated philosophical and mystical aspects of these faiths. The importance of this engagement should not be underestimated. Religious allegiance continues to play a very important role in the Indian context and due account has to be taken of it. Christians have traditionally engaged with Brahmanical Hinduism in all its aspects, specifically with the philosophical *Vedānta,* as well as with more popular forms of religiosity such as *Vaiṣṇavism.* This engagement has taken the form of translation of the texts and commentary on them, but often there has also been an attempt to grasp the significance of the tradition being mediated by the texts and to evaluate it from a Christian point of view. Furthermore, Christian writers such as Raimundo Pannikar have attempted to discern "the shape of grace" in Hinduism and to find "the mystery of Christ" there.[7]

For example, according to Bishop Lesslie Newbigin the heart of Tamil Christian spirituality is to be found in the lyrical poetry which is written, read and sung in the Tamil-speaking churches.[8] It is almost impossible to translate these lyrics into European, or even other Indian, languages without some loss of their beauty and power. At the same time, it needs saying that these lyrics have not arisen entirely *in vacuo*. They are related to their context, which is largely that of *Bhakti* Hinduism (that is, a Hinduism which emphasises personal experience of a personal god who reveals himself to human beings as loving and gracious). It is no surprise, therefore, to discover that there are notable affinities, not only of style but of content as well, between such Christian lyrical poetry and those aspects of Tamil literature which have their origins in the work of the *Alvars* (Hindu holy men who promoted the cult of *Vishnu*). The power and the beauty of the poetry comes from the distinctives of the Gospel but also from the context with which it is so closely identified.

The *ashram* is another aspect of the Hindu religious life with which some Christians have identified very closely. Originally an *ashram* was a dwelling in a forest in which a guru would live a life of meditation. Around him would gather disciples who through yogic discipline, instruction and contemplation would try to perfect their mystical experience. The Hindu movement of reform, which was, in part, a response to the challenge of the Gospel on matters such as caste and the practice of *suttee* (or window-burning), brought about a renewal of interest in *ashrams* as centres where a programmatic Hinduism could be formed and from where it could be propagated.[9]

Christians in India, of both Oriental and Western Christian traditions, have attempted to adapt the *ashram* idea to Christian use. Christian *ashrams* function as places of contemplation, renewal and engagement with traditional, as well as popular, Hinduism. Perhaps the best-known example of a Christian *ashram* is that of Kurisumala, founded by Dom Bede Griffiths. He is now the leader of the Saccidananda *ashram* at Shāntivanam in Tamil Nadu. Bede Griffiths, like so many others in India, is concerned to make Christ incarnate there. This may sound a somewhat arrogant project, especially if undertaken by a foreigner. The ancient churches of India, after all, have existed for centuries in a totally Indian milieu. What right has this foreigner to make Christ incarnate there? Part of the justification is given by Bede Griffiths himself in his *Christ in India*.[10] The country's ancient churches have integrated perfectly (too perfectly?) into the social structure of Hinduism, even to the point where they are regarded almost as a "caste" among their neighbours. It has often been noted that a relatively "high caste" status has prevented these Christians from engaging in mission until modern times. Although their Liturgy is generally now in Malayalam (though there are vestigial Syriac parts), its structure is mainly Middle-Eastern, though there are instances of inculturation even here. The ancient churches (like the younger ones) are also engaged in social service and in a great deal of educational and medical work. However, until modern times they have *not* been noted for trying to relate their faith to their *religious* context, which is largely that of Hinduism. There has not been a great deal of theological reflection and, of what there *has* been, a large proportion has been concerned with questions of classical Christian theology and of Liturgy rather than with the issues raised by inter-faith encounter.

Bede Griffiths, a Benedictine, and others like him are the heirs of the seventeenth-century Jesuits of India and China. The attempt to create distinctively Chinese and Indian rites was suppressed by Rome, and ultimately the Jesuit order itself was dissolved. The questions raised for missiology, however, remained. Was it permissible to use the religious terminology of the culture concerned to mediate Christian truth? Was it permissible for Christians to continue to observe social distinctions (such as those of caste)? In the Chinese context then (as in the African and East Asian context now), there was the question about reverence for ancestors. Was it permissible to honour one's ancestors within and outside the context of Christian worship?

The Christian *āshram* movement certainly seeks to express Christian spirituality in terms and forms familiar to Hinduism. These have do do with external matters like architecture, dress and food, with the practice of meditation and prayer and with the language used for religious discourse, both among Christians and in the context of inter-faith encounter. Even Christian iconography may assume distinctively Hindu forms.

Some (like Bede Griffiths and Raimundo Pannikar) have gone much further and have tried to discern the shape of the mystery of Christ within Hindu religious traditions themselves. Every such claim must be evaluated on its own merits, but the question remains of how *we* discern the mystery of Christ in another religious tradition. Surely it must be the Christ who is revealed in the Gospels, preached by the Church and experienced in worship who leads us to a discernment of his presence as the Eternal Word in all human endeavour, including the various religions of humankind. There is also the question of explication and fulfilment. If Christ is deemed as being present in the apprehension of truth and beauty anywhere, how is the Christian to bring about an acknowledgement of this presence, both for those in the Christian community and for others? Furthermore, how is the Christian recognition of Christ's immediate presence in the Church and with believers related to his "scattered" presence in many human communities and individuals who are completely outside the boundaries of the Church? Even more crucially, how are both of these related to the visions of the universal acknowledgement of Christ found in the Scriptures (Ephesians 1:9-10; Philippians 2:10-11; Revelation 7:9-11; 21:22-27)?

If Christian *āshrams* are an attempt to identify with Hindu religious culture in communal terms, the proliferation of Christian *sādhus,* or wandering mendicants, is an attempt to identify with the more eremitical aspect of the ascetical tradition of Hinduism. Not that *sādhus* are necessarily hermits. Many of them are active purveyors of popular devotion to the masses. It is interesting to observe that while attempts by Western Christians or by Western-educated Indian Christians to identify with Hindu religious culture often take the form of communal living in an *āshram,* for ordinary Indian Christians such attempts, if they take any form at all, take that of the *sādhu.* The best known Indian Christian *sādhu* is of course, Sundar Singh (1889-1929). Sundar was born into a wealthy Sikh family in the Punjāb. In his early life he was greatly influenced by his pious mother and by Hindu and Sikh religious teachers. Although he went to a mission school, he was hostile to Christianity and is reputed to have publicly torn up a copy of the Gospels and to have burnt it. At the age of fifteen, however, he underwent a spiritual experience during which Christ appeared to him. Sundar now found the joy and peace for which he had been looking. There was a price to pay, however. Sundar was rejected by his family, and it was only after finishing his schooling that he was baptised. Although he regarded himself as an Anglican and even studied for ordination at St John's Divinity School in Lahore, he soon came to realise that a more or less sedentary pastoral ministry was not for him, and so he set out to be a *sādhu.* Sundar's adventures as a *sādhu* are too well known to require repetition. In 1929 he left for yet another missionary journey to Tibet and was never heard of again.[12]

Stephen Neill, in an article on Sundar, remarks that he did not leave a movement behind him.[13] This is somewhat unfair on two counts. First, to be a *sādhu* is, by its very nature, to be alone and free. Secondly, numerous individuals in the subcontinent *have* emulated Sundar Singh. Hundreds of thousands of villages have, at some time or other, received a Christian *sādhu*. Sometimes these are evangelists, like Sundar himself; others see their role as that of edifying the local church. Some are opportunists and rogues, others fall into temptation, but many are saints who have been blessed with the gifts of the Holy Spirit. The Church in the subcontinent is the richer for having this spiritual tradition. We are greatly indebted to Sundar Singh for focussing for us the possibilities of this kind of spirituality.

Islām is the only world religion which has its historical origins in a largely Christian and Jewish milieu. There is a very long shared history and in many places Christians and Muslims have been part of a common culture and have spoken the same language for centuries.[14] Many of the earliest mosques in the Middle East were once Christian churches. Sometimes Muslims and Christians have even shared places of worship. In other parts of the world (such as Spain) buildings which were once mosques are now churches.[15]

The complexity of the interrelationships between Islām and Christianity is illustrated by a recent journalistic account of a Christian state funeral in the Middle East. The correspondent thought that the chanting of the Liturgy was very like the Muslim call to prayer and the *qirā'a* or recitation of the *Qur'ān*. Orientalists, however, would not have been puzzled by this phenomenon, because it is known that the chanting of the *Qur'ān* is related to the singing of the lections in oriental Christian liturgies. Indeed, the term *Qur'ān* itself is related to the Syriac *qeryana*, which means "the Scripture readings".[16] Anyone familiar with both oriental Christianity and Islām will know that they share many features, such as attitudes to worship, times of prayer, postures of reverence, dress and other matters. In some cases there is direct influence and dependence (not necessarily of the newer on the older), in others it is simply that both religions share in a common culture.

156

Identification within an Islāmic context, then, is not simply an attempt to translate the Gospel into terms and forms which are culturally appropriate. Nor is it only an attempt to discern the significance of the Muslim's pilgrimage from a Christian point of view. It is also an attempt at "recovery", at regaining, for all Christians, the ancient Christian tradition which has enriched and has been enriched by what is commonly, if somewhat erroneously, called "Islāmic" civilisation. Pākistānī Roman Catholic Christians of the Western rite, for example, have begun to chant the Liturgy in the style of the *qirā'a*. This is not simply in imitation of Muslims, as it might appear to be to an uninitiated observer. It *is* an attempt to relate to an Islāmic context but, at the same time, it is an attempt to recover a Christian oriental tradition of great significance to the Church in Pākistān. In the same way, churches are beginning to be built in architectural styles usually associated with mosques. Once again, this is recovery. Mosques have generally followed the architectonic of oriental churches, and if church buildings are now inspired by their design, this is not mere imitation but recovery.

The ordering of Christian devotional life on the pattern of the daily *salāt* (or ritual prayer) is another case of recovery. The times of the *salāt* and some of its postures are related to the ascetical practices of the Syrian and Egyptian monks. For this reason, there are still some correspondences between the *salāt* and the Christian canonical Hours. It is perfectly possible to adapt the usual daily offices in such a way that they correspond with the *salāt*. The optional *salāt* called the *tahajjud* (or "waking") corresponds to the vigils of the Christian ascetics. The idea can certainly be used for vigils by Christians today.

The similiarities between the Jesus Prayer of Orthodox Christians and the *dhikr* of the Muslim Ṣūfīs have often been noticed. Both rely on patterns of recitation and movement to bring about intense concentration in meditation. Like the term *salāt,* the term *dhikr* has rich Christian resonances. It is interesting to note that both the Jesus Prayer and aspects of the *dhikr* are beginning to be used in Christian meditative practices in Islāmic contexts.[17]

Inculturation in Liturgy, poetry and theological reflection is not, of course, limited to the religious aspects of a particular culture. It is much more wide-ranging than that. One of the greatest achievements of the *Punjābī* Church, on both sides of the border, has been the paraphrasing of the Psalms into *Punjābī* and their setting to the *rāgs* (or tunes) of Indian classical music. The value of the resource that this has provided for the worship of the Church cannot be over-estimated. The development of Christian *qawwālī* is another instance of a form of Muslim devotional life being adapted admirably for Christian use. The *qawwālī* is a type of concert, developed within Indo-Muslim culture, the ostensible purpose of which is to celebrate the person of the Prophet of Islām. Underneath, however, there is much else, ranging from experiences of mystical ecstasy to pure entertainment.

We have noticed already the relation between Tamil Christian poetry and the context in which it has arisen. In other Asian contexts too, strong traditions of Christian poetry have developed. For example, in the Urdū language there is a considerable corpus of good Christian poetry which has been inspired in form, symbolism and terminology by the traditions of Indo-Muslim and Persian poetry.[18] In Īrān, Bishop Ḥassan Dehquānī-Taftī's poetry has been set to traditional music and is regularly used in worship, including eucharistic worship. Here is a translation of one stanza of a hymn often sung at the offertory:

> *Mine the pain, yours the medication,*
> *Mine the sorrow, yours the healing,*
> *Mine the faith, yours the revelation,*
> *Mine the freedom, yours the willing.*[19]

Those engaged in the translation of the Scriptures know that intimate knowledge of their original context, languages and history is absolutely essential if they are to be faithfully translated. This is not enough, however, for intimate knowledge of the context and language *into* which the translation is to be made is also essential. In reading the Bible in Urdū or Persian, I am struck again and again by the exact correspondences that the translators have been able to discover between terms in these languages and terms in Hebrew (and, less often, in Greek). It is true, of course, that Urdū and Persian have a significant number of Arabic loan words. Arabic is very close to Hebrew, and so it is not surprising that many biblical Hebrew words correspond to words of Arabic origin in Urdū and Persian.

When William Carey arrived in *Bengāl* and began to translate the Bible into *Bengālī*, he faced a somewhat different situation. One of his first problems was deciding which of the names of the gods in the Hindu pantheon to use for the divine name of the Bible. The documents of the New Testament, which represent attempts at inculturation in the milieu of the Graeco-Roman World, provided a clue. They used the word *Theos* for God. This was a general name for divinity and could not be identified with any particular god (though it was used to refer to each of them). Carey, similarly, chose *Ishwar*, which is a general word for God in Hinduism and denotes the supreme personal being. Carey's choice has proved largely acceptable to Bengālī Christians from Hindu backgrounds as well as to Hindus reading the Bible. The case is somewhat different with Muslim Bengālīs. For them, use of the term *Ishwar* was a barrier, as it seemed to identify the God of the Bible with each or all of the "High Gods" of Hinduism – that is, with *Vishnu, Shiva* and *Brahmā.*

It was not until the 1970s that a Muslim Bengālī translation of the Bible was made. Its popularity amongst Bengālī-speaking Muslims has shown how important language and context are in the translation of the Scriptures. The term for God used in this translation is the Persian world *Khudā* (meaning "the self-existent"). The usual Muslim word for God, *Allāh,* was regarded as too specific, and so a more general term was used. *Urdū* – and Persian-speaking Christians, too, prefer to use *Khudā*, although they sometimes use *Allāh* and even *Ibn Allāh* ("Son of God"). Arabic-speaking Christians, however, habitually use *Allāh* for God, and this is the usual term both in the Arabic Bible and in the liturgies of the Arab churches. While Arab Christians have used *Allāh* for centuries, Christians in Malaysia are forbidden by law to use this term to refer to God! The translation of the Bible into *Bahasa,* published in Indonesia (which shares the language with Malaysia), uses *Allāh* for God and so has its circulation restricted in Malaysia. Other words, such as *nabī (prophet), are also forbidden, despite their origin in the religion of the Old Testament. Christians in Malaysia claim the right to express their faith in their national language without restriction.* They are also aware that many of the words of Arabic origin which are now forbidden to them have roots in the Christian and Jewish milieu in which Islām arose.

There is a tension between the need to contextualise the Gospel into specific cultures and the need to maintain its universality and the unity of the Church. A story from pre-partition India illustrate this tension clearly. A church in a large city in northern India had two clergymen attached to it. One was a distinguished scholar from a Muslim background, the other an equally distinguished scholar from a Hindu background. Each was trying to contextualise the worship of the church in his own way. For the first this meant writing verses from the Bible on the walls of the church and an emphasis on preaching and on reverence in worship. For the other it meant pictorial representation of the Trinity, garlands of flowers, incense, music and sacramental worship. The tension that these two approaches caused is still remembered by the older members of the congregation.

In multicultural situations today there are advocates of the Homogeneous Unit Principle. They support the emergence of congregations which are unicultural, unilingual and racially homogeneous. There is little in the New Testament or in the early Church to warrant the existence of such congregations. The early Christians were concerned to show in their own lives and worship how Christ had broken down the barriers of race, class and sex. It is right still to insist that the local church must manifest the diversity as well as the unity of God's people in a given area. This can be done by joining together regularly in the Eucharist and by agreeing on priorities in teaching, preaching and the mission of the Church. All the different groups must agree not to do separately whatever can be done together. There has to be joint leadership and joint planning. At the same time, people with a common cultural background have to be encouraged to meet together, within the fellowship of the wider congregation, and to celebrate their faith in terms of their own culture. They should remain open to people of backgrounds other than their own and should invite them to share in their celebration and to be enriched by it. On the other hand, they should remain open to the enrichment offered to them by the wider congregation.

What is true of a local congregation holds also for a national church and even for the Universal Church. The Gospel must become incarnate in every culture. People must experience the affirmation of their cultural roots in the worship of the Church. At the same time, the Gospel unites Christians of all ages and all places. The worship of the Church should celebrate the Faith delivered once for all to the saints and should be within the context of an awareness of the communion of the saints. A Christian from another culture should be able both to appreciate the distinctives which a particular culture imparts to worship *and* to be conscious of continuity with worship within his or her own cultural context as well as with the worship of the Church down the ages. The tension is difficult to maintain, but it is the demand of the Gospel that it should be proclaimed and lived in every possible context and culture. It is the will of Christ that Christians should be united in worship, fellowship and mission. The tension can be creative, allowing Christians in different cultures to celebrate their faith in their own way, while at the same time always keeping before them the witness of the Universal Church at all times and in all places and, in local situations, challenging them to transcend barriers of language, race and gender in a common experience of fellowship.

Ultimately, the inculturation of the Gospel and the identification of Christians and the Church with a particular people or culture is for the purpose of bringing about a transformation and renewal of that people or culture. As my late and much lamented friend, Orlando Costas has put it:

> To incarnate Christ in our world is to manifest the transforming presence of God's kingdom among the victims of sin and evil. It is to make possible a process of transformation from personal sin and corporate evil to personal and collective freedom, justice and well-being.[20]

F

CHAPTER TEN

Mission as Dialogue

As iron sharpeneth iron, so the countenance of man his fellow.
(Proverbs 27:17)

The human being is what George Steiner has called a "language-animal".[1] Human societies of different kinds throughout the course of history have sought to describe the world and their own place in it in terms of language. Thus have come about the scores of "worlds of discourse" which exist today. Modern linguistic philosophy has been fascinated with the rules which govern each of these worlds and which provide it with a character and an autonomy all of its own. It is possible, of course, for human beings to inhabit, or at least to understand more than one world of discourse. This may be because of the circumstances in which they have been nurtured or because they have chosen to try and understand or to enter a particular world of discourse.

The ability of human beings to cross linguistic and cultural boundaries is the basis for the "interface" that can exist between different, even radically different, worlds of discourse.[2] Exposure leads to mutual interrogation, discussion, persuasion and, perhaps, agreement to differ. Although different worlds of discourse are autonomous, they are not watertight. Ideas, values and fashions continually penetrate into a particular world of discourse either through gradual processes of "osmosis" brought about through commerce, emigration or politics, or through the revolutionary impact of a new ideology or religion. At the same time, "interior" dialogue within a particular tradition can also modify and renew it, sometimes in quite radical ways.

Each religious tradition is also a world of discourse. It has its own distinctive origins, beliefs and rituals. The distinctives of each religion have, therefore, to be recognised and respected. Any attempt to describe, understand or evaluate it exclusively from the standpoint of another tradition has to be resisted. At the same time, because each tradition makes at least some claims which have universal significance, there is the presumption, *mutatis mutandis,* in all of them that they will be understood by people belonging to different faith-communities as well as by those who do not belong to any faith-community at all. If, however, there is intelligibility, then there is accountability as well. Such "mutual reckoning" (a phrase coined by Kenneth Cragg) forms a significant part of the dialogue among people of different faiths.[3]

It is not surprising that many of the words for "language" among different peoples are related to conversation, discussion and dialogue. Within each tradition there is a continual conversation going on about the foundations of that tradition and the need to strengthen them, modify them, develop from them or even to replace them. Between traditions too there is a continuous interchange of influences and challenges. Within each *religious* tradition there is an internal dialogue going on about the nurture and development of that tradition. In the same way, *between* religious traditions there is encounter, conversation, polemic and dialogue. During certain periods and in particular places, one tradition may strongly challenge the beliefs or practices of another. We have seen how this happened in eighteenth and nineteenth century India, when Christians challenged certain social aspects of Hinduism – challenge which ultimately brought about not only social reform but revision and renewal within Hinduism itself. Encounter, conversation and dialogue are part of the fabric of life. Wherever and whenever people meet, they occur. This is particularly the case when people of different faiths meet.

In the New Testament, both *dialegomai* and *dialogizomai* mean "discussion" or "argument conducted for the sake of persuasion" (Acts 17:2; 18:4)[4]. The earliest Fathers, such as Justin Martyr, also used the term in this way (as in the *Dialogue with Trypho the Jew).* Indeed, this term continued to be used in this way throughout antiquity (St John of Damascus' two dialogues with Muslims are late examples of this usage). In the English-speaking world the term was still used of the Socratic (i.e. dialectical) method of argument well into modern times (as in David Hume's *Dialogues Concerning Natural Religion).*[5]

There is, therefore, an aspect of witness, of persuasion, in the Christian use of the word "dialogue". Within the ecumenical movement, however, there is a certain amount of tension about the appropriateness of dialogue as "a medium of authentic witness". A meeting of Muslims and Christians at Chambésy in 1979, called together by the World Council of Churches, insisted that dialogue must never be used for proselytization. In other words, there can be no witness within the context of dialogue which is evangelistic.[6] On the other hand, the guidelines for dialogue produced by the World Council of Churches affirm the appropriateness of dialogue as a way in which Jesus Christ can be authentically confessed today without any attempt at manipulation or seduction.[7] These guidelines have received widespread support in church councils at national and local levels.[8] At regional levels too, while it is stated clearly that dialogue must not be used in a manipulative or coercive way, its significance as a way of evangelisation is affirmed.[9] The tension continues to be felt, however, and the ambivalence of the ecumenical movement in this respect can be discerned in the documents emerging from the recent conference on World Mission and Evangelism held at San Antonio.[10]

The international and interdenominational network of Christians represented by the Lausanne Movement did not have too much to say about inter-faith dialogue at their most recent meeting in Manila in 1989. At an earlier meeting, however, they made these remarks on the subject:

> We reaffirm that dialogue is and should be an integral part of Christian mission. Some kinds of dialogue may lead to service for the sake of the Gospel. Others may lead us, either within the context of dialogue or in some other way, to a direct but sensitive sharing of the Good News with our non-Christian partner.[11]

Professor Eric Sharpe has tried to distinguish between different kinds of dialogue.[12] The first kind which he identifies in his list is *discursive dialogue.* This involves meeting people of other faiths, listening carefully to *their* account of faith and sharing with them an account of *our* faith. The danger with this kind of exercise is that it can become overly concerned with the formal doctrines of religious systems and may draw attention away from the need for a spiritual encounter, which is just as great as the need for intellectual encounter. It is to be noted that for none of the participants is this kind of dialogue value-neutral. Each comes to it with particular convictions, but if the exercise is not to be merely a "set-piece" one, then there must be opportunity for mutual challenge and debate as well as for a discovery of commonality, congruence and convergence.

Another kind of dialogue identified by Sharpe is that which occurs on the basis of *our common humanity*. When we meet someone of another faith, we are not meeting an abstract entity but a real person. Inter-faith dialogue, therefore, can never simply be a discussion of religious beliefs. It is, at a most profound level, inter-personal encounter. We meet as people with similar needs, networks of relationships, hopes for the future and fears of what might happen. At the same time, it has to be acknowledged that our humanity is formed in specific cultural and religious contexts. What we are has a great deal to do with what we believe. In other words, interpersonal encounter cannot become "whole" unless there is engagement at every level of being.

Then there is dialogue which seeks to *build community*. This can be at very basic levels, such as co-operation in self-help projects in local communities, in joint efforts at securing clean water and sanitation, or in the mounting of a joint campaign for immunisation. This dialogue may be state-sponsored. For example, in Indonesia adherents of the different religions are required to engage in dialogue based on the principles of *Panchasila* (the five principles which are the basis for the constitution). This is held to be an essential element in the promotion of national integration. The dialogue could also be at a world level, with people of different faiths meeting together to address common problems.[13]

There is also the dialogue about the *interior life* this is a sharing of mystical experiences and of the disciplines of contemplation which often are at their basis. There may indeed, as in the case of Sūfism and oriental Christian mysticism, be direct influence and interaction between different traditions. Although this kind of dialogue is far removed from discursive dialogue, there are similarities to it too. The fact of the matter is that mystical experiences not only occur but are evaluated in particular theological, psychological and philosophical ways by different religious traditions. Nor can we say that all mystical experiences are alike.

The late Professor R. C. Zaehner distinguished between different kinds of mysticism.[14] First of all, there is nature-mysticism. This is expressed in accounts of experiences where one feels "at one with nature", not simply in a generalised or vague way but in the sense of a profound identification with nature, even to the point where it involves a negation of one's individuality. Zaehner quoted the poetry of Wait Whitman as an example of this type of mysticism. Then there is monism. This is an experience of unity with the Absolute, which is usually understood as being beyond predication of any kind. The reality of the phenomenonal world, and even of the individual self, is denied and the Absolute is affirmed as the sole existent. In Buddhism, mystical experience leads to radical negation not only of the phenomenal world and the individual self but of the Absolute as well. The ultimate experience is the realisation of pure nothingness. Finally, Zaehner identifies theistic mysticism. This is an experience of God as personal, as *mysterium tremendum et fascinans.* Such an experience can be one of awe, and even of fear, or it can be an overwhelming sense of God's love and care.

Mystical experience has polarities of "union" and "separation", of "introspection" and uninhibited "expression", of a sense of "survival" and one of "annihilation". Zaehner has interpreted these in terms of the manic-depressive syndrome. Experiences of union and uninhibited expression are at the manic end, whereas experiences of aloneness and introspection are at the depressive end. The former often results in ecstasy, while the latter are often expressed in contemplation and asceticism. Some mystical traditions emphasise one aspect and some the other, while others yet again attempt to hold the different aspects together. The mediaeval Muslim mystics were already aware of the different kinds of mysticism, though, unlike Zaehner, they regarded each kind as a stage on the way to the final unitive experience, which was also an experience of personal fulfilment. Also, what they wrote about expansion *(bast)* and contraction *(qabd)* as aspects of mystical experience bears similarities to Zaehner's discussion of the manic-depressive syndrome.[15]

Mysticism is not, therefore, an undifferentiated experience which is identical in all human beings. Such a view of it is indeed congenial for those who believe that all religious expression must originate in and lead to a *philosophia perennis.* Both theological and psychological analyses lead, however, to different conclusions. Dialogue about the interior life, therefore, can lead to a "mutual reckoning" of beliefs and assumptions which underlie mystical experience and which lead to particular evaluations of it. Such dialogue can in its turn lead to dialogue with the social sciences and the humanities about the complementarity of the different ways in which human behaviour may be analysed and evaluated.

All of these kinds of dialogue have a capacity for witness. This may indeed be verbal, a sharing with our partner of our beliefs and experiences. It may also have to do with our *attitudes* to community-building, to national integration and to peace. Our *commitment* to righteousness in the affairs of individuals and nations and our *work* for equal opportunities, for just wages and for adequate levels of care for those who are vulnerable will also bear authentic witness to the Gospel. All of this, moreover, has to be done in conscious dependence on God, if it is not to become mere "Pelagian" do-gooding. Our words and deeds must point beyond ourselves to the transcendent glory of God as it is revealed in the person and work of Jesus Christ. We are but unworthy bearers of the Good News (2 Corinthians 4:5-12). We are, in the words of the Sri-Lankan theologian, D. T. Niles, beggars telling other beggars where to find bread.[16] In other words, dialogue should not be allowed to become simply a conversation between human beings. There must be an awareness of the transcendent, a sense that here we are touching holy things.

The process of dialogue greatly enriches the faith of those Christians who engage in it. New light is cast on particular matters of faith from unexpected sources. The central challenge of Islām has to do with *Tāwḥīd,* the unity of God. This alerts Christians to the biblical insistence on the divine unity and to the need to find the roots of the doctrine of the Trinity (the Triune God) in the basic doctrine of God's oneness which Christians have inherited from the Hebraic tradition. Again, it is not surprising that much contemporary reflection on the finality (or definitiveness) of Christ has come from a context where Christians are engaged in dialogue with Hindus. Hinduism is well known for its disposition to inclusivity, a tendency very welcome to modern minds. In the face of this desire not only to accept a multiplicity of divine incarnations, but to syncretise as well, Christians have to produce a theology of finality which is not arbitrary and callous but is, at the same time, definite and faithful to the normative records of divine revelation.

Eric Sharpe has pointed out that one of the benefits of dialogue, from the Christian point of view, is a deepening of Christian engagement with the values, idioms and thought-forms of cultures shaped by specific religious traditions or ideologies. To put it another way, dialogue provides the context in which inculturation takes place. The translation of the Bible and of Christian terminology, the patterns and language of worship, iconography and the "baptism" of symbols for use in rites of passage – all of these cannot be brought about without profound dialogue with the traditions of a people, including their religious traditions.[17]

In the end, of course, it is not for Christians to say how inter-faith dialogue affects those of other faiths. We cannot but note, however, that dialogue with Christians, or even their mere presence, has often brought about introspection, reform and renewal among those of other faiths (of course, this same dialogue has also had similar effects among Christians themselves). We have had occasion to note the movements of reform and renewal within Hinduism which were brought about by contact with Christianity. At the same time, we cannot fail to notice that the fertility of much contemporary Indian Christian thought arises out of its engagement with Hindu religion, culture and philosophy.

The Christian's claim that Jesus Christ is the definitive clue to the meaning and purpose of the Universe and of history does not exclude the possibility of mutual learning in dialogue between Christians and those of other faiths. It remains possible for Christians to understand themselves as pilgrims on the way of truth. There are others who are pilgrims or who seek to be pilgrims too. Carrying out Christian mission through dialogue means inviting our partners in the quest for truth to take Jesus Christ as the clue which leads to the unravelling of the mystery of our existence. As Bishop Lesslie Newbigin points out:

> When Christians affirm, as they do, that Jesus is the way, the true and living way by whom we come to the Father (John 16:4) they are not claiming to know everything. They are claiming to be on the way, and inviting others to join them as they press forward toward the fullness of truth, toward the day when we shall know as we have been known.[18]

Newbigin points out that the Gospel is not a set of timeless propositions about God, nature and human beings. It is, Christians claim, the key to the human story, to the story of God's dealings with human beings. This story has not ended. God is present and active in all human societies, families and cultures. There is, however, resistance to him too. Yet, Christians believe, God is working his purposes out to bring all things to fulfilment and fruition in Christ (Ephesians 1:10). Christians will approach dialogue, therefore, with confidence in God, who is patiently (sufferingly?) bringing about the fulfilment of his purpose. At the same time, they will be sensitive to the human capacity for rebellion, ignorance and fear. They must pray that they and their partners will be delivered from captivity to sin and that they will open their minds and hearts to God's truth and grace.

CHAPTER ELEVEN

Mission as Action

There is a growing constituency in the Christian churches which, while acknowledging the necessity for presence, identification and dialogue, believes that they are not sufficient if the wholeness of God's love is to be communicated in the contemporary world. There is a sense in which this strand in Christian thinking is not new. It is deeply rooted in the Scriptures, particularly in the prophetic commitment to justice for the poor, the strangers and the oppressed, but also in the New Testament's emphasis on interdependence (as in the Corinthian correspondence) and on the equal dignity and worth of all human beings (as in the Epistle of James). In the early Church too "love for the poor" is an important theme, and is to be found in the writings of both the Eastern and the Western Fathers of the Church. The category extends beyond the materially poor to include exiles, widows, orphans and the sick. It goes without saying that the early Christian view was developed in full awareness of Jesus' teaching on the sharing of wealth, the blessedness of the poor and his own identification with them. This last aspect of dominical teaching alerts us to another theme in early Christian writing – that of "love of poverty". This involved not only solemn warnings about the dangers of riches but exhortations to the rich to share their wealth with the poor, the alien and the sick.

Not only in the early Church, but throughout Christian history there has been a recognition of the responsibility of the Church towards the poor. It is not accidental that the Church has pioneered medical and educational work among the poor in so many parts of the world. At the same time, it has to be admitted that on many occasions and in many places, particularly during the imperial ascendancy of the West, the Church has appeared to be on the side of the oppressors. This was not *always* the Church's role even during the colonial period. Sometimes Christian leaders *were* able to be prophetic, as in the campaign against the slave trade and slavery itself. Many local and expatriate Christians made important contributions to the emergence of nationalist aspirations in many colonised lands. Many more were deeply involved in the study and promotion of the cultures, languages and literatures of oppressed peoples. It remains true, nevertheless, that wherever the Church has become implicated in a dominant "Christendom" type of arrangement, it has either become an instrument of oppression (as in Latin America) or it has been used to justify imperial or state oppression.

It is interesting, therefore, to note that numerous Christian groups have now emerged at the "grass-roots" in precisely those situations where the Church is seen as oppressive. These groups are committed to a "subversion" of this understanding of Christianity. It is a testimony to the liberating power of the Gospel that the oppressed are now using it to free themselves from the oppressors who, in many instances, brought it to them in the first place.[1]

The grass-roots groups or base communities, as they are often called, have as their aim not only the liberation of the Church from the oppressive structures in which it finds itself enmeshed, but also what is coming to be known as "the strengthening of the poor". In fact the two aspects are closely interconnected. The assumption of leadership by the poor in their own communities is a sign of the enabling work that is going on in the community as a whole. One secret of the success of these groups is the model of interdependence which they exhibit. Here it is the poor who enable the poor, the poor who plead for others who are poor, the poor who lead in worship, celebration and reflection. In this respect they represent a recovery of New Testament models of interdependence. We do not know if the Christians in Antioch who sent help to the church in Jerusalem were poor or rich (Acts 11: 27-30), but we do know that the Macedonian Christians helped that church *out of their poverty* (2 Corinthians 2:1-5). Perhaps more importantly, St Paul develops his teaching on interdependence among Christians and churches on the basis of this example set by the Macedonians.

This initiative by the poor in mission and ministry is perhaps the most remarkable development in the Christian world this century. The Church at large, however, needs to be conscientised or made aware of the dynamic ways in which the Gospel is being lived and shared by the poor in certain parts of the world. Indeed, the poor in other parts of the world need to be conscientised about the possibilities for liberation in living and sharing

171

the Gospel in this way. At the same time, there remains a ministry for the wider Church, and that is a ministry of "strengthening the poor" by providing material, educational and human resources for the local communities so that their life together is deepened and their witness strengthened.[2]

Another aspect of this ministry of the wider Church might be that of *advocacy*. In many parts of the world, Christians struggling against political oppression and economic injustice are being harassed, imprisoned and even exiled because of their commitment to freedom, justice and peace.[3] The wider Church and its leadership is often in a position to exert pressure on governments, regional associations and international organisations to bring about noticeable change in this state of affairs. Yet often the Church fails in its prophetic task at this point. The reticence of many international evangelical organisations to speak out on these issues is well known. Sometimes this reluctance is related to the fact that certain kinds of Christians who are sympathetic to these organisations are also involved with the state apparatus in their countries. The ecumenical movement, on the other hand, has been very muted in its criticism of repression in communist lands, because many of its member churches were regulated by the state, and in some cases, were officially related to it. It is a remarkable fact that the churches became central to the popular movements which brought about change in these countries. Nevertheless, the wider Church has to repent of its collaboration with the collaborators, many of whom have now, happily, gone into oblivion. International evangelical bodies too need to respond prophetically to gross violations of human rights and dignity, especially in countries where they have influential constituencies.

It is very important to point out, however, that because of significant shifts in the demography of the Christian world, it is perhaps the mission of the poor *to* the rest of the Church and to the world which is the most significant of all. This matter is somewhat difficult to understand in the West, particularly Western Europe, where the history of Christian churches in the last two hundred years or so has often been that of withdrawal from the deprived areas of the cities and of a reduced presence even in rural areas. The Archbishop of Canterbury's Commission on Urban Priority Areas records some of the evidence showing the Church of England's vulnerability in the deprived areas of the city. This trend goes back well into Victorian times.[4] The attention received by the Commission's report, *Faith in the City*, and the creation of the Church Urban Fund led to demands that a similar commission be established for rural areas. This commission has now completed its work, and it will be instructive to see which areas of need it has identified as crucial for the Church in an age of rapid decline in terms of housing, transport and agriculture. The dwindling number of full-time clergy and ageing plant, beset by numerous planning difficulties, will also need to be considered.

Paradoxically, however, the decline of the Church among the poor in the West has been paralleled by an unprecedented growth of the Church among the poor in Africa, Asia and Latin America. Vibrant, full-blooded and committed Christian faith is to be found in countless communities throughout the Two-Thirds World. Some were brought into existence as a result of mission activity from the West, others were evangelised by their own people or by someone from nearby. Whatever their origin, many of these communities have testimonies which are critical for the cause of the Gospel in the world. It is these testimonies of courage and perseverance which will, more and more, bring a response from a world which needs hope. Churches in the West and their mission agencies need to be challenged to put their resources increasingly into facilitating this witness of the poor to each other, to the Church at large and to the world.

One result of the emergence of these communities of solidarity among the poor has been the development of a new way of doing theology. Those engaged in working with the poor have begun to see that theology cannot any longer be a purely deductive science, deriving all its results from given and unalterable first principles. Nor can it be merely speculative. It must be related, more and more, to the *praxis* of local communities of Christians as they read the Word of God in their context, as they celebrate the Sacraments and live the Christian life in situations of oppression and of struggle for liberation. This approach is sometimes called "doing theology from below".[5] One part of the basis for this kind of theological reflection is undoubtedly the life of the local community. In itself this could lead to unbridled and unprincipled reflection which could become greatly distanced from its Christian origins. There is, however, another aspect to the basis. This is reflection on "Jesus among the crowds in Galilee".[6] Doing theology from below, then, has to do with reflecting on the *praxis* of the local community in the light of the *praxis* of Jesus (and of the Apostolic Church?).[7] As we have seen, it is the necessary interaction between these two which has often led theologians of Liberation to take seriously the reliability of the New Testament records, since they give us some access to the Jesus of history and to the history of the early Church.

One element in the life of Jesus which has become almost a kind of hermeneutical key for many Liberation theologians is what is often called "the Galilean Option". It is claimed that the coming of the Messiah to Nazareth and the Synoptics' placing of most of Jesus' ministry in Galilee are profoundly significant factors in our understanding of divine providence in the life of Jesus. Galilee is seen as a symbol of the oppressed. From the very earliest times it has known oppression. The first of the provinces of the Northern Kingdom to be occupied by the Assyrians, its population was displaced and people from other parts of the Assyrian Empire were settled there (hence the name, Galilee of the Gentiles).[8] Moreover, it seems that at the time of Jesus there had been significant immigration from Judah of people in search of a better life. This had created an underclass of social casualties. It is suggested that there was a disproportionate number of widows, orphans and people who were unemployed or sick.[9] Also, the people of Galilee were somewhat removed from the metropolitan centres of the ancient Middle East and were, therefore, often regarded as rude, untutored and unlettered. In Matthew's account of Peter's denial of Jesus at the trial, for example, Peter's accent gives him away as a Galilean (Matthew 26:73).

Jerusalem, on the other hand, is seen by the Liberation theologians as a place of privilege and wealth where the religious aristocracy colluded with the imperial powers and their lackeys in the oppression of the rest of the people. It is suggested, for example, that while taxes, in certain instances, were reduced for the inhabitants of Jerusalem, they were increased commensurately for the rest of the population of Palestine. In addition, the people also had to pay the Temple tax. The leaders in Jerusalem, therefore, wished to maintain the *status quo* which so favoured them and were hostile to any suggestions of radical change. Their opposition to Jesus has to be understood in this context.

It is suggested, furthermore, that when Jesus entered Jerusalem in triumph, the crowds which welcomed him were made up largely of Galilean pilgrims who had come over to Jerusalem for the Passover. The religious, political and commercial élite, on the other hand, were alarmed at the manner of his entry and by the revolutionary ardour which accompanied the cleansing of the Temple. They tried then to arrest him and to do away with him (Mark 11-12 and parallels).

Another aspect of the Galilean Option has to do with the mixed population of Galilee. It was truly a place of many cultures and many faiths. Many of Jesus' own encounters with people of other faiths, such as the Roman centurion and the Syro-Phoenician woman, took place in this area (Matthew 8:5-13 and parallels; Mark 7:24-30 and parallels). Significantly, the Great Commission, at the end of Matthew's Gospel, is also given to the apostles in Galilee. However, before this commissioning to evangelise the world, Jesus had told the disciples that he was going *ahead* of them into Galilee. Some commentators take this to mean that Jesus was to *lead* them into Galilee, others that he would already *be present* in Galilee when the disciples arrived there (Matthew 28:1-10). Whichever interpretation proves acceptable, there is the possibility of the Gospel's engagement with many cultures and many faiths here at the very heart of Christian origins. The Risen Lord promises his disciples that he is already present in the multicultural and multifaith situations to which they are called.

The other part of the basis of mission-oriented theological reflection is, as we have seen, the *praxis* of the local communities of faith. This can be the ways in which Christians live and share their faith in a context which has been shaped by a great world religion. It may be a context of rapid modernisation and industrialisation or it may be one which is rich in relationships and stories but materially poor.

Expatriate missionaries, for example, have sometimes suggested an accommodation with the caste system in India. The ancient Christian communities of India lived for a considerable period almost as a caste within the Hindu social structure. Yet the challenge of the Gospel to caste (as to slavery in other contexts) has always re-emerged in the encounter of Christians with Hinduism. Despite the assiduous fostering of missiological fashion in the name of the Homogeneous Unit Principle, the consensus among Indian Christians is that caste, as a basis for the socio-economic and political structure in modern India, is unacceptable. It is, moreover, unacceptable as a basis for organising Christian communities. Those who preach the Gospel which announces the breaking down of barriers (Galatians 3:28; Ephesians 2:11-22) must organise their corporate life in a way that reflects Gospel truth. This is not to say that barriers are broken down instantly or that prejudices are overcome immediately. Rather, it means that the structures of the Church must not be allowed to reflect an aspect of Indian culture which is not only unjust and exploitative but which presumes to judge certain people as sinners without any possibility of verification, as the sin which is supposed to have resulted in their present life as people of low caste is believed to have been committed in a previous life. In their attitudes to caste, Indian Christians reflect the consensus which is at the basis of a modern and non-communal India. But this consensus itself has, as we have seen, been shaped to a certain extent by the Gospel's encounter with Hindu culture and custom. This has led not only to the reform of Hinduism itself but to the emergence and development of significant aspects of the ideology of modern India.[10]

In the heavily industrial city of Inchon in South Korea, Christians are helping workers to acquire a sense of their own worth. This leads the Christians to support the workers' struggles to be employed in accordance with the law and for fair wages. Involvement such as this leads to an awareness of the *han* or suffering of the *Minjung,* the common people whether these are the industrial workers in the cities or the peasants in the rural areas.[11]

Minjung theology is an attempt to discern God's presence and action among the common people. The experience of the suffering masses is the context in which the Bible is to be read and understood. This is not an abstraction. The Bible has to be shown to be relevant to the daily experience of suffering which is the lot of the *Minjung.* Local communities of faith have to learn and minister in such a way that the daily needs of the people – material, social and spiritual – are met. It needs to be said, at the same time, that the Bible is the kind of book which speaks to the poor and that Christians have the spiritual resources to deal with evil in a way which brings about liberation for the *Minjung.* In their solidarity with the *Minjung,* Christians will discover a great deal about the Bible and about their faith. But is is *discovery,* not invention, that we are talking about. Another kind of book or another faith may not be able to provide the resources which are needed for the struggle. The *Minjung* may well provide the interpretive framework which is needed for the Christian tradition to be effective *in the Minjung's situation.*[12] However the Scriptures and the tradition which springs from them have a radical priority in that other people in other situations also discover resources for liberation in them. These different perspectives, moreover, are not mutually exclusive and isolated from each other. In the fellowship of the Church they are accountable to each other, and their interaction will lead to a whole view of the Bible and of Christian tradition, a view which it is not possible for any one of the perspectives to attain.

An aspect of the emergence of "people's theologies" such as *Minjung* theology, at least in Asia, has been the opening up of new areas of encounter between Christians and the cultures in which they live. For too long Christian engagement with Asian cultures has been dominated by the need to understand the great World Religions, to have dialogue with their followers and to witness among them with sensitivity and appropriateness. All of these remain important concerns. People's theologies, however, are much more interested in engagement with folk-religion and folk-culture. The histories, literatures and cults of the great religions of Asia are dominated by the concerns of the religious and social aristocracy. It is the popular music, poetry, history (perhaps in the form of legends) and religion which provide insights into the real, as well as the felt, needs of the ordinary people. Theologians who take the *Minjung* seriously reflect, in their work, on aspects of *Minjung* culture such as the famous mask-dances of Korea. These dances portray the profound sense of oppression experienced by the Korean people. At the same time, however, they achieve a "critical transcendence" by their capacity to enable the people to stand over against and beyond the entire world. This brings about conscientisation about their exploited state and also a yearning for change.[13]

James Massey, from the Punjàb in Northern India, points out that the main concerns of the movement for inculturation in India have had to do with the interpretation of the Faith in terms of Brahmanic religions and culture. Both high-caste Indian Christians and expatriate missionaries have been heavily involved in this enterprise. According to Massey, however, inculturation of the Faith into Brahmanic terms is not the concern of the vast majority of Christians who come from low-caste backgrounds. Where inculturation is concerned, their worship and spirituality is already profoundly Indian, though not Brahmanical. Their main concerns, however, along with those of other poor Indians, have to do with a recognition of their dignity as human beings made in the image of God and the need to be able to earn their living with honour and provide for a more hopeful future for their children. If a proper *dalit* theology is to emerge in India, it must take these concerns seriously. Also, it will attempt to relate to the ways in which the poor Christians have interpreted their faith in terms of traditional *dalit* spiritualities.[14] A new kind of Church history will need to be written – a history which is not limited to the origin and survival of the usually high-caste ancient Christian communities, nor to the histories of the various churches which have come into being as a result of Western mission work, but is the history of the ways in which *dalit* peoples have responded to Christ and his challenge of discipleship.

It is perhaps worth remarking that Massey refers to a disquieting body of evidence which suggests that expatriate missionaries, as well as leading Indian Christians, discouraged the conversion of *dalits* in many cases. Part of the reason for this was the fear that their conversion would prevent the evangelisation of the higher castes. The *dalits* were an embarrassment to the Church, and this prevented its full involvement in addressing their needs. All this needs to be revised now if *dalits* are to play a full part in the life of the Church and if Christianity is to be credible to the large number of *dalits* outside the Church. An authentic *dalit* theology can only emerge out of a full commitment to and engagement with the *dalits* by the Church.

There are signs that such an engagement is beginning to happen. Numerous programmes for conscientisation, development and income-generation now relate directly to the *dalits*. Theological colleges offer courses on their history and culture. Some even encourage their students to get directly involved in issues related to the emancipation and empowerment of *dalits*. They are now emerging as Christian leaders and are involved in setting the priorities of their churches. It seems that *dalits* and their concerns will become more and more crucial to the life and mission of the churches in India.

Christian encounter with Islām too has concentrated, from the very earliest times, on the Qur'ān, on *Kalām* or formal theology or on the poetry and manuals of discipline of Şūfism or Islamic mysticism. Christians are only gradually coming to a consciousness that there is a very significant substratum to almost every aspect of Islām which may be termed popular. Some of the needs which make popular Islām so pervasive are undoubtedly psychological. They arise from feelings of inadequacy and the need to depend on an authoritative, even authoritarian, figure. An important factor in popular Islām is the guide in spiritual and moral matters known as the *pīr* or *murshid*, although such figures are also common in "official" Islām. Participation in the cult of the saint and of his living representatives, moreover, provides an escape from the harsh economic and social realities of life. This is particularly true of repressed groups such as women. At shrines they are often allowed to behave in ways which are generally unacceptable in society at large. Ecstatic dancing is common at many shrines. As Myrtle Langley has shown, spirit-possession too, as understood in folk-Islām, releases women from the inhibitions which convention normally imposes on them in Islamic societies.[16] Another important aspect of folk-Islām, particularly associated with the shrine cult and the *pīr*, is that it provides an alternative to medicine. In this function, like many other alternatives to technology, it has a magical aspect. Also, there are certain elements in folk-Islām which are designed to provide care for those who have been damaged emotionally. Finally, it needs to be noted that these descriptions of the ways in which folk-Islām functions are not meant to be exhaustive and there remains a residue of the supernatural in many manifestations of popular Islām which cannot easily be explained away.[17]

It will have been noticed that popular Islām meets many of the real and felt needs of the people. A careful distinction has to be made between the need and the way it is met. Also, Christians will have to acknowledge that in some ways, especially in communal matters, folk-Islām provides authentic and constructive means for the expression of solidarity and mutual concern. What of Christian mission and ministry, then? Christians must continue to work for social and family structures which are *both* supportive and liberating. Aspects of folk-religion which are pathological manifestations of the desire to escape repression will disappear gradually as repression gives way to a more open and affirmative society. In the case of women, for instance, Christians will want to identify with the struggles of those Muslim women who believe that Islām does not necessarily involve a limitation on their freedom of expression, education and association.

Again, Christians need to be involved in the development of proper preventative and community medicine, perhaps using the insights of traditional medicine, especially in remote and severely deprived areas. So much of the recourse to degraded forms of the shrine cult is for illnesses which are caused by poor sanitation, hygiene and health awareness. Christian communities need particularly to be equipped with skills in pastoral care for those who have been hurt emotionally. Such skills must be seen now as an essential part of programmes which deal with community transformation. Mental health care is rare even in those places where comparatively adequate curative and preventative facilities are available. The supernatural (or preternatural) aspects of folk-Islām cannot be ignored, however. After social and psychological explanations have been exhausted, their remain instances of oppression, dependence and fear which cannot be explained adequately in terms of scientific world-views. Indeed, many psychologists, psychiatrists and anthropologists now allow that certain kinds of human behaviour are not amenable to conventional therapy and that in such cases spiritual help needs to be sought.[18] The ministry of exorcism is widely sought after in the Muslim world. Properly exercised by authorised ministers of the Church, it can come as a healing and liberating experience. Gifts of healing are given to some in the Church by the Holy Spirit (1 Corinthians 12:9). These gifts can be exercised among Muslims, bringing to them not only physical and mental healing but also an opportunity to hear the Good News.

In the Islāmic context it is entirely right to emphasise Jesus' rejection of *temporal* power as a way of bringing about a society obedient to God's will. The ministry of Jesus, of the early Church and of countless Christians since provide examples, however, of *spiritual* power. Such power is entirely the gift of God and is given for the building up of the Church and for the deliverance of men and women from evil, whether that evil is experienced as embodied in human structures or, more directly, in terms of spiritual oppression.

Much thought has gone into addressing the vexed question of how programmes for inculturation relate to the practices of folk-Islām. The music of folk-Islām has already deeply affected popular Christian music in many parts of the world. The practice of bringing pieces of cloth, veils, carpets, candles and even livestock as an offering before, after or during divine service is another instance of inculturation. The Roman Catholic

Church, in many countries, is actively encouraging the emergence of a "Christian shrine cult" as a response to the popularity of the shrines of Muslim saints. At the other end of the spectrum, there are more dubious forms of inculturation. For example, the Bible is sometimes treated as a talisman. Also, many itinerant "healers" are patently fraudulent. As in all areas of inculturation, there is tension between the view that the local church is a manifestation of the universal Church and the perception that the local church needs to be firmly rooted in its own context. On the one hand, any local church must manifest the universal Christian tradition, normatively witnessed to in the Scriptures and explicated in the life of the Church down the ages and across the world. On the other hand, every local church needs to order its worship and discipline in a way which is sensitive to the local culture.[19] Inculturation of Christian worship within the context of popular Islām is necessary if the Gospel is to be allowed to address people where they are. We must be sure, however, that it *is* the Gospel which is addressing people in a particular situation and that Christian worship and witness have not simply become reflections of the prejudices and superstitions of the culture in which a local church is set. Inculturation involves critical engagement with a culture, and cannot be simply an endorsement of any and every culture. This is particularly so in the case of popular Islām. The world-views of ordinary Muslims in many lands remain close to the world-views reflected in the Bible. The Bible's witness to divine providence, to human solidarity in community, to the spiritual character of individuals, societies and indeed the universe, finds a ready response among Muslims. There is also, however, a resistance to the Bible's challenge to superstition, the improper veneration of human beings or locations and the downright substitution for God and the things of God with the occult.[20]

Great discernment is needed, therefore, in the process of inculturation. Constant reference back to the Scriptures and to the teaching and practice of the early Church is necessary if inculturation is to be authentic and faithful and not merely syncretistic. Such reference is all the more necessary and profitable because both the Bible and the early Church reflect contexts very similar to that of popular Islām.[21] The ways in which the biblical writers or the Fathers deal with aspects of their cultures can provide substantial guidance for those engaging with cultures where folk-Islām is influential.

CHAPTER TWELVE

Mission as Evangelism

We have seen that the Church exercises her missionary vocation in a number of different ways – through presence, identification, dialogue and service. We have seen also that the Church's public worship, the reading and exposition of the Scriptures and the celebration of the Sacraments have a missionary significance. In short, all that the Church is and does has significance for mission. Presence, identification, dialogue, service and worship, moreover, all have an evangelistic dimension in that they bring the Gospel into encounter with individuals and communities. Such an encounter results in the Gospel challenging, transforming and enabling human beings and the communities in which they live.

It is extremely important for congregations, dioceses, conferences and councils to keep under review all their various activities from this point of view. We need constantly to be asking ourselves, "What is the evangelistic aspect of this activity?" This is not to say, of course, that there are no other aspects to a particular activity. One activity may be simply a response to human need, another may be a means of bringing members of the congregation closer together and yet another may be related to the nurture and deepening of faith. Yet all will have an evangelistic aspect to them, whether in direct outreach or in the preparation of members for outreach. In some parts of the World Church this happens quite naturally. In the course of ministering to human need, the Gospel is quietly commended. As communities are helped to obtain clean water for themselves or to get their children immunised, as they discover better ways of tending their crops and herds or of obtaining tools and machinery for their trades, they come to realise that Christians have become involved in these matters because of their faith in Christ. There is no proselytism here, no compulsion for people to hear the Gospel or to become Christians. Christian involvement and commitment are unconditional, but they should also be transparent. Men and women should know why Christians are involved in attempts to bring about social and economic transformation in so many communities around the world.

In more settled situations, the Church's involvement in the community sometimes gets distanced from its worship and witness. The hall of a parish church in England, for example, may be used for numerous community occasions ranging from weddings and youth clubs to committee meetings. The congregation and the parochial church council have to ask themselves how these occasions can also be opportunities for Christian witness.[1]

An Anglican parish in Australia, for example, has a playgroup for mothers and toddlers which has become a place of ministry to women who are often lonely in the midst of affluence. Committed Christians from the congregation go to the group regularly and make friends there. While the children are looked after, there is an imaginative presentation of the Christian Faith or else some contemporary issue is examined from a Christian point of view. Good use is made of audio-visual material and visiting speakers are chosen carefully. Through this a number of families have been reached who could not have been reached in any other way.

The ways in which churches and their facilities are furnished and decorated often have a significant impact on Christian witness in the area. If they are seen as open and welcoming, a good start will have been made. Stuffiness and a preoccupation with tradition will tend to alientate all except the enthusiasts.[2] Pictures, icons, sculpture and literature can all be used effectively for witness. The attitudes of voluntary and paid staff are also crucial if effective witness is to be made.

In Chapters 3 and 8 we saw how the Franciscans distinguished between presence and preaching. They regarded presence in a particular place as a necessary preparation for the task of preaching, which was attempted only when the time was right. If evangelisation is to be incarnational, then presence, identification, dialogue and service are all essential. But they are not enough. It is true that the whole mission of the Church has an evangelistic dimension in that the Gospel is commended by how Christians respect and serve their fellow human beings. However, a stage is reached in Christian engagement with the world when a *kairos* is discerned regarding the verbal communication of the Gospel. The advent of this *kairos* will vary from place to place and from time to time. In some situations it will be appropriate to proclaim the Gospel sooner rather than later. In other cultures a longer period of preparation may be necessary. It is perhaps salutary to remember that the communication of the Gospel in the New Testament is understood as proclamation *(kēryssō)*, which is closely related to the essential meaning of the Gospel *(kērygma)*. In other words, the essential meaning and demand of the Gospel is disclosed in its proclamation. If this is so, it is clear that evangelism, in the sense of proclamation, is essential if the Church herself is to understand the Gospel and if she is to communicate it to others.

Proclamation, however, does not necessarily mean *declamation*. It need not be wedded to any particular style or method of evangelism. It is not only in mass rallies and in the mass media that the proclamation of the Gospel takes place. An expression which is gaining currency in conciliar circles is "faith-sharing". There is an increasing realisation among church leaders, synods and councils that congregations, families and individuals have to be prepared to "give a reason for the hope that is in them" with sensitivity and gentleness (1 Peter 3:15). In order that they be able to do this, a great deal of work needs to be done on the production of apologetic material – not only literature but audio-visual and display material as well. Such material would be useful for training Christians, and at least some of it would be useful for evangelistic purposes too. Evangelical organisations such as Scripture Union have done a great deal of very good work in this area. I am not able to detect a commensurate concern for this kind of engagement in ecumenical bodies, though some of the work done by the World Association for Christian Communication on conscientisation issues also carries apologetic undertones in relation to Gospel values.

Faith-sharing, necessarily, has an aspect of testimony to it. An individual testifies to God's work in his or her life; a community can do the same. Such a testimony, whether by word or deed, is a necessary and valuable part of evangelism. How we live our lives, how we serve our fellow human beings, the primacy of love in the Christian community – all of these are important in Christian witness. But they are not enough. Christians discover sometimes that although they have invested a good deal of effort in serving their fellows and in leading lives that are committed to love and reconciliation, their interlocutors have misunderstood their reasons for living as they do. They have certainly *not* understood such a style of life and service to be witnessing to Christ. Therefore, whatever our lifestyles, whatever our acts of service, whatever the example we think we are, whatever our testimony, evangelism is *more* than any or all of these. An essential aspect of it must be a point away from ourselves to what God has done in Jesus Christ. There is a transcendent aspect to evangelism which makes it different from an invitation to join a church or even a personal testimony or example. This is also why silent witness cannot be enough in the long run – although, admittedly, it may be necessary for a period in certain contexts.[3] There is the great and ever-present danger of Pelagianism in this area of Christian life, as in so many others. Evangelism is not about how good we are, or even how good the Church is, it is about how good God is, to us and to the world. Indeed, every act of authentic witness will lead us to a realisation of our own sinfulness and unworthiness as bearers of the Good News (2 Corinthians 4:7).

Authentic models for evangelism will vary from place to place and from context and context. What is appropriate in one context will not be appropriate in another. It is perhaps instructive, however, to survey a few models of evangelism which claim authenticity in particular contexts. Raymond Fung of the World Council of Churches' Evangelism desk has put us all in his debt with his monthly letter on evangelism. These letters have, in the past, explored such sensitive issues as the relationship between evangelism and proselytism, the principles of church growth, the interaction between incarnational ministry and evangelism and so on – the list is long. In recent private correspondence, Fung has put forward a model for evangelism which is based on a congregation's commitment to justice. This is an unusual and creative initiative which brings two streams of Christian witness together into one strategy. Fung's idea is that a congregation committed to the Bible's teaching on justice would invite others, through public and personal invitation, to join with it in addressing these issues both on a local and a global scale. It is hoped that this would involve such people in the life of the congregation and, eventually, in its worship as well. There is, obviously, much to commend in this model. The dangers are somewhat obvious; people may well join in with a Christian congregation on a particular issue such as *apartheid* in South Africa or human rights in Irān but their involvement may stop there. If a model such as this is to be successful, great care must be taken that the work involved in addressing justice issues is integrated with the nurturing, teaching, praying and celebrating aspects of the congregation's life.[4]

The Episcopal Church in the USA consists largely of congregations which may rightly be described as "gathered". That is to say, they do not, on the whole, draw their membership from a clearly defined geographical area. The congregations tend to be eclectic in the sense that people *choose* to belong to a particular church. In such situations, it is not surprising that strategies for evangelism are closely related to the growth of congregations.[5] This, in itself, is not a bad thing. When the Good News of God's love in Christ is shared, people are, quite naturally, drawn into the fellowship of those who have experienced this love. In the New Testament, conversion is closely linked to baptism, which is seen as solidarity with Christ in his death and resurrection (Romans 6:1-11). To speak about those who are "in Christ" is, moreover, a way of speaking about the Church. In baptism we are baptised into the Body of Christ, the Church (1 Corinthians 12:12-13). As Professor Moule has put it,

> New Testament Christianity is nothing if not social: the Semitic traditions on which it arose are themselves strong in corporate sense; and, still more, it was quickly found to be impossible to describe Christ himself otherwise than as an inclusive, a corporate personality. To become a Christian, therefore, was *ipso facto* to become an organ or limb of that Body, and the Christian Church is essentially the household of God.[6]

In contexts where individualism is dominant and community is under threat, it is right to emphasise the communal nature of Christianity. At the same time, evangelism should not be confused with church growth. Evangelism has to do with the sharing of God's purposes for us as individuals, as families and as communities. The Gospel brings comfort as well as challenge, the opportunity to belong to a community as well as a call, perhaps, to cross frontiers, assurance as well as judgement. Some churches, undoubtedly, grow as a consequence of authentic evangelism. People are challenged, converted, baptised and incorporated into the fellowship of a believing and worshipping community. Others, however, may grow for a whole number of reasons, some of them good, some neither good nor bad and some definitely bad. It is well known, for example, that expatriates from Christianised cultural backgrounds tend to gather around a chaplaincy, even if they had little connection with the Church at home. This is a splendid opportunity for the Church to evangelise, to teach and to root such people into the Faith. Such a flocking to church, however, should not be seen as a result of evangelism! Again, people may attend church because their social status is seen as requiring it or because the church is seen as symbolic of a particular national or racial grouping. The leadership in the church may simply reinforce such behaviour, or it may use people's attendance at church as a way of leading them on in discipleship.

Once again, the mere fact of attendance cannot be confused with evangelism. There is, arguably, too much written these days which makes for just such a confusion. Ultimately then, evangelism must be about the transformation of individuals and communities, *not* about adding to the membership of congregations, though this will be a consequence, one might even say a necessary consequence, of evangelism.[7]

Hospitality has been identified as yet another way of evangelisation. Here the basic unit is not so much the congregation as the family. In certain cultures it is still possible to have effective open-air evangelism as well as door-to-door visitation. In other cultures, for reasons of climate, the increasing privatisation of life and the consequent breakdown of community, these are not credible options. Sadly, privatisation and the breakdown of community also often result in the impoverishment of values such as those of hospitality, even among Christians. Yet the exercise of Christian hospitality can surely be an occasion for evangelism. Congregational, deanery and even diocesan missions can be structured in such a way that the home becomes a focus for befriending people, for meeting their spiritual and material needs and for the sharing of the Gospel. If people are shy about direct sharing, carefully chosen literature and audio-visual material can be used to challenge both the hosts and their guests. In the early stages it is not even necessary that such literature and other material should be explicitly Christian. Much poetry and music, many novels and even some books on travel raise pointed questions about life and death, the purpose of human existence, suffering and joy and many other matters crucial in the task of evangelisation. In contexts where there has been a large-scale breakdown in community, there could be a happy congruence between the use of hospitality in the rebuilding of community and evangelisation. Hospitality to our neighbour is not only our *response* to the divine hospitality, it can also be a *witness* to it and an *invitation* to others to partake of it.[8]

Raymond Fung, in several of his newsletters, has drawn our attention to the great importance of ministries of healing and exorcism in the evangelisation of China:

> Lay evangelists and itinerant preachers spread the word and lay the hand on the sick and the disturbed. The gospel is understood largely in terms of liberation from evil spirits which wound the body and the soul. People in rural China expect this of Christianity and when they see certain signs in that direction, they respond. For people who had no contact with organised church life for some twenty years, no Bible, no Christian literature and very little teaching, living isolated in the midst of suffering, poverty and hardship, their most solid catechism must be the vivid memory of Jesus walking the earth, driving out the demons and healing the sick.[9]

Fung goes on to point out that it is not only in rural China that the ministry of healing is so effective in outreach. In the great metropolitan centres of the world too, people flock to services of healing and, notoriously, millions "participate" in cults of healing through the mass media. Fung is well aware of the great diversity which is to be found in ministries of healing. Some he clearly finds to be dubious. Others, he acknowledges, have been effective in outreach as well as faithful to the Gospel.

In my own experience, while many flock to services of healing and, perchance, hear the Gospel preached, not many are challenged to commit themselves to following the Christian way. They may be in awe of the power of the Gospel, they may treasure a reverence for Jesus in their hearts, but of outward commitment there is little indication. Another difficulty has to do with the ambivalence inherent in the phenomenon of healing. We have noticed already the many doubtful characters, among the genuine ones, who claim to have a gift of healing. Additionally, there are the psychosomatic aspects of illness and the need people have to be told that they are well after all. There is, of course, a place for deliverance from fear and anxiety in Christian healing, but we need to be clear about the nature of the problem being addressed. Even in cases where there is a clear deliverance from physical or mental disease, the claims of the

**FIGURE TO BE INSERTED
INTO THIS PAGE**

Gospel cannot be coercive. God has created humans as free beings, and if their response to him is to be authentic, it cannot be coerced. Having entered these caveats, however, one can say that it is clear that the ministry of healing is an important occasion for evangelism.

In some contexts, particularly Islâmic ones, evangelistic literature can be very helpful. Muslims generally are people of the word and often respond to written material. Such literature can take several forms. One of the most popular is the apologetic, where the Christian Faith is presented in terms which are intelligible to the reader and where care is taken to avoid unnecessary offence. Sometimes Muslim forms of literature are used. The life of Christ, for example, may be presented in the form of a *sīra* (an account of the life of a prophet, particularly Mûhammad).[10] Muslim poetical styles may be used to convey a Christian message, and even calligraphy is used to share Christian truth with Muslims. This latter can simply be verses of Scripture or prayers written in calligraphic script, or else the script may be used in such a way that the letters become symbolic of the Holy Spirit, the Cross, the Ascension and so on. In this way, an attempt is made to overcome the culture's resistance to iconography.[11]

Perhaps Scripture distribution is the most widespread form of the use of literature in evangelism in the Muslim world. Again and again, Christians find that unaided reading of the Scripture, or even of just a portion of it, has made a significant impact on an individual or a family. The "immediate felt authority" of Scripture is often experienced. While Christians will always seek to explain what Scripture means in the life of the Church, its immediate impact on a diversity of individuals and situations cannot be underestimated. It is necessary, or course, if Scripture is to have this kind of impact, that its language is such that its readers understand it easily and are not unnecessarily offended by it. In recent years the Bible Societies and other organisations have done a great deal to ensure that translations fulfil this condition. The original languages of the Bible have a special significance in the Islâmic context. Muslims are used to reading the *Qur'ân* in Arabic and even translations of it are often interlinear. In such contexts, to have translations of the Bible which also reproduce the original texts is expecially helpful.

At the same time, however, care must be taken to explain to our Muslim friends that the way in which the text of a book in the Bible is established is very different from the way in which the text of the Qur'ān is established. Christian scholars work on a variety of texts and other authorities to produce a critical text which can then be translated. The Muslim community, on the other hand, has deliberately destroyed all variants of the Qur'ānic text, and the contemporary text is the descendant of a single recension. Behind all this lies a different view of scripture in each community. Christians believe, on the one hand, that human faculties, as well as the process of history, are profoundly involved in the appropriation and mediation of divine revelation. Muslims, on the other hand, tend to believe that revelation is *ipsissima vox Dei* ("the very voice of God"), immediate and separate from human culture and its strengths and weaknesses.[12]

There are some who still ask why proclamation is necessary if Christians are faithful in presence, identification, dialogue and action. Is this not enough as the agenda for Christian witness? In preparation for its Conference on World Mission and Evangelism, which was held at San Antonio in 1989, the WCC turned its attention to this question. Some forty church leaders, scholars and evangelists, from both the ecumenical and the evangelical constituences, were invited to reflect on why intentional or invitational evangelism remains an important part of Christian Mission today. The *Stuttgart Statement,* which was issued at the end of the consultation, seeks to build on previous WCC statements in this area, particularly on *Mission and Evangelism – an Ecumenical Affirmation.*[13] First, it is pointed out that a verbal sharing of the Gospel focuses its demand for *repentance* – a demand which is, nevertheless, inherent in all Christian Mission. Repentance or *metanoia,* moreover, is not simply being sorry for personal sin. It is a complete change of direction, a renewal of the inner person. It has profound implications for our relations with fellow-believers, with other human beings and with the impersonal social structures among which we live. The Gospel's concern for repentance can certainly be apprehended to a certain extent in witness through service, dialogue and presence. But it is experienced precisely as *demand* and as needing an *urgent* response in an encounter with Christ, not merely with Christians. This encounter can occur in a variety of ways, but is often a consequence of some kind of articulation of the Gospel.

Secondly, the proclamation of the Gospel brings the Word of God in Jesus Christ into an encounter with a knowledge of the Word that is *implicit* in all human beings (John 1:9). Evangelism in this sense is *educative* in the strict meaning of the word, as it brings out and makes *explicit* what is already there. It is important to note, however, that while the Gospel affirms and confirms certain areas of human experience, it also questions and challenges others (Hebrews 4:12-13).

The Scriptures tell us that God has not left himself without witness anywhere (Acts 14:17) and, indeed, that different religious traditions have discerned the existence and purposes of God to a greater or lesser extent (Acts 17:22-31). At the same time, we are to note that the Scriptures also tell us that such knowledge of God has been overlaid by human sin, both personal and corporate, "secular" and religious (Romans 1:18-23). The coming of the Word in Jesus is a cleansing and purifying experience, but it is also a *fulfilling* one. Since the time of Irenaeus, the Church has believed, on the authority of texts such as Ephesians 1:10 and Colossians 1:15-20, that in Christ all that is authentic in humanity's quest for meaning and spirituality is fulfilled. Authentic evangelism, therefore, brings about the fulfilment of the genuine aspirations of human beings, whether these are expressed in a religious tradition, in social action or in literature and drama.

Evangelism is also seen as bringing *comfort* and assurance to those who, "without prior explicit knowledge of Jesus Christ, the only Saviour and Lord" have, nevertheless, realised their own inadequacy and sin and have thrown themselves on the mercy of God. Sir Norman Anderson, the well-known evangelical Anglican, has said that such an attitude must be the result of the Holy Spirit's work of convicting people of sin, righteousness and judgement (John 16: 7-11). He believes that it leads to a recognition of Christ, either before death or after it.[14] Bishop Newbigin is surely correct when he tells us that we cannot fully know God's final purpose and intention.[15] We know that he wants all to be saved and yet, if human freedom is to be taken seriously, we must allow for those who choose to remain obdurate even in the face of God's suffering love and limitless mercy. The most that we can do is to hope that God will show the same mercy to others which he has shown to us, unworthy as we are. Whatever our beliefs about the possibility of God's revelation to those who die without an explicit knowledge of Christ, surely we are obliged to bring the comfort and assurance of the Gospel to those who have come to repentance as a result of the work of the Holy Spirit. Since we do not know who these people are, we are obliged to reach out to all. It is also true, of course, that in many cases such a reaching out will itself bring about repentance and then faith.

It is true that the Church's evangelistic activity is directed primarily at those outside the boundaries of the visible Church. Anglicans and Roman Catholics have, however, also pointed to the necessity of "evangelising the baptised". By this they mean not only those who have been baptised and have then lapsed in terms of regular worship, Bible study and prayer, but also those who worship regularly and are full participants in the life of their church. All Christians need continually to be formed by the Gospel and by its challenge and its comfort, until they have attained to "the mind of Christ" (1 Corinthians 2:16; Philippians 2:5; Colossians 3:1 – 3). Nor is it only the baptised, faithful or lapsed, who are to be evangelised. The evangelist too needs to be evangelised by the Gospel which he or she preaches. Kenneth Cracknell calls this "the purest missionary motive of all". The evangelist shares the Gospel with others so that he or she may himself or herself be blessed by it (1 Corinthians 9:23).[16] The sharing of the Gospel with our neighbour enriches our own understanding of it, provided that we have been sensitive in our listening and in our witnessing.

> *The world is hearing the good news from heaven,*
> *There is now a community of love and salvation!*

Asīr[17]

CHAPTER THIRTEEN

Mission and Unity

> Behold, how good and joyful a thing it is, brethren, to dwell together in Unity!
>
> (Psalm 133:1, from the Liturgy of the Church of Pākistān)

The longing among Christians for unity is deeply rooted in the consciousness that Christ wills unity for his Body, the Church, and that division, however worthy the reasons for it, is at least less than ideal and therefore ultimately unacceptable. The main theme of Christ's High-Priestly Prayer in St John's Gospel is the unity of the disciples and of those who were to follow them. This unity, moreover, is compared to the unity which exists between the Father and the Son and for the sake of the world. The Church is to be united, says Jesus, "so that the world may believe that thou hast sent me" (John 17:21). The credibility of the Gospel which Christians preach and live is adversely affected by disunity. As Father Pierre Duprey of the Vatican's Council for Christian Unity put it in his address to the Lambeth Conference, the "message of reconciliation is perhaps more pressing in the world today than it was nineteen centuries ago. The ministry of the Church is and must be seen to be a ministry of reconciliation. But for that to be so, must not we be reconciled, and must not we be seen to be reconciled? Reconciled with God and with one another."[1] The Archbishop of Canterbury, in his opening address, to which Fr Duprey's was a response, also emphasised the necessity for unity if the Church was to be faithful in reconciling human beings to God and to one another: "neither conflicting Churches, nor competitive Churches, nor co-existing Churches, will be able to embody effectively the Gospel of reconciliation while the Churches themselves remain unreconciled."[2] Both the Archbishop and Fr Duprey were echoing the 1958 Lambeth Conference, which affirmed that "A divided Church cannot heal the wounds of a divided world."[3]

The Edinburgh Conference of 1910 was a focus for the growing realisation that Christian disunity inhibits Christian Mission. Churches and missionary societies were impelled into a new era of co-operation and trust. Comity arrangements were consolidated, there were more joint projects, especially in higher and theological education, and a new impetus was given to the emergence of what became National Christian Councils. For some participants, however, this was not enough. Cheng Ching-yi, a Chinese delegate, said in unambiguous terms, "speaking plainly, we hope to see in the near future a united Christian Church without any denominational distinctions . . . The Church of Christ is universal, not only irrespective of denominations, but also irrespective of nationalities."[4] Although Potter tells us that remarks such as these caused consternation among the majority of delegates of European origin, there are signs that the words were heeded. Not only did Edinburgh 1910 lead to the establishment of the International Missionary Council, it also resulted in the Life and Work and the Faith and Order Conferences. All three of these movements were ultimately to be subsumed into the World Council of Churches.

The Edinburgh Conference resulted in a host of new initiatives in what we now call ecumenism. There was, for example, the famous "Appeal to all Christian People", issued by the Lambeth Conference of 1920. It was said of the Appeal at the time of its publication that it was "the most remarkable document since the Reformation". The Appeal was eirenical in tone, and while it continued to insist that the provisions of the Lambeth Quadrilateral (Scripture, Creeds, Sacraments and the Historic Ministry) must be the basis for Christian reunion, it acknowledged the spiritual fruitfulness of the ministries of non-episcopal churches. It was marked by humility too in its willingness to accept a wider commissioning of Anglican clergy for ministry in a united Church. It hoped also that clergy from the non-episcopal churches would, similarly, not be averse to receiving an episcopal commission so that their ministry would be equally acceptable in every part of the Church. The Appeal led to both the ill-fated Malines conversations with the Roman Catholic Church and also to talks with nonconformists.[5]

Even before the 1920 Lambeth Conference, unity discussions between Anglicans and certain non-episcopal churches had begun in South India. They were the harbingers of the plethora of schemes of church union which emerged at national and regional levels. In the end, organic union was achieved only in the South Asian subcontinent with the emergence first of the Church of South India and then of the Churches of North India, Pakistan and Bangladesh. In several other places it was prevented from coming to fruition for non-theological and even frivolous reasons. The South India scheme took some of its inspiration from the series of conferences which followed the Lambeth Appeal of 1920. The conferences were held in Britain and were attended by bishops of the Church of England and nonconformist leaders.[6] Their influence is particularly discernible in the CSI's decision that all ordinations *after* union would be episcopal but that existing non-episcopal ministries would be incorporated into the new church without any act of reconciliation or unification which could be interpreted as re-ordination. It is well known that this decision made the CSI scheme very unpopular in many of the Provinces of the Anglican Communion. Communion between them and the CSI was restricted, and it is only now that the CSI is beginning to be fully represented in such Anglican *fora* as the Lambeth Conference, the Primates' Meeting and the Anglican Consultative Council. This change is only partially a result of widespread Anglican acceptance of the CSI model of union. It is also due to the fact that the interim period is now nearly over, so there are very few non-espicopally ordained ministers left in the CSI. It remains true, nevertheless, that the CSI has been hugely influential in the work of liturgical revision which has been undertaken by many denominations, though it has to be noticed that the CSI Liturgy is itself influenced by the oriental Christian tradition of the ancient churches of India.

The rough ride given to the South India scheme by some in the Anglican Communion ensured that subsequent schemes such as the North India and Pakistan one and the ill-fated Anglican-Methodist scheme in England had to give greater attention to the reconciliation of ministries and also to doctrinal matters. South Indian negotiators had been made aware of Catholic Anglican unease about the dangers of doctrinal "dilution" in the process of union, and the new schemes devoted greater attention to the matter. The Negotiating Committee of the churches involved in the North India scheme, for example, issued a supplement to the Plan for Union which set out the doctrinal bases of the uniting churches as the standards for the united church.[7] Plans such as the North Indian and the Nigerian ones, which provided for a Service of Reconciliation and

Unification, stood in the tradition of the Lambeth Appeal, which had proposed the acceptance of a wider commissioning or recognition of all ministers by representatives of all the churches involved and of partner churches, including, of course, bishops in the historic succession.[8] Inevitably, questions arose as to whether an act of unification could be understood as an ordination. For some, particularly on the Evangelical side, such a commissioning was not necessary, as the acknowledged fruitfulness of the ministry was evidence of its validity. Catholics, on the other hand, were concerned about the alleged ambiguity of the Service. They wanted it to be understood clearly as an ordination.[9] The failure of the Anglican-Methodist Scheme in England was due to the Evangelical and Catholic parties uniting against it, though each was opposed to it for very different reasons. It is perhaps worth noting that the scheme had problems peculiar to it which are not necessarily found in other schemes.

In the united Churches the act of unification is now regarded as a commissioning to a wider ministry to which all ministers coming to work in the churches from outside submit, whether they are episcopally or non-episcopally ordained. The churches of the Anglican Communion have often entered into full communion with the United Churches on the understanding that the act of unification constitutes, legally, at any rate, episcopal ordination for those who have not received it before.[10] Such anomalies will continue to exist until all the Provinces of the Anglican Communion are in organically united churches, and will perhaps exist even after that. Further acts of unification may become necessary when the stage of union with other ancient episcopal churches of the East and the West is reached. In any case, it is perhaps appropriate for an act of commissioning to take place when a minister arrives from elsewhere and seeks to minister in the local church.

The failure of so many schemes of union at the regional and national levels has led to renewed emphasis on unity at the local level and on international bilateral and multilateral ecumenical conversations. The alternative plan for unity set out in *Growing into Union* seeks to begin with unity at the local level, especially in areas of new housing. Such places are regarded as mission areas and the sponsoring denominations are seen as delegating authority to a local united church or "diocese". It is hoped that such united churches will grow and will be joined by other groups such as long-established Local Ecumenical Projects and, later on, by congregations which have hitherto had denominational affiliations. As the new "dioceses" grow as more and more churches and groups "accede" to them from the denominations they will divide and divide again until they form a network of local churches in communion with each other. Thus a fully united regional or national church will emerge.[11]

The authors are perhaps too sanguine about the reluctance of denominational establishments to allow their constituency to "leak away" in this manner. The possibilities of ecclesiastical and civil litigation are also underestimated. Although the plan ensures that the principle of there being one congregation in each place is respected, the problem of adjacent, if not parallel, Anglican and united episcopates in many areas remains a serious one – *unless* the plan is taken to mean that in areas of mixed denominational affiliation "accessions" to the united church would be acceptable only if they were contiguous with each other and with one of the "dioceses". This would, of course, retard the growth of a united church quite considerably. There are drawbacks to any plan of union, and this one is no exception. Its great merit is that it relates Christian unity to the mission of the Church and recommends that such unity should begin in areas which are, from the mission point of view, the most needy.

There are now scores of Local Ecumenical Projects in Britain with Anglican, Reformed, Methodist and (sometimes) Baptist participation. Some of these have existed for many years and have developed a common life. In many cases there is provision for joint oversight by the denominations concerned. Often there are joint rites of initiation and even common eucharistic celebrations. The Consultative Committee for Local Ecumenical Projects in England, which was founded in 1973 and, until recently, functioned under the aegis of the British Council of Churches, has done valuable work in preparing guidelines for such projects. These have now been accepted by the church bodies involved in CCLEPE (including the Roman Catholic Church). There is also a wider forum for discussion and inspiration which meets periodically. It is to be hoped that in future those involved in LEPs will be able to come together in ways which ensure that their witness to unity is heard by the membership and leadership of the various denominations, particularly in the context of the new ecumenical instruments. The emergence of so many LEPs has not only a local but national significance. It is also to be hoped that a critical stage will be reached at which there will be enough LEPs to warrant the re-emergence of schemes for unity at the national and regional levels.

The Inter-Church Process and the wider and greater unity involved in it is, perhaps, the harbinger of even greater things. The Second Vatican Council heralded the full participation of the Roman Catholic Church in the Ecumenical Movement. For all those who long for the unity of Christ's Church, this is a matter for profound thanksgiving and praise. The arrival of the Roman Catholic Church as a partner in ecumenical dialogue has, however, changed some of the emphases and direction of ecumenism. The focus has been not so much on national or regional schemes of union, nor even on Local Ecumenical Projects; it has been, very largely, on international bilateral or multilateral dialogue. The Roman Catholic Church has been in dialogue on doctrinal and ecclesial issues with a range of other churches and even with groups which are not strictly churches, such as the World Evangelical Fellowship and the ERCDOM group.[12] The phenomenon of inter-church dialogue is not limited to ecumenical endeavour where there is Roman Catholic participation. The Anglican Communion has been party to numerous such dialogues with Christian communions other than the Roman Catholic. The Report of the 1988 Lambeth Conference, for example, lists resolutions on dialogue with the Lutherans, Reformed, Methodist, Baptist, Orthodox and Oriental Orthodox families of churches. In addition, there is dialogue with the Roman Catholic Church and participation in multilateral dialogue organised by the World Council of Churches.[13]

International dialogue between families of churches has been very beneficial in clarifying matters of doctrine and practice which have divided churches for a long time. A particularly gratifying example is that of the dialogue between the Chalcedonian (or Eastern) Orthodox and the Non-Chalcedonian (or Oriental) Orthodox Churches which took place under the aegis of the World Council of Churches. Agreement appears to have been reached on the Person of Christ, a matter which has divided these churches for nearly fifteen hundred years.[14] Much still remains to be done before communion is restored between the two families, but the achievement of dialogue between them is a great step forward. Similarly, Anglican—Roman Catholic dialogue in recent years has produced agreement not only in areas of sacramental belief and ministerial priesthood but also in matters which were at the heart of the separation in the sixteenth century, such as justification by faith, the sanctification of believers, the relation between those two doctrines and their relation to that of Christ's perfect sacrifice on the cross.[15] There has also been significant agreement in this area between Lutherans and Roman Catholics, based on a detailed review of the scriptural evidence. This review can serve as a model for the use of Scripture in ecumenical discussion.[16]

It is undoubtedly the case that international dialogue, with or without Roman Catholic participation, has been beneficial for the World Church. It needs to be noted, nevertheless, that this kind of dialogue is particularly suited to the central organs of the Roman Catholic Church. These have a vested interest in the continuing centralisation of that church, and it is manifest that dialogue conducted on a world-wide basis is amenable to central ecclesiastical control. It was encouraging, for example, that the *ARCIC Final Report* was referred to National Episcopal Conferences for response. The Catholic Church, in is local manifestation, was truly involved in the decision-making, it seemed. At the same time, it appeared that there was an attempt to influence, if not to pre-empt, the decisions of the Conferences by the issuing of *Observations* on ARCIC by the Vatican's Congregation for the Doctrine of the Faith.[17]

While international bilateral and multilateral dialogue remains important for the churches, the real energy for ecumenism must come from the grass-roots, when Christian men and women in the various churches realise that division among them hurts the cause of the Gospel they love. It is at the grass-roots, in congregations, study groups, missionary groups and the like that the connection between mission and unity is felt. However the bureaucracies of denominations organise their working, this central truth must not be forgotten. In the case of one local ecumenical group in the heart of England, which is attended by lay men and women from the churches in its area, some of the clergy have asked not to be involved – perhaps they fear the consequences of involvement! In such cases it is clearly the duty of the laity to form a vanguard for unity which, by its dedication to study, prayer and common action, challenges those who, because of vested interests, fear of ecclesiastical discipline or scruples of conscience, are dragging their feet. In some areas, churches have entered into a covenant for unity with each other. In certain cases, this has become a useful basis for joint mission to the community. We have noted already the importance of the formally constituted LEPs and their significance for mission.

Despite the failure of many regional and national schemes for church union, this is a model for unity which should not be forgotten. There is good evidence for the organisation of the early Church into Provinces, even though these were not as close a unity as a congregation or several congregations gathered around their bishop, presbyters and deacons.[18] We know, for example, that matters of discipline, unity and communion were particularly provincial concerns.[19] The emergence of nation-states and of regional alliances makes it desirable that the Church too should combine to find an expression at these levels. A common cultural and linguistic heritage, together with a common concern for mission in a particular context, should bring Christians of varying traditions together in their search for a common expression of the Faith, so that there can be common engagement in mission. At the national level, it has been noticed again and again that Christian disunity is often exploited by those who restrict freedom of religion or are uneasy about the work of the churches among the disadvantaged. Even a shown of unity, in the form of a council or association of churches, can go a long way in strengthening the hand of the Christian presence in a country. A truly united Church would be a great advantage in dealing with governments on matters such as human rights, a just allocation of resources and freedom of movement for individuals or groups. So many of the political and economic decisions which affect us all are made at regional and national levels. It is necessary, therefore, for Christian unity to be expressed, in terms of visible structures and a common programme, at these levels too.

It is interesting to observe that in some parts of the world, such as Papua New Guinea, where there is close co-operation between the Roman Catholic Church and other churches, such as the Anglican, the Roman Catholic Church has begun to explore the possibility of unity at the provincial or national level. This is indeed a welcome development, but all parties need to be reminded that many schemes for Church union in the past have made provision for the *continuing* communion of the united Church with *all* the families of churches to which the parties in the scheme of union belong. It would be a great pity if union at the local level meant a diminution, or even a rupture, of communion at other levels. The situation reveals the interdependence between local and national efforts at unity and international ecumenical dialogue. Local schemes can be greatly assisted by the fruits of international dialogue, whereas the latter needs constantly to be in contact with the grass-roots and the urgency of unity there.

Bishop Azariah of Dornakal, commending the South India scheme, has this to say:

> We must have *one* Church, a Church of India which can be our spiritual home, where Indian religious genius can find natural expression, a living branch of the Holy, Catholic, Apostolic Church, the visible symbol of unity in a divided land, drawing all to our Blessed Lord. Unity is vital to the Church in mission.[20]

Church union should never be at the expense of catholicity. Rather, a united Church should, by drawing on the different traditions which have joined together, embody catholicity more fully. Such a consiousness of having preserved and indeed enhanced catholicity will lead the Church to seek communion with all Christians on the basis of a common Faith and a universally accepted Order. In the meantime, it will accept the ministry of those ordained in other churches, provided they submit to its discipline and accept a form of commissioning which enables them to minister in such a wider context. If the ministry of a united Church is so constituted that it results in the widest possible recognition, this will enable its ministers to work in denominations which are outside their own context but which, nevertheless, recognise them and in which they can bear witness to the unity they have experienced. The laity from other churches will be welcomed too, on the basis of their baptism and their assent to the Faith and Order of the united Church, while laity from the united Church, on the basis of their initiation into the Universal Church, should be welcomed in other churches, where they too can witness to their experience of unity.

Ubi Christianus, ibi Christus: ubi Christus, ibi Ecclesia!
(Where there is a Christian, there is Christ:
Where there is Christ, there is the Church!)[21]

CHAPTER FOURTEEN

Mission, the Congregation and the Community

There is considerable debate these days as to whether the Church should concentrate on strengthening its own liturgical and devotional life or whether its priorities should be in the area of service and witness to the community. Those who have experience of Christian community at the grass-roots will perceive at once that this is a somewhat false dichotomy. It is true that there are some Christian communities which are so preoccupied with their worship, its ritual and the internal organisation of their communities that they have very little time left for the world outside. On the other hand, there are Christians who are so heavily engaged in a campaigning or caring ministry that they are in danger of "burn-out" because their ministry is not being nurtured by full participation in the life of a congregation.

On the whole, however, many will recognise that it is the Christian *community* in a particular place which has a special responsibility for engagement with the wider community around it. Also, those individuals who are called to specific ministries related to the wider community will need to be carefully nurtured and trained for their tasks. Bishop Lesslie Newbigin calls the Christian congregation a "hermeneutic of the Gospel". That is to say, the meaning, the challenge and the invitation of the Gospel become clear when men and women observe Chrisian communities believing and living the Gospel. Newbigin lists six leading characteristics of such a community. It will be a eucharistic community, he says, a community of thanksgiving and praise. It will be a community of truth, committed to a recovery of truth rather than to the perpetuation of propaganda and prejudice. It will be a community that lives for others and prays for others. It will be a community where there is sharing at every level. And it will be a community of hope – a hope, moreover, which can be mediated to the wider community.[1]

This is a very comprehensive description and there are numerous Christian communities which patently lack some, or even all, of these characteristics. If Christian Mission is to be effective, they must be renewed. In particular, there needs to be a commitment to the systematic study of the Bible. In many parts of Asia, Africa and Latin America, Theological Education by Extension (TEE) has been a remarkable instrument in the promotion of Bible study among people at every level of literacy.[2] We have seen already how attention to the Scriptures, in the light of their own context, is an important aspect of the Base Communities. In other parts of the World Church, however, there is considerable unfamiliarity with the Scriptures and their use in Liturgy, devotion and reflection remains marginal. Such communities, whatever their numerical strength and spiritual heritage, cannot be effective in mission unless they are exposed to the Bible, its demands and its comfort.

Many cultures continue to be "sacramental" in the sense that people find it easy to believe that the supernatural can be mediated through the material and social. In such cultures it is possible to express and to mediate the Christian Faith in symbol, movement and corporate celebration while, at the same time, avoiding the temptations of superstition. In other cultures, however, de-sacralisation has gone so far that the mystery at the heart of worship is no longer apprehended. There is a kind of flatness about worship. This has less to do with the language of the Liturgy or of the Bible than with dominant world-views and what Newbigin, quoting Berger, calls "plausibility structures".[3] "Scientific" views of the Universe which are mechanical in inspiration and insist on seeing the Universe as a closed system of material cause and effect leave no room, logically, for human freedom, let alone divine initiative. The dominance of "the paradigim of Physics" in even the life sciences and the social sciences has led to widespread scepticism about the possibility of a *telos* or final end for which the Universe was created or indeed for which we were created. This has given rise to a whole genre of moral and political thought and literature which is governed by the assumption that ultimately life is meaningless.[4]

Renewal in worship cannot be merely about tinkering with words, tunes or ritual. All these are important, but they must be the means to an end. That end can be nothing else than encounter with the *mysterium tremendum et fascinans,* the aweful majesty as well as the beauty of God! The death of Christ recalled and made present for the believer in the Eucharist must be experienced as the source of new life. The wounded

Christ is also Christ the Healer. To be sure, this cannot be understood in the crude sense of mere physical healing. It must be a restoration to *wholeness,* with or without healing of bodily ailments (2 Corinthians 12:7-10). The congregation needs to experience the diverse gifts of the Spirit, as well as the fruit of the Spirit, in its corporate life.

Word and Sacrament need to be kept together. The Word of God has to be communicated authoritatively. This does not of necessity mean preaching, though there is still a great deal of room for thematic, exegetical or expository preaching.[5] In modern times the Word can be communicated through audio-visuals, drama, dance and music. The Word has to be related to contemporary situations and needs to be communicated in ways which are pastorally sensitive.

A congregation which experiences worship in these ways will undoubtedly have something to say to a needy world. An encounter with God's power and love cannot be manufactured or induced. God's grace is prior. He reveals himself to men and women, but many of the barriers to an experience of this grace are the result of human blindness, arrogance and impoverishment. In short, they are due to sin. We need in humility to open our lives to God's grace and love and be prepared to receive his Word in whatever way he chooses to reveal him.

Only a congregation deeply aware of the Faith will be able to share its faith with others. Much of the uncertainty attending the Decade of Evangelism and how to respond to it, in some parts of the Church, has to do with a lack of knowledge of the Christian Faith *among church-people.* Unless there is systematic preparation of congregations in this area, Christians will be unable to share their faith effectively. In the same way, only Christians who have encountered "the wounded Healer" in Word and Sacrament and have been touched by his healing hand can take this healing to the world around them, whether this takes the form of medical or community care, shelter for the homeless or more "charismatic" ministries of healing. In the absence of such an encounter, such work can become extremely burdensome and sterile. We need constant renewal and healing ourselves if we are to minister wholeness to others.

Christian advocacy of the poor and disadvantaged and campaigning for social and economic justice is a crucial aspect of the prophetic ministry to which Christians are called. It must, however, spring from the intercessory prayer of the Church. In its turn, such prayer will be informed by stories emerging from Christian engagement with injustice, poverty and war.[6]

When people say that the Church is for the community and not simply for itself, they sometimes mean that it has a place in folk-memory and that its buildings have aesthetic value in the community. Such a view gives the Church a place in society and some marginal influence in its decision-making. By the above expression people can also mean that the Church must serve the community in which it is placed, putting this service before its own life of worship, prayer and learning.

The result quite often is that the resources of the Church are placed at the disposal of the community, but little attempt is made to relate such a disposal of resources to *Christian* mission. How Christian witness is made in the Church's *diakonia* remains an urgent question. Another consequence is that the burden of service to the community is placed on the clergy and lay leadership of a congregation without commensurate participation by the rest of the laity. Such a burden is often hard to bear and, what is more, retards the proper development of a congregation. The 1988 Lambeth Conference rightly put the emphasis on "every-member ministry". The whole congregation needs to be involved in mission to the community in which it is placed, as well as to the rest of God's world, in appropriate ways. If such a vision is to come to fruition, there needs to be a great deal of "formation" of the People of God in local contexts so that they can engage in mission. The clergy need to understand their role as one of preparing and enabling, rather than one of being substitutes for the rest of the Church.[7]

There is no necessary contradiction, therefore, in emphasising the importance of a strong congregational life, where Christians are nurtured in the Faith and are supported by a strong sense of fellowship, and stressing the need for congregations to be mission minded. It is, of course, possible for congregations to be entirely "turned-in" on themselves. This is pathological and clearly undesirable. On the whole, however, nurture and fellowship, if they are authentic to the Gospel, will lead to a strong commitment to mission. Without such nurture and fellowship, mission runs the risk of being just another instance of "do-gooding" and of ultimately becoming sterile. Being "in Christ" as members of his Body is to partake of his death and resurrection. Such participation breaks us and then remakes us. This new life is not just for us—it overflows into the world, re-creating men and women in the image of their Creator, thus fulfilling the purpose of their creation. As John V. Taylor has said, "The *koinōnia* of the Church is nothing less than the most literal partaking in the suffering and the resurrection of Christ in order to make up the balance of what has still to be endured in order to unlock the kingdom for others to enter in."[8]

CHAPTER FIFTEEN

Mission: From Everywhere to Everywhere

David Barrett is his *World Christian Encycolpaedia* points out that during this century the demography of the Christian world has changed dramatically. There are now some 300 million Christians in Africa alone, and there can be little doubt that Africa will be the next great Christian continent. There is rapid growth in East and North-East Asia too, with countries like Singapore and South Korea reporting significant increases in their Christian populations. In other areas of Asia such as Indonesia and East Malaysia there is considerable growth as well. This has not been much publicised, largely because of the sensitivities of the Muslim majorities in those countries. Even in India, where several other World Faiths remain strong, the number of Christians and "adherents" who are not formally converts continues to grow. Some regions, such as the north-east, are now heavily Christianised. Latin America remains strongly Christian, despite the emergence of anti-clerical political movements. Movements for Liberation and the Base Communities have revitalised the Christian presence there. Primary evangelism also continues among the indigenous people. In North America too, despite the existence of a pluralist sociey, churchgoing and the outward signs of an adherence to Christianity remain strong. Only in Europe and some of its derivative societies, it seems, is the "withdrawing roar" of the Sea of Faith to be heard. To be sure, the Middle East, the cradle of Christianity, causes concern, for while many of the ancient churches are experiencing renewal, there is a worrying increase in Christian emigration from the area because of political instability and special difficulties for Christians. This is not, however, a crisis of faith such as that experienced by Europe.[2]

The number of Christians in Asia, Africa, the Pacific, the Caribbean and Latin America now exceeds the number of Christians elsewhere, and the trend is that an increasing proportion of Christians will be found in these areas of the world. In such a world context, it is not surprising that many initiatives in Christian Mission, both within cultures and across cultural boundaries, are now coming from churches and Christians in these parts. In countries such as Nigeria, India and Korea there are strong mission organisations which prepare and send considerable numbers of Christians to live and work in cultures not their own, whether within national boundaries or across them. There have been allegations that they are merely surrogates of Western missionary organisations and receive funds from them.[3] However, many are very independent in terms of policy and some have strict rules about not accepting financial assistance from outside sources.

The ancient churches of Africa and Asia too are taking a renewed interest in mission. We have seen that some of these churches have glorious mission histories. They are now drawing upon this heritage and sending people across cultural and national frontiers. In some cases, they are more acceptable to national governments and even churches because of their lack of colonial baggage, and because they are seen as indigenous to Africa and Asia.

Even at the height of the Western missionary movement, the Gospel was often communicated by indigenous Christians to their families, tribes and nations. Samuel Adjai Crowther, Apolo Kivebulaya and 'Abdul Masíh are only the bestknown examples of an army of ordained and lay people in Africa and Asia who were at the interface of the Church's mission to the myriad cultures of these continents. Now, however, perhaps for the first time in centuries, Christian Mission is not going along in the same direction as economic, technological, cultural and political influence. Certainly, a great deal of cross-cultural mission is sent from the South to other parts of the South. This in itself is a challenge to the usual North-South flow of information, skills and money. There is, however, evidence that Christians in the South are increasingly interested in mission to the *North*.

Some sophisticated Christian leaders in the North remain unconvinced that such a mission can be effective. They point to the immensely complex problems which the Church faces in Northern contexts and ask how Christians from the South can address them. There is resistance also from those of particular political orientations, who dislike the strong emphasis that Christians from the South place on social, economic and political involvement. There are signs, though, that parish and mission clergy and the faithful are now ready to recieve mission-input from the South. They are tired of the somewhat vacillating attitudes in their churches and are beginning to feel that continual indecision is not the only possible response to complexity. They are aware, moreover, that Christian expression and commitment in the South also takes place in immensely complicated situations – situations of racial tension and discrimination, of economic and social exploitation and of political repression. Despite all this, Christians are able to witness clearly in these contexts. Nor is such witness entirely irrelevant in Northern contexts. In many of these contexts too the Church is faced with questions of justice and freedom. People need to hear that the Gospel of Jesus Christ can transform lives, that it can give us courage to face adversity with confidence and even joy and that it can bring about real change in our societies.

Of course, like people anywhere preparing for cross-cultural mission, those coming from the South need careful preparation both by the sending and the receiving churches. They need to be formed in their vocation, their spirituality has to be challenged and deepened and they need to engage with the anthropology and sociology of the cultures to which they have been called. Some facilities for such formation already exist in the South, particularly in Kenya, India, Korea and Singapore, but they need to be extended and developed. In other parts of the world, where no facilities exist, there needs to be concerted effort on the part of the World Church to develop them. Such facilities can be used not only for the prepartion of those who are to be involved in South-South or South-North interchange but also for partners coming from the North to participate in mission in the South. They would form an important part of the receiving church's contribution to the formation of its mission partners. Equally, institutions for mission formation in the North, which were developed primarily to prepare people for mission in the South, can be used for the further formation of those coming from both North and South, whose vocation is mission in the North.

One matter needs urgent clarification. Those who come from the South for mission in the North must not be restricted to the margins of the Church's missionary endeavours. All too often one hears expressions like "The mission-field has come to us" or "The mission-field is now on our doorstep". Often this does *not* mean that the greater part of the population has become unchurched and retains only residual belief, if that. More often than not, it refers to the new presence of ethnic minorities in Northern countries. Some of these belong to other World Faiths or to traditional religions but many come from strongly Christian backgrounds. Now it is true that churches in Northern countries need the assistance of the World Church in relating to such minorities. In the fields of community relations, inter-faith dialogue and religious education churches and Christians in the South have a great deal to offer churches in the North. In the end, however, the seriousness of the Northern churches regarding partnership with the churches of the South will be fully tested only when the Northern churches realise their need for Southern partners in mission to the *indigenous* populations of their countries. To say this is not to deny the continuing existence of folk-religion with a Christian veneer in many Northern countries. Nor is it to deny that this can be used as a bridge to reach people and to bring them to greater understanding and commitment. These, however, are missionary tasks. The Church cannot be content simply to endorse half-beliefs and folk-religion as an adequate expression of the spiritual aspect of humanity.

Partnership in mission must mean partnership in the *whole* of mission. Churches in the South need to be involved with the North in the identification and articulation of mission issues as much as in addressing them. Indeed, part of the value of partnership is precisely that our partners may discern issues in our context which we cannot discern. If this is to be authentic, as well as comprehensive, it is important that mission partners are exposed to the whole of a pastoral and missionary situation and not restricted to bits of it.[4]

Mission agencies in the North have a crucial role to play in conscientising their churches about the World Church and the resources for mission which are now available. They have an important role too in assisting in the identification of appropriate mission partners for churches in the North and in their formation and enabling. At the same time, they need to continue to identify mission partners in the North for service in the South. Such service will often be at the request of churches in the South and in partnership with them. However, both in the North and the South there may well be pioneer situations where the institutional church is not active and where the partnership may be with a forward movement of Christians or even with groups which are not exclusively Christian. Such a partnership will be entered into only after consultation with the nearest local church, though in extreme situations Christians sometimes *have* to act, for reasons of conscience, *contra mundum* and even *contra ecclesiam*.

An important aspect of the work of Northern agencies will surely be the promotion and facilitation of South-South interchange. Many churches in the South are now ready for such interchange but lack information and other resources to bring it about. Mission agencies have long experience of the Church in many lands and also the resources to make this kind of interchange possible. If such a task is to be addressed seriously, the agencies will need to restructure themselves in significant ways and also to undertake a massive exercise in the education of their constituencies. It is a task, however, which cannot be avoided if the agencies care for the World Church and wish mission to prosper.

There is currently a great deal of talk about the internationalising of mission. If by this it is meant that intra-cultural and cross-cultural mission must be encouraged and enabled in a diversity of locations and contexts, then such talk is to be welcomed. Great care has to be taken, however, that internationalisation does not in practice mean the imposition of certain kinds of structure and mission-thinking on the World Church. It is to be expected that in different contexts there will be different responses. In some, the churches themselves will establish and operate mission structures, on a denominational or ecumenical basis. In others there will be voluntary movements which mobilise Christians for mission and enable those who are engaged in it. Both are authentic repsonses to the challenge of mission and are not mutually exclusive even in the same context.

Where the voluntary principle is concerned, we should note that one of the lessons which the Base Communities are teaching us is that the Church is not simply hierarchy or parochial and diocesan structures.[5] Every movement of the People of God, every communal expression of the Body, is Church. Movements in the Church, whether local, national or international, which have as their aim the furtherance of the Gospel can also be Church. They are not *solely* the Church, of course, and they are related to other manifestations of it. We have seen how the local congregation and the province are important in this respect. In an episcopal context, the bishop is understood as the focus of unity, and every local ecclesial movement which understands itself as Church will relate to him. The bishop, on the other hand, is not to be regarded as the sole repository of all responsibility but, rather, must be seen as an enabler of the mission of the pilgrim people. The bishop's authority, moreover, is to be understood in the light of the Gospel's demand. It cannot, therefore be absolute but must be interpreted by the Gospel. Movements which understand themselves as Church, moreover, must seek to relate to that communion of churches which is a manifestation of the Catholic Church at the universal level (the Catholic Church is also fully, but differently, manifested at the local level in a variety of ways). Once again, such a relationship should be liberating rather than constricting and should be understood in the context of the Gospel's demand.

It is vital for the Church's mission that Christian leaders understand themselves as servants and enablers, not lords and masters. Ever since Constantine's bestowal of magisterial and judicial powers on bishops, Christian leaders have been wont to acquire the patterns of authority which are dominant in their particular culture.[6] In contemporary contexts the temptation, in some parts of the world, is to model Christian leadership on the leadership of a tribal chief. Apart from inherent dangers such as pride and corruption, this is greatly divisive. The pattern, by its very nature, is owned only by a specific group, leaving others with a feeling of alienation. The multiplication of dioceses on tribal lines, for example, is a matter of urgent concern for the Church.

The feudal model is another way which is sometimes emulated by Christian leaders. Its classical expression was in the "prince" or "baron" bishops of mediaeval Europe, but there are contemporary expressions of it, particularly in societies which remain agrarian or are emerging from an agrarian economy into an industrial one. It is perhaps worth observing that in the latter leadership in industry is also exercised along paternalistic, feudal lines. Once again, the Church's resources are treated as a personal fiefdom and individuals are denied the freedom which they need for growth.[7]

The uncritical acceptance of forms of church government which are based on adversarial debate rather than consensus and the emergence of ecclesiastical bureaucracy which is modelled on the civil service is also a cause for concern in this respect.[8]

The teaching of Jesus is quite clear. Only leadership which is rooted in service of God, of his Church and of the world is authentically Christian. It is in such service that Christian leadership must be recognised, and it is in such service that it must be exercised (Luke 22:24-27).[9]

Humility is, of course, an aspect of holiness and is not, therefore, limited to leaders. It is a calling of all the saints, of all the People of God. If humble leaders are to emerge, they must emerge from a humble *laity*. From the earliest days, Christian leaders have been recognised by popular acclamation (this survives vestigially in the ordinals).[10] It is good that procedures for choosing leaders, at least in some churches, are becoming more and more democractic. We need to ensure, however, that the constituency which elects such leaders is well prepared spiritually so that it can recognise qualities such as integrity, humility and sympathy and will not be misled by glamour, ambition, mere learning or the ability to dispense patronage.

We need to pray earnestly that humble men and women of God will emerge as Christian leaders – leaders whose authority is derived from their humility and service; who persuade but do not coerce; who free Christians to exercise the gifts which the Holy Spirit has given them; who make the Gospel attractive to the millions who need to believe but are sceptical of the Church's structures; who are concerned that the poor should hear God's Word and receive his blessings. Such leaders would truly forward God's mission in this world.

> Authority is that kind of structured reality, whether social or personal, which through nurture and cultivation enables individuals to become truly centred selves or persons, and thus, relatively free beings.
>
> John E. Skinner[11]

Notes

CHAPTER ONE

1. *De Trinitate* VI:7.
2. Ibid., XIV; of. *Confessions* XIII:11.
3. Ibid., XV.
4. *Confessions* XIII:6f., referring to Genesis 1:2.
5. See further John V. Taylor, *The Go-Between God* (New York, 1979), pp. 25ff.
6. The present writer's "The Gospel Offer of Wholeness" in *Frontiers in Muslim-Christian Encounter* (Regnum, 1987), pp. 61ff.
7. H. Wheeler Robinson, *The Religious Ideas of the Old Testament* (London, 1913), pp. 48ff.
8. There is an interesting testimony to the recovery of this aspect of biblical prophecy, as a result of an engagement with Liberation Theology, by Rabbi Dan Cohn-Sherbok in *On Earth as it is in Heaven* (Orbis, 1987), pp. 36ff., 112ff.
9. John Goldingay, *Theological Diversity and the Authority of the Old Testament* (Eerdmans, 1987), pp. 66f.
10. Norman K. Gottwald, *The Tribes of Yahweh: A Sociology of the Religion of Liberated Israel* (Orbis, 1979), p. 611.
11. Op. cit., p. 67.
12. *The People of God and the State: An Old Testament Perspective,* an unpublished paper, pp. 8-9.
13. Kenneth Cracknell, *Towards a New Relationship* (Epworth, 1986), pp. 50, 53ff.; cf. Sir Norman Anderson, *God's Law and God's Love* (Collins, 1980), pp. 32-33, 128.
14. See my concluding essay in *Towards a Theology for Inter-Faith Dialogue* (ACC, London, 1986), pp. 44-45. See also Georges Khodr, "Christianity in a Pluralistic World – The Economy of the Holy Spirit" in *The Ecumenical Review* vol. XXIII, April 1971, No. 2, pp. 118-128.
15. M. M. Thomas, *The Achnowledged Christ of the Indian Renaissance* (London, 1969), and in *Secular Man and Christian Mission* (ed. P. Leoffler, New York, 1968), pp. 19-23.
16. "Islam and Incarnation" in *Truth and Dialogue* (ed. John Hick, London, 1974), pp. 6ff., 12; cf. *Frontiers of Muslim-Christian Encounter,* pp. 21-22.
17. Cohn-Sherbok, op. cit., pp. 13f.
18. *Epistle to the Ephesians,* VII:2.
19. *The Wreck of the Deutschland.*
20. *Epistle to the Trallians,* IX:1.
21. *De Incarnatione 20;* cf.Hebrews 2:14f.
22. See further Karl Barth, *Church Dogmatics* II, "The Doctrine of God" 2 (ET, Edinburgh, 1959).
23. So C. K. Barrett, *The Gospel According to St. John* (London, 1967), p. 475.
24. Ibid., p. 475.
25. Op. cit., p. 44.
26. For the evidence see Charles Bigg, *The Epistles of St. Peter and St. Jude* (Edinburgh, 1902), p. 134.
27. See the present writer's *Islam: A Christian Perspective* (Paternoster, Exeter, 1983), Chap. 8, "The Christian Presence", pp. 142ff.

CHAPTER TWO

1. See further, Wayne A. Meeks, *The First Urban Christians* (New Haven, 1983), pp. 9ff. and Derek Tidball, *An Introduction to the Sociology of the New Testament* (Paternoster, Exeter, 1983), pp. 23ff.

2. Cf. I. H. Marshall, *Acts* (Eerdmans, Grand Rapids, 1980), pp. 19f.

3. Henry Chadwick, *The Early Church* (London, 1967), p. 285.

4. Ibid., p. 62.

5. Ibid., p. 17, 62.

6. See further *Islam: A Christian Perspective*, pp. 10f., 15.

7. *Patriarch, Shah and Caliph*, (Rawalpindi, 1974).

8. N. Turner, "The Language of the New Testament", pp. 659ff. and B. M. Metzger, "The Early Versions of the New Testament", p. 672 in *Peake's Commentary on the Bible* (ed. Matthew Black, London, 1962).

9. R. C. D. Jasper and G. J. Cuming, *Prayers of the Eucharist: Early and Reformed* (London, 1975), pp. 26f.

10. P. Bedjan, *Acta Martyrum et Sanctorum* (Leipzig 1890-1895), 2:136.

11. *Ecclesiastical History* 2:14 in W. G. Young, *Handbook of Source Materials for Students of Church History* (Madras, 1969), p. 280.

12. Young, *Patriarch, Shah and Caliph*, pp. 27ff.

13. Ibid., pp. 78ff.

14. Ibid., pp. 38ff.

15. Juhanon Mar Thoma quoted in Alexander Mar Thoma, *The Mar Thoma Church: Heritage and Mission* (Tirvalla, 1985), p. 3.

16. *Acts of the Holy Apostle Thomas* in M. R. James (ed.), *The Apocryphal New Testament* (OUP, 1924), pp. 364ff.

17. See further John Rooney, *Shadows in the Dark* (Rawalpindi, 1984), pp. 29ff. See also G. N. Bannerjee, *Hellenism in Ancient India* (Delhi, 1961), pp. 124ff.

18. W. G. Young, *The Life and History of the Church in Pakistan* (Islamabad Lecture, 1971), p. 3.

19. Rooney, op. cit., pp. 44-45.

20. Iris H. ElMasry, *Introduction to the Coptic Church* (Cairo, 1977), p. 20f.

21. W. H. C. Frend, *The Early Church* (London, 1965), pp. 200ff. and Chadwick, op. cit., pp. 174ff.

22. Masry, op. cit., p. 22; "Life of St. Athanasius" in the *De Incarnatione*, pp. 21f.; Frend, op. cit., pp. 202f.

23. An example of a Coptic theologian of this period would be the famous exegete Hibat Allah Iln Al^c Assâl. See further K. E. Bailey, *Poet and Peasant* (Eerdmans, 1976).

24. Maurice Assad, "Mission in the Coptic Church: Perspective, Doctrine and Practice" in *Mission Studies*, "The Journal of the IAMS", vol. IV-I, 1987, p. 31.

25. Marshall, op. cit., p. 162.

26. Colin Battell, "The Ethiopians" in *Light from the East* (Henry Hill ed., Toronto, 1988), pp. 62ff.

27. Calvin E. Shenk, "The Ethiopian Orthodox Church's Understanding of Mission" in *Mission Studies*, "The Journal of the IAMS", vol. IV-1, 1987, pp. 4ff.

28. Young, *Patriarch, Shah and Caliph*, pp. 55f.

29. The present writer's *Martyrs and Magistrates: Toleration and Trial in Islam* (Nottingham, 1989), p. 14 for, at times, conflicting evidence.

30. Young, *Patriarch, Shah and Caliph*, pp. 38ff., et al.; Hill, op. cit., pp. 10ff.; Igor de Rachewiltz, *Papal Envoys at the Court of the Great Khans* (London, 1971). For a contemporary account of Christian disunity in mission see J. Pettifer and Richard Bradley, *Missionaries* (BBC, 1990).

31. Alexander Mar Thoma, op. cit., passim; also Hill, op. cit., pp. 82ff.

32. Op. cit., p. 4.

33. *For the Sake of the Kingdom,* "A report of the Inter-Anglican Theological and Doctrinal Commission" (London, 1986), pp. 38f.

34. See further Anthony Thiselton, *The Two Horizons* (Paternoster, Exeter, 1980). See also J. Andrew Kirk, *Liberation Theology* (Marshalls, London, 1979), pp. 185ff.

35. See further Charles Bigg, *The Epistles of St. Peter and St. Jude* (Edinburgh, 1961), pp. 269f.

36. J. Goldingay, *Theological Diversity and the Authority of the Old Testament* (Eerdmans, Grand Rapids, 1987), pp. 29ff.

37. The Emmaus Report: *A Report of the Anglican Ecumenical Consultation* (ACC, London, 1987), pp. 29ff; *The Final Report: The Anglican-Roman Catholic International Commission* (CTS/SPCK, London, 1982), "Authority in the Church I", pp. 52ff.

38. For the debate see the present writer's *Islam: A Christian Perspective*, pp. 156ff. and *The Pasadena Consultation: Homogeneous Unit Principle* (Wheaton, 1978), a Lausanne occasional Paper.

CHAPTER THREE

1. Stephen Neill, *A History of Christian Missions* (Penguin, London, 1964), pp. 99ff.; J. M. Gaudeul, *Encounters and Clashes* Vol. I (Rome, 1984), pp. 125ff.; R. W. Southern, *Western Views of Islam in the Middle Ages* (Cambridge, Mass., 1962); the present writer's *Islam: A Christian Perspective*, pp. 71f. and *Frontiers in Muslim-Christian Encounter*, p. 18.

2. J. Rooney, *The Hesitant Dawn* (Rawalpindi), pp. 68f.

3. Neill, op. cit., p. 170.

4. Penguin, London, 1968, pp. 47f.

5. Neill, op. cit., p. 170f.

6. Ibid., p. 221.

7. G. Warneck, *Protestant Missions* (Edinburgh, 1906), p. 8.

8. Ibid., pp. 8-9.

9. Neill, op. cit., p. 221.

10. Warneck, op. cit., pp. 19f.; Neill, op. cit., p. 222.

11. Warneck, op. cit., p. 20; D. W. Bebbington, *Evangelicalism in Modern Britain* (London, 1989), p. 41.

12. Warneck, op. cit., pp. 20f cf. Neill, op. cit., pp. 222-223.

13. Timothy Ware, *The Orthodox Church* (Penguin, London), pp. 180ff. See also an older and fascinating work, recently republished: Eugene Smirnoff, *Russian Orthodox Missions* (Welshpool, Powys, 1986).

14. See further Ion Bria (ed.), *Martyria/Mission, The Witness of the Orthodox Churches Today* (WCC, Geneva, 1980) and *Go Forth in Peace, Orthodox Perspectives on Mission* (WCC, Geneva, 1986).

15. Ion Bria (ed.), *Go Forth in Peace*, pp. 57f.; John Meyendorff, "The Orthodox Church and Mission, Past Present and Perspectives" in G. H. Anderson and T. F. Stransky (eds.), *Mission Trends No. 1* (Eerdmans, Grand Rapids, 1974), p. 65f.

CHAPTER FOUR

1. An early work by David L. Edwards was entitled *Not Angels but Anglicans.*
2. Neill, op. cit. pp. 223ff.
3. Op. cit., pp. 40f.
4. Ibid., p. 41.
5. Warneck, op. cit., p. 21.
6. Op. cit., p. 232.
7. Ibid., p. 233.
8. David L. Edwards, *The Futures of Christianity* (London, 1987), pp. 94f. See also the present writer's "The Vocation of Anglicanism", *Anvil*, Vol. 6, No. 2, 1989.
9. Bebbington, op. cit., p. 73.
10. See the present writer's "Church, Culture and Change", in R. Draper (ed.), *Communion and Episcopacy (Cuddesdon, 1988), pp. 99f.* and also in *Anvil*, Vol. , No. 2, 1988, pp. 127f.
11. Leonardo Boff, *Church, Charism and Power* (SCM, London, 1981), pp. 125ff and *Ecclesio-Genesis* (Orbis, London, 1986).
12. Boff, *Church, Charism and Power*, p. 126.
13. Edwards, op. cit., pp. 89f.
14. Bebbington, op. cit., pp. 72f.
15. Ibid., p. 40.
16. See the present writer's *Liturgical Development in the Anglican Communion: A View (LC, 1988), pp. 4f.* and J. Dowden, *The Scottish Communion Office 1764* (OUP, 1922).
17. Kenneth Stevenson and Michael Perham, *Anglican Liturgy Today* (LC, 1988), pp. 2f.
18. David Nicholls and Rowan Williams, *Politics and Theological Identity* (Jubilee, London, 1984), pp. 20ff. and 34ff.
19. John D. Davies, *The Faith Abroad* (Blackwells, 1983), p. 2.
20. Cf. Rowan Williams, op. cit., pp. 19f.
21. The remarkable story of this community is well related in Peter Mayhew's *All Saints: Birth and Growth of a Community* (Society of All Saints, 1987).
22. Davies, op. cit., pp. 44f.
23. Nicholls and Williams, op. cit., pp. 30f. and "Christianity and Politics" in R. Morgan (ed.), *The Religion of the Incarnation: Anglican Essays in Commemoration of Lux Mundi* (Bristol, 1989), pp. 178f.
24. Alexander Mar Thoma, op. cit., p. 14f.; Hill, op. cit., p. 91f. See further E. Stock, *The History of the Church Missionary Society* Vol. I (London, 1899), pp. 231ff. and 324ff.
25. See the present writer's *Liturgical Development in the Anglican Communion*, pp. 3f. and C. O. Buchanan, *Modern Anglican Liturgies 1958-1968* (OUP, 1968).
26. Hill, op. cit., pp. 112f.
27. Ibid., pp. 91f.
28. Ibid., pp. 79f.
29. See *The Emmaus Report*, op. cit., pp. 10ff.

CHAPTER FIVE

1. "Mission and Ministry" in Michael Nazir-Ali and W. D. Pattinson (eds.), *The Truth Shall Make You Free*, the Report of the Lambeth Conference 1988 (London, 1988), p. 32, quoting from *Giving Mission its Proper Place*, the Report of the Mission Issues and Strategy Advisory Group of the ACC (London, 1984), p. 9.

2. Nazir-Ali and Pattinson, op. cit., p. 32.

3. Ibid., pp. 34f.; cf. Pastoral Letter 7: *On the Gospel and Transformation*, pp. 326f. of the Lambeth 1988 Report.

4. Nazir-Ali and Pattinson, op. cit., pp. 32f.

5. See further Vinay Samuel and Chris Sugden, *Lambeth: A view from the Two-Thirds World* (SPCK, London, 1989).

6. *Evangelisation and Culture: Primary Evangelism in Northern Kenya* (Lambeth Conference, 1988).

7. For a magisterial but controversial survey of this growth see D. B. Barrett, *Schism and Renewal in Africa: An Analysis of 6000 Contemporary Religious Movements* (Nairobi, 1968).

8. *Evangelisation and Culture: An Asian Case* (Lambeth Conference, 1988).

9. Boff, *Church, Charism and Power*, pp. 125f., 130. Also *Ecclesio-Genesis*, pp. 10ff., 61ff.

10. An interesting account of this situation may be found in Elsie Hinkes, *A Respectable Occupation* (Oxford, 1988).

11. *Love in any language*, the Report of the First International Conference of Young Anglicans (Belfast, 1988), pp. 16f.

12. *The Truth Shall Make You Free*, pp. 132f.; *The Emmaus Report*, pp. 35f.

13. See, for example, *The Report of the First Day Conference on Church Planting in the Church of England* (London, 1987).

14. D. B. Barrett, *World Christian Encyclopaedia* (Oxford, 1982), cf. David Liao (ed.), *World Christianity: Eastern Asia* (Monrovia, 1979).

15. See, for example, the special edition (for the centennial of Korean Christianity) of the *International Review of Mission* (Suh David Kwang-Sun, ed.), Vol. LXXIV, No. 293,January 1985.

16. Vivienne Stacey, *Henry Martyn* (Hyderabad, India, 1980). See also the somewhat romantic biography by K. M. Finnie, *Beyond the Minarets*, (Bromley, 1988).

17. In this connecton, see the report of an excellent symposium organised by the theological commission of the (Anglican) Council of the Church of East Asia, *In Search of a Relevant Anglicanism in East Asia Today* (Quezon City, Philippines, 1987).

18. E.g. A. J. Ayer, *Language, Truth and Logic* (Gollancz, 1946).

19. See further Roland Robertson (ed.), *Sociology of Religion* (Penguin, Baltimore, 1969) and Peter L. Berger, *A Rumour of Angels* (Penguin, Baltimore, 1969).

20. Ibid., pp. 63f.

21. Ibid., pp. 41f.

22. For an early critique of science's inability to recognise its limitations, particularly in relation to teleology, see James Ward, *The Realm of Ends* (CUP, 1912).

23. See further Hugh Montefiore, *The Probability of God* (SCM, London, 1985). Montefiore, however, appears to use the term 'the anthropic principle' in the more restricted sense of an egocentric view of the universe (p. 130).

24. The title of a book by Paul Van Buren, *The Secular Meaning of the Gospel* (SCM, 1963).

25. SCM, 1965.

26. E.g. Thomas J. J. Altizer, *The Gospel of Christian Atheism* (Collins, 1967); Alistair Kee, *The Way of Transcendence* (Penguin, 1971).

27. Cf. Bertrand Russell, *A Free Man's Worship* (Unwin, 1976) pp. 10 ff.

28. W. Freytag, *The Gospel and the Religions* (SCM, 1957).

29. Boff, *Church, Charism and Power*, pp. 32ff.

30. J. Macquarrie, *20th Century Religious Thought* (SCM, 1971), pp. 324f.

31. Wayan Mastra, *"Christology in the Context of the Life and Religion of the Balinese"* in Vinay Samuel and Chris Sugden (eds.), *Sharing Jesus in the Two-Thirds World* (Bangalore, 1983), pp. 229 ff.

32. Kwame Bediako, *"Christian Tradition and the African God Revisited"* in David Gitari and Patrick Benson (eds.), *The Living God* (Nairobi, 1986), pp. 77ff.

33. Neill, op. cit., pp. 164-165, 191-193.

34. On this question see further, Vincent Donovan, *Christianity Rediscovered: An Epistle from the Masai* (SCM, 1978).

35. Guillermo Cook, *The Expectation of the Poor* (Orbis, New York, 1985), pp. 43ff. and J. B. Libanio, "BECs in Socio-Cultural Perspective" in *Transformation,* July/Sept 1986, Vol. 3, No. 3, pp.7 ff.

36. Neill, op. cit., p. 232.

37. Ibid. pp. 279, 291 and passim.

38. This seems to be the burden of certain missiologies. See further R. D. Winter, "The Highest Priority: Cross-Cultural Evangelism" in D. A. Fraser (ed.), *The Church in New Frontiers for Mission* (MARC, Monrovia, 1983), pp. 85ff.

CHAPTER SIX

1. Charge to the *St Augustine's Seminar* at the Church Army's Wilson Carlisle College, Blackheath, London, 29th July–7th August 1987.
2. Walter Hollenweger, *The Pentecostals* (Minneapolis, 1972).
3. A powerful testimony to the gift and ministry of healing in the Roman Catholic Church is to be found in Francis McNutt, *Healing* (Ave Maria, 1974). See also Edward O'Connor, *The Pentecostal Movement in the Catholic Church* (Ave Maria, 1971).
4. Josephine Bax, *The Good Wine: Spiritual Renewal in the Church of England* (CHP, London, 1986), pp. 46f., 135f.
5. For a summing up see M. Harper, *This is the Day* (London, 1979), pp. 58ff.
6. Ibid., pp. 60f.
7. D. W. Bebbington, *Evangelicalism in Modern Britain*, pp. 229ff.; D. L. Edwards, *The Futures of Christianity*, pp. 330f.; E. Willems, "Religious Pluralism and Class Structure" in Roland Robertson (ed.), *Sociology of Religion*, pp. 195ff.
8. Bebbington, op. cit., pp. 232ff.
9. See further Roger Forster, "What Can Charismatics and Evangelical Social Activists Learn from Each other?" and D. W. Dayton, "Pentecostal/Charismatic Renewal and Social Change", both in *Transformation*, Vol. 5, No. 4, Oct-Dec 1988, pp. 3ff. and 7ff.
10. E. Willems, op. cit., pp. 209ff., 214f.
11. M. Harper, "These Stones Cry Out" in Colin Craston (ed.), *Open to the Spirit* (ACC, London, 1987), pp. 18ff,; cf. Norberto Saracco, "Charismatic Renewal and Social Change: A Historical Analysis from a Third World Perspective" in *Transformation*, op. cit., pp. 14ff.
12. Saracco, op. cit., p. 16.
13. Dayton, op. cit., pp. 11f.
14. Saracco, op. cit., pp. 17f.; P. G. Leavenworth, "Good News for the Poor" in *Transformation*, op. cit., pp. 32ff.
15. Op. cit. p. 18.
16. Moses Tay, "The Charismatic Movement: A Way or The Way of Renewal?" in *Open to the Spirit*, pp. 44f.
17. Ibid., pp. 47f.
18. In a private paper by Roger Hooker entitled *CMS and Other Faiths – Some Lessons From Our History*, (Smethwick, 1987), pp. 8f.
19. *The Go-Between God*, op. cit, p. 181.
20. Georges Khodr, "Christianity in a Pluralistic World – the Economy of the Holy Spirit" in Constantin G. Patelos (ed.), *The Orthodox Church in the Ecumenical Movement* (Geneva, 1978), pp. 304f.
21. See Moses Tay's very helpful tabulation, op. cit., p. 44.
22. In *Open to the Spirit*, op. cit., pp. 27f.
23. Op. cit., p. 47.
24. For an account of the roots and development of Christian existentialism see A. C. Thiselton, *The Two Horizons: New Testament Hermeneutics and Philosophical Description* (Paternoster, Exeter, 1980).
25. Norman K. Gottwald, *The Tribes of Yahweh*, op. cit., is an example of this approach.
26. See W. Bruggemann, *The Prophetic Imagination* (Fortress, 1978).

27. *Theological Diversity and the Authority of the Old Testament*, op. cit., pp. 69ff., 84ff.
28. *The People of God and the State*, op. cit., pp. 15ff.
29. Ibid., pp. 20ff.
30. For a useful discussion of this perspective see J. Andrew Kirk, *Liberation Theology* (MMS, London, 1979), ch. 7, pp. 73ff. Also Enio Mueller, *The Interpretation of the Bible in Latin American Liberation Theology* (unpublished paper, Oxford Centre for Mission Studies, 1988).
31. Kirk, op. cit., ch. 17, pp. 169ff.
32. For an example of such an approach see Jon Sobrino, *Christology at the Crossroads: A Latin American Approach* (Orbis, Maryknoll, 1978).
33. See further Rene Padilla, "Christology and Mission in the Two-Thirds World" in V. Samuel and C. Sugden (eds.), *Sharing Jesus in the Two-Thirds World* (Bangalore, 1983), pp. 17ff.
34. J. P. Migne (ed.), *Patrologia Graeca* (Paris, 1857-66), Vol. LXVI 9-1020. *Voice from the East*, the journal of the Church of the East, is currently serialising some of Theodore's writings. See the issue for Jan-March 1988. Vol. 7, No. 1.
35. K. Y. Bock (ed.), *Minjung Theology: People as the Subjects of History* (CCA, Singapore, 1981). See also Choan-Seng Song, *Third-Eye Theology: Theology in Formation in Asian Setting* (Orbis, Maryknoll, 1979).
36. J. H. Strawley, *The Liturgical Movement: Its Origin and Growth* (Alcuin Club, London, 1954); H. E Chandlee, "The Liturgical Movement" in J. G. Davies (ed.), *A New Dictionary of Liturgy and Worship* (SCM, London, 1986), pp. 307ff.
37. A convenient collection of the various eucharistic rites may be found in R. C. D. Jasper and G. J. Cuming, *Prayers of the Eucharist, Early and Reformed* (Collins, London, 1975).
38. The present writer's *Liturgical Development in the Anglican Communion: A View*, op. cit., pp. 2f.
39. Phyllis Tribble, *God and the Rhetoric of Sexuality* (Fortress, 1978); Letty M. Russell (ed.), *Feminist Interpretation of the Bible* (Westminster, Philadelphia, 1985).
40. The late Bishop Lakshman Wickremsinghe in a submission to the Inter-Anglican Theological and Doctrinal Commission, p. 1.
41. Ibid., p. 1.
42. R. R. Ruether, *"Feminist Interpretation: A Method of Correlation"* in Letty Russell (ed.), op. cit., p. 115.
43. E. S. Fiorenza, *"The Will to Choose or to Reject: continuing our critical work"*, ibid., pp. 130ff.
44. *For the sake of the Kingdom*, op. cit., pp. 40f.
45. The present writer's *The Vocation of Anglicanism* op. cit., p. 118.
46. Preface to the *Book of Common Prayer of 1662* and the *Thirty-Nine Articles of Religion*, especially art. 34.
47. The present writer's *"Church, Culture and Change"* in J. Draper (ed.), *Communion and Espicopacy*, op. cit., pp. 97ff.
48. Camilo Marivoet, "Principles of Inculturation" in *Focus*, Multan, September 1985, p. 284.
49. *Sacrosanctum Concilium* 21 and 37, quoted in Evarist Pinto, "Localising the Liturgy", *Focus*, op. cit., p. 328.

H

50. Report of the *National Liturgical Commission (Islamabad, 1984).*

51. Professor Nicholas Lash of Cambridge, a "laicised" priest, would like the term "magisterium" to denote *function,* not *functionaries.* He points out, however, that to an increasing extent the term is being used to refer to officials at the Vatican rather than to the teaching office of bishops. In *The Unity We Seek,* an address to the Seventh Meeting of the Anglican Consultative Council (Singapore, 1987).

52. Ion Bria (ed.), *Go Forth in Peace, pp. 25f.*

53. See Paul Avis, *Anglicanism and the Christian Church* (T. and T. Clark, Edinburgh, 1989), pp. 6ff.

54. Barrett, *Schism and Renewal in Africa,* op. cit.

55. See further Bruce J. Nicholls, *Contextualisation: A Theology of Gospel and Culture* (Paternoster, Exeter, 1979).

56. Marshall, *Acts,* op. cit., pp. 84-85.

57. M. A. Smith, *From Christ to Constantine* (London, 1971), pp. 102-103.

58. F. F. Bruce, *I and II Corinthians* (NCBC, Eerdmans, Grand Rapids, 1986), pp. 157-158.

59. See, for example, Margaret E. Thrall, *I and II Corinthians* (CUP, 1965), pp. 160f.

60. See, for example, M. Toal (ed.), *The Sunday Sermons of the Great Fathers* (London, 1963), A Nygren, *Agape and Eros* (SPCK, 1939) and D. F. Winslow, "Gregory of Nazianzus and Love for the Poor" in *Anglican Theological Review,* Vol. XLVII, No. 4, Oct. 1965, pp. 348ff.

61. Bebbington, *Evangelism in Modern Britain,* op. cit., pp. 69, 123-124.

62. See further, *Deacons in the Ministry of the Church,* a report to the House of Bishops of the General Synod of the Church of England, (CHP, London, 1988).

63. *The Place of Women in the Orthodox Church* (Rhodes, 1988), pp. 10-11.

64. C. Ceccon and K. Paludan (eds.), *My Neighbour-Myself: Visions of Diakonia* (WCC, Geneva, 1988). The *Guidelines for Sharing* produced by the WCC concultation on resource-sharing at El Escorial are an instance of the kind of thinking which is now current in ecumenical circles.

65. See for example, Stuart Brown (ed.), *Meeting in Faith,* especially ch. II. I, *"Christian Mission and Islamic Da^cwah* (WCC, Geneva, 1989), pp. 73ff.

66. M. M. Thomas, *The Acknowledged Christ of the Indian Renaissance* (London, 1969) and S. J. Samartha, *The Hindu Response to the Unbound Christ* (Madras, 1974).

67. Boff, *Ecclesio-Genesis,* op. cit., pp. 2ff.

68. Ibid., pp. 23f.

69. Ibid., pp. 62.

70. *Bonds of Affection: ACC-6* (ACC, London, 1984), pp. 67; *Many Gifts, One Spirit: ACC-7* (ACC, London, 1987), pp. 57f.; *The Truth Shall Make You Free,* Report of Lambeth 1988 (ACC, London, 1988), p. 73.

71. Op. cit., p. 63.

72. TEE, of course, is more than ministerial formation; it is also about the formation of the laity. See further, F. Ross Kinsler (ed.), *Ministry by the People* (WCC, Geneva, 1983).

73. Op. cit., p. 23.

74. David Sheppard, *Bias to the Poor* (Hodder, London, 1983); *Faith in the City,* Report of the Archbishop of Canterbury's Commission on Urban Priority Areas (CHP, London, 1985); Lourdino A. Yuzon (ed.), *Mission in the Context of Endemic Poverty* (CCA, Singapore, 1983).
75. Gustavo Guttierrez at the Lambeth Conference, 1988. Quoted in the *Report,* op. cit., "Mission and Ministry", Sec. 36.

CHAPTER SEVEN

1. In Robert Morgan (ed.), *The Religion of the Incarnation: Anglican Essays in Commemoration of the Lux Mundi* (Bristol, 1989), p. 173.

2. See further J. Goldingay, *Theological Diversity and the Authority of the Old Testament,* (Eerdmans, Grand Rapids, 1987), pp. 29ff.

3. E. A. Pratt, *Can we pray with the unconverted?* (CPAS, Rushden, 1971).

4. J. N. D. Anderson, *Christianity and Comparative Religion* (Tyndale, 1970), pp. 91ff., *God's Law and God's Love* (Collins, London, 1980); cf. Kenneth Cracknell, *Towards a New Relationship* (Epworth, London, 1986), pp. 63-64.

5. The first phrase is taken from John Bowker's *The Sense of God: Sociological, Anthropological and Psychological Approaches to the Origin of the Sense of God* (Oxford, 1973). The second is taken from Emil Brunner.

6. See Justin's *First Apology* and *Second Apology* and Clement's *Stromateis.*

7. See A. Rudvin, *The Gospel and Islam: What sort of Dialogue is Possible;* (*Al-Mushir,* Autumn, 1979), pp. 111f.

8. Cracknell, op. cit., pp. 101f.

9. Oscar Cullman is usually regarded as the main protagonist for Salvation-History in the post-war period. See his *Christ and Time* (London, 1951) and *Salvation as History* (London, 1967).

10. *Towards a Theology for Inter-Faith Dialogue* (ACC, London, 1986), pp. 16-17.

11. Ibid., pp. 25-26.

12. The late Bishop Lakshman Wickremsinghe of Kurunegla, Sri Lanka, was in the process of developing such a theology before his untimely death.

13. Jerram Barrs, *Christian Standards in a Pluralistic Society: Salt and Light,* a consultation on Christian Social Action (1988), p. 1.

14. A term used by Dr Bong-Ho Son of the Seoul National University, Korea.

15. "The Humanitarian Theory of Punishment", reprint from "Res Judicate" in *Churchmen Speak* (Marcham Manor Press, 1966), pp. 39f.; cf. Michael Nazir-Ali, *Frontiers in Muslim-Christian Encounter* (Regnum, Oxford, 1987), "Retaliation: A Response", pp. 146ff.

16. Michael Nazir-ali and W. D. Pattinson (eds.), *The Truth Shall Make You Free,* Report of the Lambeth Conference, 1988, (ACC, London), pp. 82ff. Also, *For the Sake of the Kingdom,* a report of the Inter-Anglican Theological and Doctrinal Commission (ACC, London, 1986) pp. 38ff.

CHAPTER EIGHT

1. See further the present writer's *Martyrs and Magistrates: Toleration and Trial in Islam* (Grove Books, Nottingham, 1989), pp. 11f.
2. See, for example, Maurice Assad, "Mission in the Coptic Church", in *"Mission Studies"*, op. cit., pp. 24f.
3. Quoted in Sergei Hackel, "Orthodox Worship" in J. G. Davies (ed.), *A New Dictionary of Liturgy and Worship* (SCM, 1986), pp. 420f.
4. For an account of Valeri Barinov's life see Lorna Bordeaux, *Trumpet Call* (Marshall Pickering, London, 1985).
5. There is a great deal of literature on the subject. See, for example, the present writer's *Islam: A Christian Perspective*, op. cit., pp. 60ff.; Erica Hunter, "Isaac of Nineveh: The Persian Mystic", *Iqbal Review* (Winter, 1988, Lahore), pp. 90ff. An early but unsurpassed work is Margaret Smith's *Studies in Early Mysticism in the Near and Middle East* (London, 1931). Also Muhammad Iqbal, *The Development of Metaphysics in Persia* (Lahore, 1964), pp. 77ff.
6. For a mediaeval Sūfī view of Jesus the ascetic, see Jalāluddīn Rūmī, *Fihi mā Fīhi* (Tehran, 1959), p. 182, tr. by A. J. Arberry as *Discourses of Rumi* (London, 1961). Also *Islam: A Christian Perspective*, p. 18 for views of Sūfī poets such as Sānā'ī.
7. Iris El-Masry, *Introduction to the Coptic Church*, op. cit., pp. 20f. See also the present writer's "Christian Worship, Witness and Work in Islamic Contexts: Directions in Mission", *International Review of Mission* (WCC, Geneva, January 1987), pp. 33f. and *Frontiers in Muslim-Christian Encounter*, op. cit., pp. 9ff.
8. Faber, London, 1962.
9. See further V. Stacey, *Thomas Valpy French* (in Urdu), (MIK, Lahore, 1979), pp. 120ff.

CHAPTER NINE

1. J. A. T. Robinson, *The Body* (SCM, London, 1952), pp. 46, 68 and passim; C. F. D. Moule, *The Birth of the New Testament* (A & C Black, London, 1971), pp. 99 and 135. See also his *The Epistles to the Colossians and to Philemon* (CUP, 1980), pp. 87ff.; F. F. Bruce, *Romans: An Introduction and Commentary* (Tyndale, London, 1971), pp. 135ff.

2. The establishment of the parochial system in the C. of E. we owe to Theodore of Tarsus (602–690), the only Archbishop of Canterbury of Asian origin!

3. David Nicholls, "Two Tendencies in Anglo-Catholic Political Theology" in R. Williams and D. Nicholls, *Politics and Theological Identity* (London, 1984), pp. 30ff.

4. As, for example, in Luther. See Paul Avis, "Luther's Theology of the Church", *Churchman,* Vol. 97, No. 2, 1983, pp. 104f.

5. Michael Barnes S. J., *Religions in Conversation: Christian Identity and Religious Pluralism* (SPCK, London, 1989), p. 167.

6. The Church of North India now has a theological college which aims to teach in the vernacular (Hindi) and uses this method of "immersion" in its ministerial formation.

7. See, for example, *The Unknown Christ of Hinduism* (DLT, London, 1981).

8. In *The Open Secret* (SPCK, London, 1978), pp. 170f.

9. See further, M. M. Thomas, *The Acknowledged Christ of the Hindu Renaissance* (London, 1969), and S. J. Samartha, *The Hindu Response to the Unbound Christ* (Madras, 1974). Also, Hans Staffner S. J., *The Significance of Jesus Christ in Asia* (Gujarat, 1985).

10. New York, 1966, pp. 56f. Among his other works are *Return to the Centre* (London, 1976) and *The Marriage of East and West* (London, 1982).

11. Stephen Neill, *A History of Christian Missions,* op. cit., pp. 183ff.

12. A. J. Appasamy, *Sundar Singh* (Madras, 1966).

13. *Concise Dictionary of the Christian World Mission,* eds. S. Neill, G. H. Anderson, J. Goodwin (London, 1970) p. 576.

14. *Islam: A Christian Perspective,* op. cit., ch. 1 and passim.

15. Ibid., pp. 84f.; *Frontiers in Muslim-Christian Encounter,* op. cit., pp. 80f.

16. R. Bell, *The Origin of Islam in its Christian Environment* (London, 1968), pp. 90f.

17. See further the present writer's "A Christian View of Muslim Spirituality and Prayer" in D. A. Carson (ed.), *Teach us to Pray* (Paternoster, 1989). See also Constance Padwick, *Muslim Devotions* (SPCK, London, 1961), pp. 19f and Timothy Ware, *The Orthodox Church* (London, 1973) pp. 174f.

18. See also *Frontiers in Muslim-Christian Encounter,* op. cit., pp. 43-44 and p. 162, footnote 25.

19. *Tartībī barā'ī ʿishā muqaddas rabbānī,* Eucharistic Liturgy of the Episcopal Church in Iran, p. 40.

20. *Christ Outside the Gate: Mission Beyond Christendom* (Orbis, New York, 1982), p. 16.

Notes

CHAPTER TEN

1. *Real Presences* (Faber, London, 1989), p. 59.
2. See further Lesslie Newbigin, *The Gospel in a Pluralist Society* (SPCK, London, 1989), ch. 5, pp. 55ff.
3. K. Cragg, *Muhammad and the Christian: A Question of Response* (DLT, London, 1984), pp. 12f. See also the present writer's "That which is not to be found but which finds us" in *Towards a Theology for Inter-Faith Dialogue* (ACC, London, 1986), p. 44.
4. I. H. Marshall, *Acts*, op. cit. p. 293.
5. Richard Wollheim (ed.), *Hume on Religion* (Collins, London 1971), pp. 99ff.
6. WCC Muslim-Christian Meeting (Chambésy, 1979), p. 1, No. 7.
7. *Guidelines on Dialogue with People of Living Faiths and Ideologies* (Geneva, 1979), p. 11.
8. See, for example, *Relations with People of Other Faiths: Guidelines on Dialogue in Britain* (BCC, London, 1981).
9. L. Yuzon, *Communicating the Christian Message* (CCA, N.D.), pp. 55f. For a full discussion see *Islam: A Christian Perspective*, pp. 145ff. and *Frontiers in Muslim-Christian Encounter*, pp. 85ff, 105ff.
10. Section I: *Turning to the Living God; 4: Witness Among People of Other Living Faiths*, paras 31-33.
11. *Christian Witness to Muslims:* Report of a Consultation held at Pattaya, Thailand (Wheaton, Ill., 1980), p. 23.
12. In J. Hick (ed.), *Truth and Dialogue: the relationship between world religions*, pp. 77ff.
13. See, for example, Stuart E. Brown (ed.), *Meeting in Faith: Twenty Years of Muslim-Christian Conversations* (WCC, Geneva, 1989).
14. *Mysticism, Sacred and Profane* (Oxford, 1957) and *Concordant Discord* (Oxford, 1970). See also *Our Savage God* (Collins, London 1974).
15. *Islam: A Christian Perspective,* op. cit. pp. 65f.
16. *A Testament of Faith* (Epworth, London, 1972), p. 206.
17. Sharpe, op. cit., pp. 90f.
18. The Gospel in a Pluralist Society, op. cit. p. 12.

231

CHAPTER ELEVEN

1. In some ways, this is the burden of the document known as *The Road to Damascus: Kairos and Conversion* (London, 1989), which is a statement by Chritians from certain countries in the Two-Thirds World.
2. *To Strengthen the Poor* (Christian Aid, London, 1987).
3. These struggles as well as the harassment and persecution that ensue are chronicled in Charles Elliot's *Sword and Spirit* (BBC, London, 1989).
4. *Faith in the City* (CHP, London, 1985), ch. 2.
5. Rene Padilla, *Christology and Mission,* op. cit. p. 44.
6. See Norberto Saracco, "The Liberating Options of Jesus" in V. Samuel and C. Sugden (eds.), *Sharing Jesus in the Two-Thirds World* (Bangalore 1983), pp. 50ff.
7. Andrew Kirk, *Liberation Theology,* p. 195, ff.
8. Otto Kaiser, *Isaiah 1–12* (SCM, London, 1983), pp. 204ff.
9. Saracco, op. cit. p. 51.
10. V. Samuel and C. Sugden (eds.), *The Gospel among our Hindu Neighbours,* Bangalore 1983. Also S. J. Samartha, *The Hindu Response to the Unbound Christ,* Madras 1974 and M. M. Thomas, *The Acknowledged Christ of the Indian Renaissance,* London 1969. See also a recent publication, Vishal Mangalwadi, *Truth and Social Reform* (Nivedit, Delhi, 1989).
11. Elliott, *Sword and Spirit,* op. cit. pp. 39ff. See also Leon Howell, *People are the Subject* (WCC, Geneva, 1980), ch. 6.
12. See further K. Y. Bock (ed.), *Minjung Theology* (CCA, Singapore, 1981).
13. Ibid., pp. 29ff, 43ff.
14. It is interesting, in this context, to reflect that a survey done on the use of the Psalms among Pākistānī Christians of similar background revealed that the most popular were the ones which dealt with the human experience of suffering!
15. James Massey, "Christians in North India: Historical perspective with special reference to Christians in the Punjab", *Religion and Society,* Vol. XXXIV, No. 3, sept. 1987, pp. 88ff.; also *Ingredients for a Dalit Theology* (place and date of publication unknown).
16. "Spirit-Possession, Exorcism and Social Context: An Anthropological Perspective", *Churchman,* Vol. 94, No. 3., 1980, pp. 226ff.
17. See further Philip Lewis, *Pirs, Shrines and Pakistani Islām,* Christian Study Centre, Rawalpindi, 1985; Bill Musk, *The Unseen Face of Islām* (MARC, Eastbourne, 1989); Paul Hiebert, "Power Encounter and Folk-Islām" in J. D. Woodberry (ed.) *Muslims and Christians on the Emmaus Road* (MARC, Monrovia, 1989), ch. 3. pp. 45ff.
18. An association of priests and psychiatrists in the UK, called the Christian Exorcism Study Group, encourages inter-disciplinary contact in this area. See further Michael Perry (ed.), *Deliverance* (SPCK, London, 1987).
19. Report of the National Liturgical Commission of the Roman Catholic Church in Pakistan, *Focus,* Multan, Vol. 4, No. 5, Sept/Oct 1985, pp. 292ff.
20. Musk, op. cit. pp. 249f.
21. A. Rudvin, *The Holy Spirit and World Evangelisation,* a paper read to the joint meeting of the Evangelical Fellowship in the Anglican Communion and SOMA prior to the 1988 Lambeth Conference.

CHAPTER TWELVE

1. David Winter, officer for Evangelism, speaking on the Diocese of Oxford's priorities for the forthcoming *Decade of Evangelism,* 24th November 1989.

2. *Faith in the City* points out, for example, the extent to which "hierarchically-arranged rented pews" alienated the working people of England in the nineteenth century, op. cit., pp. 28f.

3. This is the burden of Vincent Donovan's *Christianity Rediscovered: An Epistle from the Masai,* SCM, London 1982.

4. Raymund Fung, 5th October 1989 (used with permission).

5. See, for example, Arlin J. Rothauge, *Sizing up a Congregation for New Member Ministry,* Episcopal Church Centre, N.Y.N.D.

6. C. F. D. Moule, *The Birth of the New Testament,* A & C Black, London 1971, p. 135.

7. See "The Gospel and Tranformation" *in Trustworthy and True: Pastoral Letters from the Lambeth Conference 1988,* CHP, 1988, pp. 20f. The Bishop of Durham's presentation at the Conference is also a testimony to such "transformative evangelisation".

8. "Showing the Hospitality of God" in *Trustworthy and True,* op. cit., pp. 15f.

9. Nos. 3/4, March/April 1989.

10. E.g. *Sīrat Al-Masīḥ bi-lisān ᶜArabī faṣīḥ,* Cyprus 1987 (Arabic); *Injīl-i-Masīḥ* (no date or place of publication), a new diatessaron in Persian. See also Dennis E. Clark, *The Life and Teaching of Jesus the Messiah* (Dove, Ill., 1977).

11. An effective example of this work is to be found in the art of Fr Siddique Mark Sundei, a Dominican from Pākistān. See *USPG Network,* July 1988, pp14-15 (used with permission).

12. "The Place of Holy Scripture in Muslim-Christian Encounter" in the present writer's *Frontiers in Muslim-Christian Encounter,* op. cit. pp. 45ff. See also the findings of a joint Muslim and Christian research group, *The Challenge of the Scriptures: The Bible and the Qur'ān,* Stuart W. Brown (tr.), Orbis (New York, 1989), p. 66.

13. The Stuttgart Statement is most conveniently to be found in V. Samuel and A. Hauser (eds.), *Proclaiming Christ in Christ's Way: studies in integral evangelism,* Regnum (Oxford, 1989), pp. 212–225.

14. *God's Law and God's Love* (Collins, London 1980), pp. 32–33 and 128.

15. *The Gospel in a Pluralist Society,* op. cit., pp. 176f.

16. *Towards a New Relationship,* op. cit., p. 29 and p. 41.

17. Hārūn Asīr, *Lahū kā Rang,* Lahore 1984, p. 73 (translated by the present writer).

CHAPTER THIRTEEN

1. In *The Truth Shall Make You Free: The Lambeth Conference 1988,* op. cit., Appd. 2, p. 280.
2. Ibid., p. 21.
3. *Lambeth Conference 1958* (SPCK, London, 1958). p.1.29.
4. Philip Potter, "From Edinburgh to Melbourne" in *Your Kingdom Come,* a report of the CWME Conference in Melbourne, 1980 (WCC, Geneva, 1980), p. 19.
5. Alan Stephenson, *Anglicanism and the Lambeth Conferences* (SPCK, London, 1978), pp. 128ff.
6. Ibid., p. 153.
7. *Statements of Faith of the Uniting Churches in North India and Pakistan* (CLS, Madras, 1965).
8. E.g. *Forward to Union: The Church of North India* (ISPCK, Delhi, 1968), pp. 71f.
9. For a joint statement of the Evangelical and Catholic case see C. O. Buchanan, E. L. Mascall, J. I. Packer and Graham Leonard, *Growing into Union* (SPCK, London, 1970).
10. See, for example, the debate in the Proceedings of the General Synod of the Church of Enland, 13th July 1971, Vol. 2, No. 1, pp. 302 – 315 and 325 – 332. See also GS37, *Report on Full Communion with the Churches of North India and Pakistan,* MECCA 1971.
11. Op. cit., pp. 123ff.
12. E.g. Basil Meeking and J. R. W. Stott (eds.), *The Evangelical-Roman Catholic Dialogue on Mission* (Exeter, Paternoster, 1986).
13. *Report,* op. cit. pp. 201ff.
14. See further, Paulos Gregorios, W. H. Lazareth and N. A. Nissiotis (eds.), *Does Chalcedon Divide or Unite?* (Geneva, 1981).
15. *ARCIC: The Final Report,* CTS/SPCK, London 1982 and *ARCIC II: Salvation and the Church,* CTS/CHP, 1987.
16. *Justification by Faith, Origins:* N. C. Documentary Service, October 1983 and J. Reumann, *Righteousness in the New Testament: Justification in Lutheran – Catholic Dialogue* (Philadelphia/New York, 1982).
17. *Towards a Church of England Response to BEM and ARCIC,* CIO, 1985, pp. 8 – 9 and passim; *Observations,* Sacred Congregation for the Doctrine of the Faith, CTS, London 1982. See also *Anglican Orders: A New Context* (CTS, London, 1986), p. 6.
18. E.g. Ignatius, *Epistle to the Philadelphians* (SPCK, London, 1954), Section IV, p. 35.
19. Cyprian of Carthage, Letter 67:5 in J. T. Lienhard S. J., *Ministry: Message of the Fathers of the Church,* Delaware 1984, p. 139 and R. B. Eno, S.S., *Teaching Authority in the Early Church,* Delaware, 1984, pp. 84-96.
20. Carol Graham, *Azariah of Dornakal* (SCM, London, 1946), p. 110.
21. *The Church Missionary Society: A Manual Outlining its History, Organisation and Commitment* (London, Highway, 1961), p. 9.

CHAPTER FOURTEEN

1. *The Gospel in a Pluralist Society,* op. cit., pp. 222ff.
2. See further F. Ross Kinsler (ed.), *Ministry by the People* (WCC, Geneva, 1983).
3. Op. cit., p. 53.
4. The matter is brilliantly explored by George Steiner in *Real Presences,* op. cit.
5. J. R. W. Stott, *I believe in Preaching* (Hodder, London, 1982).
6. Charles Elliot, *Praying the Kingdom* (DLT, London, 1985).
7. *Report,* op. cit., pp. 44ff.
8. "The Church Witnesses to the Kingdom" in *Your Kingdom Come,* a report of the CWME Conference at Melbourne, Australia (WCC, Geneva, 1980), p. 137.

CHAPTER FIFTEEN

1. OUP, 1982.
2. "Who are the Christians in the Middle East?" *MECC Perspectives,* Beirut, Oct. 1986, pp. 23f.
3. E.g. Julian Pettifer in the *Open Air* programme on *Missionaries,* BBC1, 26th February, 1990.
4. See my CMS Newsletter, *A Servant of the Servants of God,* No. 492, January/February 1990.
5. Boff, *Ecclesio-Genesis,* op. cit., pp. 23ff.
6. Henry Chadwick, *The Role of the Christian Bishop in Ancient Society* (Colloquy 35 of the Centre for Hermeneutical Studies, Berkeley, California, 1980), pp. 6-7.
7. The present writer's "Church, Culture and Change" in J. Draper (ed.), *Communion and Episcopacy,* Cuddesdon, 1988, p. 100.
8. See, for example, the Archbishop of Canterbury's opening address at the 1988 Lambeth Conference, *Report,* p. 20.
9. *Frontiers in Muslim-Christian Encounter,* op. cit., pp. 70ff.
10. Chadwick, op. cit., p. 1 and *The Early Church* (London, 1967), pp. 47ff.
11. *The Meaning of Authority,* Lanham, Maryland, 1983, p.6 and also Stephen W. Sykes (ed.), *Authority in the Anglican Communion* (Toronto, 1987), p. 35.

Bibliography

THEOLOGY OF MISSION

Assad, Maurice, *Mission in the Coptic Church*, Mission Studies, Vol. IV:1, 1987.

Bria, Ion (ed.), *Martyria/Mission, The Witness of the Orthodox Churches Today*, WCC, Geneva, 1980.

Buren, Paul Van, *The Secular Meaning of the Gospel*, SCM, 1963.

Cox, Harvey, *The Secular City*, SCM, 1965.

Donovan, Vincent, *Christianity Rediscovered: An Epistle from the Masai*, SCM, 1978.

Go Forth in Peace: Orthodox Perspectives on Mission, WCC, Geneva, 1986.

Newbigin, Bishop Lesslie, *The Gospel in a Pluralist Society*, SPCK, London, 1989.

————*The Open Secret*, SPCK, London, 1978.

Staffner, Hans, S. J., *The Significance of Jesus Christ*, Gujarat, 1985.

Taylor, Bishop John V., *The Go-Between God*, New York, 1979.

The Pasadena Consultation: Homogeneous Unit Principle, Wheaton, 1978 (a Lausanne Occasional Paper).

Your Kingdom Come, CWME Conference in Melbourne, WCC, Geneva, 1980.

MISSIOLOGY

Fraser, D. A. (ed.), *The Church in New Frontiers for Mission*, MARC, Monrovia, 1983.

CHURCH AND MISSION HISTORY

Bebbington, D. W., *Evangelicalism in Modern Britain*, London, 1989.

Bedjan, P., *Acta Martyrum et Sanctorum*, Leipzig, 1890-95.

Chadwick, Henry, *The Early Church*, London, 1967.

————*The Role of the Christian Bishop in Ancient Society*, Colloquy 35 of the Centre for Hermeneutical Studies, Berkeley, California, 1980.

Davies, John D., *The Faith Abroad*, Oxford, 1983.

de Rachewiltz, Igor, *Papal Envoys at the Court of the Great Khans*, London, 1971.

Edwards, David L., *The Futures of Christianity*, London, 1987.

El Masry, Iris, *Introduction to the Coptic Church*, Cairo, 1977.

Frend, W. H. C., *The Early Church*, London, 1965.

Hill, Henry (ed.), *Light from the East*, Toronto, 1988.

Hollenweger, Walter, *The Pentecostals*, Minneapolis, 1972.

James, M. R. (ed.), *The Apocryphal New Testament*, OUP, 1924.

Kahl, Joachim, *The Misery of Christianity*, Penguin, London, 1968.

Neill, Stephen, *A History of Christian Missions*, Penguin, London, 1964.

Mar Thoma, Alexander, *The Mar Thoma Church: Heritage and Mission*, Tiruvalla, 1985.

Meeks, Wayne A., *The First Urban Christians*, New Haven, 1983.

Meyendorff, John, *"The Orthodox Church and Mission, Past and Present Perspectives"* in G. H. Anderson and T. F. Stransky (eds.), *Mission Trends No. 1*, Eerdmans, Grand Rapids, 1974.

Bibliography

Rooney, John, *Shadows in the Dark,* Rawalpindi, 1984.
─────*The Hesitant Dawn,* Rawalpindi, 1984.
Smirnoff, Eugene, *Russian Orthodox Missions,* Welshpool, Powys, 1986.
Smith, M. A., *From Christ to Constantine,* London, 1971.
Stock E., *The History of the Church Missionary Society,* London, 1899.
Ware, Timothy, *The Orthodox Church,* Penguin, London, 1969.
Warneck, G., *Protestant Missions,* Edinburgh, 1906.
Young, Bishop William G., *Handbook of Source Materials for Students of Church History,* Madras, 1969.
─────*The Life and History of the Church in Pakistan,* Islamabad Lecture, 1971.
─────*Patriarch, Shah and Caliph,* Rawalpindi, 1974.

HISTORY

Bannerjee, G. N., *Hellenism in Ancient India,* Delhi, 1961.

PATRISTIC MATERIAL

Athanasius, St., *On The Incarnation,* Mowbray, 1953.
Augustine, St., *Confessions,* Airmont, New York, 1969.
─────*De Trinitate,* in J. P. Migne (ed.), *Patrologia Latina,* Vol. 42 pp.819–1098, 1841-42.
Clement of Alexandria, St., *Stromateis,* in J. P. Migne (ed.), *Patrologia Graeca,* Vol. 8, pp.685–1382, 1857.
Eno, R. B. SS, *Teaching Authority in the Early Church,* Delaware, 1984.
Ignatius, St., *The Epistles of St. Ignatius,* London SPCK, 1954.
Lienhard, J. T. S. J., *Ministry: Message of the Fathers of the Church,* Delaware, 1984.
Martyr, Justin, St., *First and Second Apology,* Migne's Patrologia Graeca, Vol. 6, 1857.
Nygren, A., *Agape and Eros,* SPCK, 1939.
Theodore of Mopsuestia, in J. P. Migne (ed.), *Patrologia Graeca,* Vol. 66, Paris, 1857–1866.
─────*Voice from the East,* Journal of the Church of the East, Vol. 7, No. 1., Jan–Mar 1988.
Toal, M. (ed.), *The Sunday Sermons of the Great Fathers,* London, 1963.
Winslow, D. F., *Gregory of Nazianzus and Love for the Poor,* Anglican Review, Oct. 1965.

LITURGY

Buchanan, C. O., Modern Anglican Liturgies, OUP, 1968.
Davies, J. G. (ed.), *A New Dictionary of Liturgy and Worship,* SCM. London, 1986.
Dowden, J., *The Scottish Communion Office,* OUP, 1764.

Jasper, R. C. D. & Cuming, G. J., *Prayers of the Eucharist: Early and Reformed,* Collins, London, 1975.

Nazir-Ali, Michael J., *Liturgical Development in the Anglican Communion,* A View, Lambeth Conference, 1988.

Stevenson, Kenneth & Perham, Michael, *Anglican Liturgy Today,* Lambeth Conference 1988.

Strawley, J. H., *The Liturgical Movement; Its Origin and Growth,* Alcuin Club, London, 1954.

BIBLICAL MATERIAL

Bailey, K. E., *Poet and Peasant,* Eerdmans, 1976.

Barrett, C. K., *The Gospel According to St. John,* London, 1967.

Bigg, Charles, *The Epistles of St. Peter and St. Jude,* Edinburgh, 1902.

Bruce, F. F., *I and II Corinthians,* NCBC, Eerdmans, Grand Rapids, 1986.

————*Romans: An Introduction and Commentary,* Tyndale, London, 1971.

Brueggemann, W., *The Prophetic Imagination,* Fortress, 1978.

Goldingay, John, *Theological Diversity and the Authority of The Old Testament,* Eerdmans, Grand Rapids, 1987.

Gottwald, Norman K., *The Tribes of Yahweh: A Sociology of the Religion of Liberated Israel,* Orbis, 1979.

————*Injil-i-Masih,* no date of publication, a new diatessaron in Persian.

Kaiser, Otto, Isaiah 1–12, SCM, London, 1983.

Marshall, I. H., *Acts,* Eerdmans, Grand Rapids, 1980.

Moule, C. F. D., *The Birth of the New Testament,* A & C Black, London, 1971.

————*The Epistles to the Colossians and to Philemon,* CUP, 1980.

Nygren, A., *Agape and Eros,* SPCK, 1939.

————*Sirat Al-Masih bi-Lisan ᶜArabi Fasih,* Cyprus, 1987, (Arabic).

Thiselton, A. C., *The Two Horizons: New Testament Hermeneutics And Philosophical Description,* Paternoster, Exeter, 1980.

Thrall, Margaret, E., *I and II Corinthians,* CUP, 1965.

Tidball, Derek, *An Introduction to the Sociology of the New Testament,* Paternoster, Exeter, 1983.

Wheeler Robinson, H., *The Religious Ideas of the Old Testament,* London, 1913.

Wright, Chris, *The People of God and the State; An Old Testament Perspective,* Unpublished Paper.

CHRISTIAN DOCTRINE

Altizer, Thomas J. J., *The Gospel of Christian Atheism,* Collins, 1967.

Barth, Karl, *Church Dogmatics,* ET, Edinburgh, 1959.

Cullmann, Oscar, *Christ and Time,* London, 1951.

————*Salvation as History,* London, 1967.

————*For the Sake of the Kingdom,* Report of the Inter-Anglican Theological and Doctrinal Commission, London, 1986.

Gitari, David & Benson, Patrick, *The Living God,* Nairobi, 1986.

Kee, Alistair, *The Way of Transcendence,* Penguin, 1971.

Macquarrie, J., *20th Century Religious Thought,* SCM, 1971.

Morgan, R. (ed.), *The Religion of the Incarnation:* Anglican Essays in Commemoration of Lux Mundi, Bristol, 1989.

Pratt, E. A., *Can we pray with the unconverted?* CPAS, Rushden, 1971.

Robinson, J. A. T., *The Body,* SCM, London, 1952.

THEOLOGIES OF LIBERATION

Bock, K. Y. (ed.), *Minjung Theology,* CCA, Singapore, 1981.

Boff, Leonardo, *Church, Charism and Power,* SCM, London, 1981.

————————*Ecclesio-Genesis,* Collins, London, 1986.

Choan-Seng Song, *Third-Eye Theology: Theology in Formation in Asian Setting,* Maryknoll, Orbis, 1979.

Cohn-Sherbok, Dan, Rabbi, *On Earth as it is in Heaven,* Orbis, 1987.

Cook, Guillermo, *The Expectation of the Poor,* Orbis, New York, 1985.

Elliot, Charles, *Sword and Spirit,* BBC, London, 1989.

Howell, Leon, *People are the Subject,* WCC, Geneva, 1980.

Kirk, Andrew, *Liberation Theology,* Marshalls, London, 1979.

Libanio, J. B., *"BECs in Socio-Cultural Perspective",* Transformation, July–Sept 1986.

Mangalwadi, Vishal, *Truth and Social Reform,* Ninedit, Delhi, 1989.

————————*The Road to Damascus: Kairos and Conversion,* London, 1989.

————————*To Strengthen the Poor,* Christian Aid, London, 1987.

Samuel, Vinay & Sugden, Chris (eds.), *Sharing Jesus in the Two-Thirds World,* Bangalore, 1983.

Sobrino, Jon, *Christology at the Crossroads: A Latin American Approach,* Maryknoll, Orbis, 1978.

Yuzon, Lourdino A. (ed.), *Mission in the Context of Endemic Poverty,* CCA, Singapore, 1983.

POLITICAL THEOLOGY

Nicholls, David & Williams, Rowan, *Politics and Theological Identity,* Jubilee, London, 1984.

PASTORAL THEOLOGY

Ceccon, C. & Paludan, K. (eds.), *My Neighbour-Myself: Visions of Diakonia,* WCC, Geneva, 1988.

————————*Deacons in the Ministry of the Church:* A Report to the House of Bishops of the General Synod of the Church of England, CHP, London, 1988.

Langley, Myrtle, *"Spirit-Possesson, Exorcism and Social Context: An anthropological perspective",* Churchman, 1980–3.

J

McNutt, Francis, *Healing*, Ave Maria, 1974.
Perry, Michael (ed.), *Deliverance*, SPCK, London, 1987.
Stott, J. R. W., *I believe in Preaching*, Hodder, London, 1982.

FEMINIST THEOLOGY

Russell, Letty M. (ed.), *Feminist Interpretation of the Bible*, Westminster, Philadelphia, 1985.
Tribble, Phyllis, *God and the Rhetoric of Sexuality*, Fortress, 1978.

URBAN THEOLOGY

Cox, Harvey, *The Secular City*, SCM, 1965.
Faith in the City, Report of the Archbishop of Canterbury's Commission on Urban Priority Areas, CHP, London, 1985.
Sheppard, David, *Bias to the Poor*, Hodder, London, 1983.
Sheppard, D., and Worlock, D., *Better Together*, Hodder, 1988.

PRAYER AND MYSTICAL THEOLOGY

Elliot, Charles, *Praying the Kingdom*, DLT, London, 1985.
Hunter, Erica, *"Isaac of Nineveh: The Persian Mystic"*, *Iqbāl Review*, Lahore, 1988.
Iqbāl, Muhammad, *The Development of Metaphysics in Persia*, Lahore, 1964.
Nazir-Ali, M. J., *Teach Us to Pray*, (ed.), D. A. Carson, Paternoster, 1989.
Padwick, Constance, *Muslim Devotions*, SPCK, London, 1961.
Rūmi, Jalāluddin, *Fihi mā Fihi*, Tehran, 1959.
Smith, Margaret, *Studies in Early Mysticism in the Near and Middle-East*, London, 1931.
Zaehner, Prof. R. C., *Concordant Discord*, Oxford, 1970.
———*Mysticism, Sacred and Profane*, Oxford, 1957.
———*Our Savage God*, Collins, London, 1974.

RENEWAL

Bax, Josephine, *The Good Wine: Spiritual Renewal in the Church of England*, CHP, London, 1986.
Craston, Colin, *Open to the Spirit*, ACC, London, 1987.
O'Connor, Edward, *The Pentecostal Movement*, Ave Maria, 1971.

INCULTURATION

Griffiths, Bede, *Christ in India,* New York, 1966.
————*Return to the Centre,* London, 1976.
————*The Marriage of East and West,* London, 1982.
Marivoet, Camilo, *Principles of Inculturation in Focus,* Multan, 1985.
Nicholls, Bruce, J., *Contextualisation: A Theology of Gospel and Culture,* Paternoster, Exeter, 1979.

PHENOMENOLOGY OF RELIGION

Bowker, John, *The Sense of God: Sociological, Anthropological and Psychological Approaches to the Origin of the Sense of God,* Oxford, 1973.

SOCIOLOGY

Berger, Peter L., *A Rumour of Angels,* Penguin, Baltimore, 1969.
Bottomore, T. B. and Rubel, M. (eds.), *Karl Marx: Sociology and Social Philosophy,* Pelican, London, 1961.
Robertson, Roland (ed.), *Sociology of Religion,* Penguin, Baltimore, 1969.
Tidball, Derek, *An Introduction to the Sociology of the New Testament,* Paternoster, Exeter, 1983.

PHILOSOPHY

Ayer, A. J., *Language, Truth and Logic,* Gollancz, 1946.
Russell, Bertrand, *A Free Man's Worship,* Unwin, 1976.
Steiner, George, *Real Presences,* Faber, London, 1989.
Ward, James, *The Realm of Ends,* CUP, 1912.

NEW RELIGIOUS MOVEMENTS

Barrett, D. B., *Schism and Renewal in Africa: An Analysis of 6000 Contemporary Religious Movements,* Nairobi, 1968.

CHRISTIAN DEMOGRAPHY

Barrett, D. B., *World Christian Encyclopaedia*, Oxford, 1982.
————————"Who are the Christians of the Middle-East?", *MECC Perspectives*, Beirut, 1986.
————————*World Christianity*, series, Marc, Monrovia, 1979–1981.

EVANGELISATION

Gitari, David, *Evangelisation and Culture: Primary Evangelism in Northern Kenya*, L.C., 1988.
Jiwan, Bashir, *Evangelisation and Culture: An Asian Case*, L.C. 1988.
Rothauge, Arlin J., *Sizing up a congregaton for New Member Ministry*, Episcopal Church Centre, New York.
Rudvin, A., *The Holy Spirit and World Evangelisaton*, paper read to the Joint Consultation of the Evangelical Fellowship in the Anglican Communion and SOMA prior to the 1988 L.C.
Samuel, Vinay & Hauser, A., (eds.), *Proclaiming Christ in Christ's Way: Studies in integral evangelism*, Regnum, Oxford, 1989.
————————*The Report of the First Day Conference on Church Planting in the Church of England*, London, 1987.

ANGLICANISM

Avis, P., *Anglicanism and the Christian Church*, T & T Clark, Edinburgh, 1989.
————————*Bonds of Affection*, ACC, London, 1984.
Draper, R. (ed.), *Communion and Episcopacy*, Cuddesdon, 1988.
Hinkes, Elsie, *A Respectable Occupation*, Oxford, 1988.
————————*In Search of a Relevant Anglicanism in East Asia Today*, Theological Commission of the (Anglican) Council of the Church of East Asia, Quezon City, Philippines, 1987.
————————*Love in Any Language*, Report of the First International Conference of Young Anglicans, Belfast, 1988.
Morgan, R. (ed.), *The Religion of the Incarnation: Anglican Essays in Commemoration of Lux Mundi*, Bristol, 1989.
Nazir-Ali, Michael J., *The Vocation of Anglicanism*, Anvil, 1989.
Nazir-Ali, Michael J. & Pattinson, W. D. (eds.), *The Truth Shall Make You Free*, The Lambeth Conference, 1988.
————————*Trustworthy and True*, Pastoral Letters from the L.C., 1988.
Samuel, Vinay, & Sugden, Chris, *Lambeth: A view from the Two-Thirds World*, SPCK, London, 1989.
Skinner, John E., *The Meaning of Authority*, Lanham, Maryland, 1983.
Stephenson, Alan,*Anglicanism and the Lambeth Conferences*, SPCK, London, 1978.
Sykes, Stephen, W. (ed.), *Authority in the Anglican Communion*, Toronto, 1987.

ECUMENISM

Anglican Orders: A New Context, CTS, London, 1986.

ARCIC II: Salvation and the Church, CTS/CHP, 1987.

The Emmaus Report, A Report of the Anglican Ecumenical Consultation, ACC, London, 1987.

Buchanan, C. O., Mascall, E. L., Packer, J. I., Leonard, Graham, *Growing into Union*, SPCK, London, 1970.

Forward to Union: The Church of North India, ISPCK, Delhi, 1968.

Justification by Faith, Origins: N. C. Documentary Service, 1983.

Lash, Nicholas, *The Unity We Seek*, address to the Seventh Meeting of the ACC, Singapore, 1987.

Meeking, Basil, & Stott, J. R. W. (eds.), *The Evangelical-Roman Catholic Dialogue on Mission*, Paternoster, Exeter, 1986.

Observations, Sacred Congregation for The Doctrine of the Faith, CTS, London, 1982.

Patelos, Constantin (ed.), *The Orthodox Church in the Ecumenical Movement*, Geneva, 1978.

Righteousness in the New Testament: Justification in Lutheran-Catholic Dialogue, Philadelphia/New York, 1982.

The Final Report, Anglican-Roman Catholic International Commission, CTS/SPCK, London, 1982.

Towards a Church of England Response to BEM and ARCIC, CIO, 1985.

APOLOGETICS

Montefiore, Hugh, *The Probability of God*, SCM, London, 1985.

BIOGRAPHY

Appasamy, A. J., *Sundar Singh*, Madras, 1966.

Finnie, K. M., *Beyond the Minarets*, Bromley, 1988.

Graham, Carol, *Azariah of Dornakal*, SCM, London, 1946.

Stacey, Vivienne, *Henry Martyn*, Hyderabad, India, 1980.

————*Thomas Valpy French*, (in Urdu), MIK, Lahore, 1979.

OTHER FAITHS

Anderson, J. N. D, *Christianity and Comparative Religion*, Tyndale, 1970.
————*God's Law and God's Love*, Collins, 1980.
Barnes, Michael, *Religions in Conversation: Christian Identity and Religious Pluralism*, SPCK, London, 1989.
Bell, R., *The Origin of Islam in its Christian Environment*, London, 1968.
Brown, Stuart, (ed.), *Meeting in Faith*, WCC, Geneva, 1989.
Brown, Stuart, (trans.), *The Challenge of the Scriptures: The Bible and the Qur'ān*, Orbis, New York, 1989.
Christian Witness to Muslims: Report of a Consultation held at Pattaya, Thailand, Wheaton, 1980.
Cracknell, Kenneth, *Towards a New Relationship*, Epworth, 1986.
Cragg, Kenneth, *Muhammad and the Christian: A Question of Response*, DLT, London, 1984.
Freytag, W., *The Gospel and the Religions*, SCM, 1957.
Gaudeul, J. M., *Encounters and Clashes*, Rome, 1984.
————*Guidelines on Dialogue with People of Living Faiths and Ideologies*, Geneva, 1979.
Hick, John, (ed.), *Truth and Dialogue*, London, 1974.
Hooker, Roger, *CMS and Other Faiths – Some Lessons from our History*, Smethwick, 1987.
Khodr, George, *The Ecumenical Review*, 1971.
Lewis, Philip, *Pirs, Shrines and Pakistani Islam*, Christian Study Centre, Rawalpindi, 1985.
Musk, Bill, *The Unseen Face of Islam*, MARC, Eastbourne, 1989.
Nazir-Ali, Michael J., *Frontiers in Muslim-Christian Encounter*, Regnum, 1987.
————*Islam: A Christian Perspective*, Paternoster, Exeter, 1983.
————*Martyrs and Magistrates: Toleration and Trial in Islam*, Nottingham, 1989.
————*Towards a Theology for Inter-Faith Dialogue*, ACC, London, 1986.
Pannikar, Raimundo, *The Unknown Christ of Hinduism*, DLT, London, 1981.
Relations with People of Other Faiths, Guidelines on Dialogue in Britain, BCC, London, 1981.
Rudvin, Arne, Bishop, *The Gospel and Islam: What sort of Dialogue is Possible?* Al-Mushir, Rawalpindi, 1979.
Samartha, S. J., *The Hindu Response to the Unbound Christ*, Madras, 1974.
Samuel, Vinay & Sugden, Chris (eds.), *The Gospel among our Hindu Neighbours*, Bangalore, 1983.
Southern, R. W., *Western Views of Islam, in the Middle-Ages*, Cambridge, Mass., 1962.
Thomas, M. M., *The Acknowledged Christ of the Indian Renaissance*, London, 1969.
Woodberry, J. D. (ed.), *Muslims and Christians on the Emmaus Road*, MARC, Monrovia, 1989.

THEOLOGICAL EDUCATION BY EXTENSION

Kinsler, F. Ross, (ed.), *Ministry by the People*, WCC, Geneva, 1983.

Index

250

253

257

Mosque(s): 126, 135, 156, 157.

Moule, C. F. D.: 186.

Mount Kenya East, diocese of: 67, 68.

Mughals, the: 47.

Muhammad, Prophet of Islam: 141, 158, 190.

Murshid (Ptr): 179.

Music: 69, 79, 82, 89, 92, 100, 102, 103, 107, 109, 128, 140, 158, 160, 177, 180, 187, 205.

Muslims: 29, 30, 39, 40, 117, 126, 130, 133, 135, 136, 147, 156, 157, 158, 159, 160, 163, 166, 180, 181, 190, 191, 208.

Mylapore: 25.

Mysticism: 165f.

N

Naaman the Syrian: 126.

Nabi: 159.

Nabion(s): 10, 82, 84, 85, 95, 103, 117, 129, 131, 144, 160, 167, 187, 195, 201, 209.

National Apostasy: 52.

National Christian Councils: 195.

Nationalism: 107, 165, 167, 171.

Nazareth: 174.

Near East School of Theology: 28.

Neill, Stephen: 41, 43, 47, 48, 156.

Nepal: 33, 147.

Nestorian Tablet, the: 31.

Newbigin, L.: 152, 168, 192, 203, 204.

New Religious Movements: 83.

New Testament: 10, 20, 22, 23, 24, 56, 74, 95, 96, 104, 113, 125, 126, 127, 128, 131, 132, 135, 149, 159, 160, 163, 170, 171, 173, 184, 186.

Newton, J.: 48.

Nicaea: 25.

Nicholls, David: 124.

Nigeria: 126, 196, 209.

Nile, the: 28.

Niles, D. T.: 167.

Nineveh: 13.

Nigeria: 126, 196, 209.

Nomads: 66, 68.

Non-Jurors: 51.

North, the: 115, 116, 209, 210, 211, 212.

North America: 104, 124, 208.

Nubia: 28.

O

Oath of the Coonan Cross: 32.

Occult, the: 181.

Old Catholic Church: 60.

Old Testament, the: 10, 11, 15, 16, 19, 34, 96, 104, 112, 113, 125, 130, 131, 159.

Omnipotence, divine: 15.

Omniscience, divine: 15.

Ordinal(s): 214.

Ordination: 48, 54, 68, 114, 119, 120, 155, 196, 197, 202.

Oriental (or Non-Chalcedonian) Orthodox Churches: 29, 44, 57, 108, 109, 141, 145, 153, 154, 196, 197, 199, 208, 209.

Origen: 28.

Orthodoxy: 17, 26, 33, 45, 66, 92, 109, 140, 141, 142, 143.

Ottoman Empire, the: 142.

Oxford: 40.

Oxford Movement: 52, 53.

P

Pacific, the: 67, 208.

Padroado: 40, 41, 42, 46.

Paganus: 22.

Pagan(s): 42, 67, 74, 132, 142.

Pakistan: 26, 68, 135, 145, 157.

Palestine: 56, 111, 145, 174.

Panchasila: 165.

Pannikar, R.: 152, 154.

Pantaenus: 28.

Papua New Guinea: 201.

Parable(s): 15, 112.

Parish, the: 50, 51, 67, 68, 69, 70, 71, 72, 107, 114, 121, 149, 183, 209, 212.

Parliament: 51.

Parousia: 19.

Parson's Freehold: 72.

Parthian Empire, the: 23, 24.

Partnership in Mission: 49, 55, 84, 113, 115, 210f.

Passion, the: 18, 19, 20, 40, 139, 149, 186, 204, 206, 207.

Passover, the: 174.

Pastoral Care: 48, 65, 68, 70, 71, 72, 109, 118, 120, 125, 149, 155, 179, 180, 211.

Pastoral Epistles, the: 113.

Pastoral Measure, the: 72.

259

Scriptural References

QU'RAN